Rick

SNAPSHOT

Nice & the French Riviera

D0208977

CONTENTS

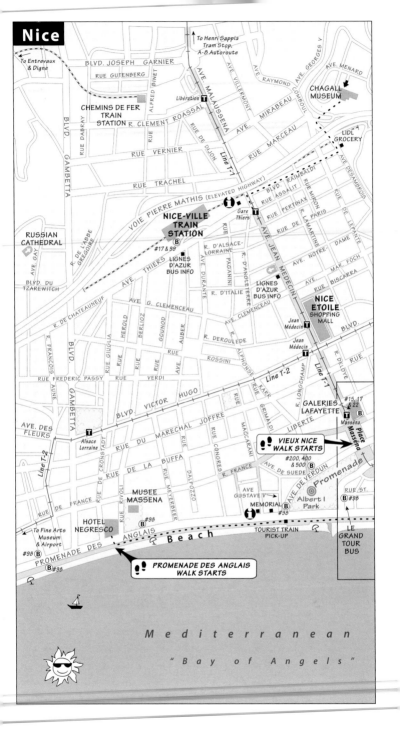

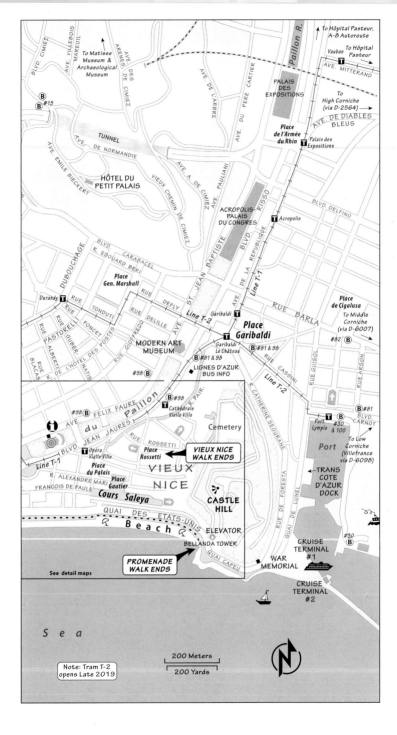

Promenade des Anglais Walk

Legend:
1. Hôtel Negresco
2. Villa Masséna
3. Bay of Angels
4. Palais de la Méditerranée
5. Albert I Park
6. Steel Girders Sculpture
7. Metal Winch

Vieux Nice Walk

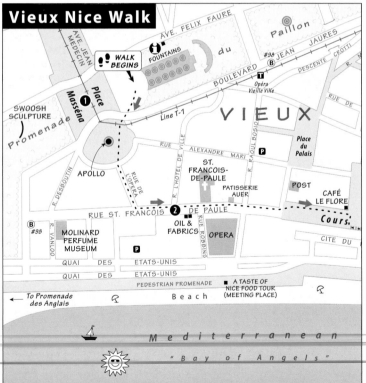

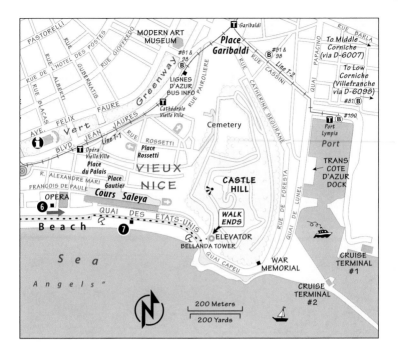

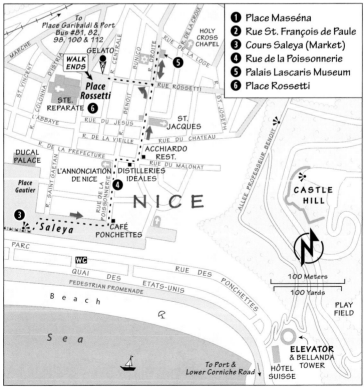

❶	Place Masséna
❷	Rue St. François de Paule
❸	Cours Saleya (Market)
❹	Rue de la Poissonnerie
❺	Palais Lascaris Museum
❻	Place Rossetti

INTRODUCTION

The French Riviera is an intoxicating bouillabaisse of enjoyable cities, warm stone villages, contemporary art, and breathtaking coastlines steaming with sunshine and stirred by the wind. There's something about the play of light in this region, where natural and man-made beauty mingle to dazzle the senses and nourish the soul. It all adds up to *une magnifique* vacation.

The Riviera stretches along France's southeast Mediterranean coast from St-Tropez to Monaco and rambles inland into the Alps. Much of the Riviera is about the sea and money—it's populated by a yacht-happy crowd wondering where the next "scene" will be. Yet Nice feels downright Italian—with fresh-Parmesan-topped pasta and red-orange, pastel-colored buildings.

This book covers the predictable biggies, from jet-setting beach resorts to famous museums, but it also mixes in a healthy dose of Back Door intimacy. Along with the urban bustle of Nice, I'll introduce you to my favorite villages and scenic walks. Marvel at ancient monuments, take a journey along the greatest canyon in Europe, and settle into a shaded café on a made-for-movies square. Claim your favorite beach to call home, and at day's end dive headfirst into a southern France sunset.

To help you have the best trip possible, I've included the following topics in this book:

• **Planning Your Time,** with advice on how to make the most of your limited time

• **Orientation,** including tourist information (abbreviated as TI), tips on public transportation, local tour options, and helpful hints

• **Sights** with ratings:

▲▲▲—Don't miss

▲▲—Try hard to see

▲—Worthwhile if you can make it

No rating—Worth knowing about

• **Sleeping** and **Eating,** with good-value recommendations in every price range

• **Connections,** with tips on trains, buses, and driving

Practicalities, near the end of this book, has information on money, staying connected, hotel reservations, transportation, and more, plus French survival phrases.

To travel smartly, read this little book in its entirety before you go. It's my hope that this guide will make your trip more meaningful and rewarding. Traveling like a temporary local, you'll get the absolute most out of every mile, minute, and dollar.

Bon voyage!

THE FRENCH RIVIERA

THE FRENCH RIVIERA

La Côte d'Azur

A hundred years ago, celebrities from London to Moscow flocked to the French Riviera to socialize, gamble, and escape the dreary weather at home. Today, budget vacationers and heat-seeking Europeans fill belle époque resorts at France's most sought-after fun-in-the-sun destination.

The region got its nickname from turn-of-the-20th-century vacationing Brits, who simply extended the Italian Riviera west to France to include Nice. Today, the Riviera label stretches even farther westward, running from the Italian border to St-Tropez. To the French, this summer fun zone is known for the dazzling azure color of the sea along this coast: La Côte d'Azur. All of my French Riviera destinations are on the sea, except for a few hill towns and the Gorges du Verdon.

This sunny sliver of land has been inhabited for more than 3,000 years. Ligurians were first, then Greeks, then Romans—who, as usual, had the greatest impact. After the fall of Rome, Nice became an important city in the Kingdom of Provence (along with Marseille and Arles). In the 14th century Nice's leaders voted to join the duke of Savoy's mountainous kingdom (also including several regions of northern Italy), which would later evolve into the Kingdom of Sardinia. It was not until 1860 that Nice (and Savoy) became a part of France—the result of a plebiscite. (The "vote" was made possible because the King of Sardinia had to trade the region to France as a quid pro quo for Napoleon III's support of the Italian states that wanted to break away from Austria to create modern Italy).

Nice has world-class museums, a splendid beachfront promenade, a seductive old town, and all the drawbacks of a major city (traffic, crime, pollution, and so on). The day-trip possibilities are easy and exciting: Monaco offers a royal welcome and a

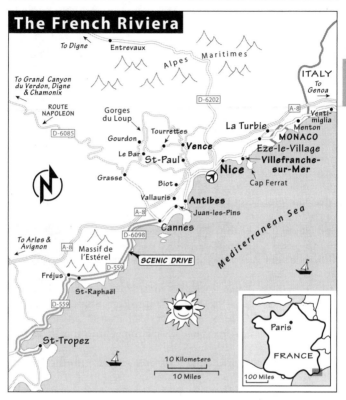

fairy-tale past; Antibes has a thriving port and silky sand beaches; and image-conscious Cannes is the Riviera's self-appointed queen, with an elegant veneer hiding...very little. Yacht-happy St-Tropez swims alone an hour west. The Riviera's overlooked interior transports travelers to a world apart, with cliff-hanging villages, steep canyons, and alpine scenery—a refreshing alternative to the beach scene.

CHOOSING A HOME BASE

My favorite home bases are Nice, Antibes, and Villefranche-sur-Mer.

Nice is the region's capital and France's fifth-largest city. With convenient train and bus connections to most regional sights, this is the most practical base for train travelers. Urban Nice also has museums, a beach scene that rocks, the best selection of hotels in all price ranges, and good nightlife options. A car is a headache in Nice.

Nearby **Antibes** is smaller, with a bustling center, a lively night scene, great sandy beaches, grand vistas, good walking trails, and a stellar Picasso museum. Antibes has frequent train service to Nice and Monaco, and good connections by train or car to Grasse. It's the most convenient overnight stop for drivers, with light traffic and easy hotel parking.

Villefranche-sur-Mer is the romantic's choice, with a serene setting and small-town warmth. It has sand-pebble beaches; quick public transportation to Nice, Monaco, and Cap Ferrat; and a small selection of hotels and good restaurants in most price ranges.

PLANNING YOUR TIME

Ideally, allow a day and a half for Nice itself, an afternoon to explore inland hill towns, a full day for Italianesque Villefranche-sur-Mer and lovely Cap Ferrat, a day for Monaco and the Corniches (including Eze-le-Village), and—if time allows—a day for Antibes and maybe Cannes. If you must do St-Tropez, visit it while traveling to or from destinations farther west (such as Cassis, Aix-en-Provence, and Arles) and avoid it on weekend afternoons, as well as all summer.

Monaco is radiant at night, and Antibes works well by day (good beaches and hiking) and night (fine choice of restaurants and a lively after-hours scene). Hill-town-loving naturalists should add a night or two inland to explore the charming hill-capping hamlets near Vence.

Depending on the amount of time you have in the Riviera, here are my recommended priorities:

3 days:	Nice, Villefranche-sur-Mer with Cap Ferrat, and Monaco
5 days, add:	Antibes and hill towns near Vence
7 days, add:	Grand Canyon du Verdon and/or just slow down

HELPFUL HINTS

Medical Help: Riviera Medical Services has a list of English-speaking physicians all along the Riviera. They can help you make an appointment or call an ambulance (tel. 04 93 26 12 70, www.rivieramedical.com).

Sightseeing Tips: Mondays and Tuesdays can frustrate market lovers and museumgoers. Closed on Monday: Nice's Modern and Contemporary Art Museum, Fine Arts Museum, and Cours Saleya produce and flower market; Antibes' Picasso Museum and market hall (Sept-May). Closed on Tuesday: Chagall, Matisse, Masséna, and Archaeological museums in Nice; Renoir Museum in Cagnes-sur-Mer. Matisse's Chapel of the Rosary in Vence is closed Sunday and Monday and in the morning on Wednesday and Saturday.

The **French Riviera Pass** includes entry to many Riviera

sights and activities, including Nice's Chagall Museum, Monaco's Oceanography Museum, and Villa Ephrussi de Rothschild on Cap Ferrat (€26/24 hours, €38/48 hours, €56/72 hours, tel. 04 92 14 46 14, http://en.frenchrivierapass.com). This pass is worth paying for if you have an aggressive sightseeing plan or want to do some bigger-ticket items like the included Le Grand Tour Bus in Nice (see page 22) or the Trans Côte d'Azur cruise (see page 23).

A €10 **combo-ticket for Nice** covers all of the city's museums, except the Chagall Museum.

Events: The Riviera is famous for staging major events. Unless you're actually taking part in the festivities, these occasions give you only room shortages and traffic jams. Here are the three biggies: **Nice Carnival** (two weeks in Feb, www.nicecarnaval.com), **Cannes Film Festival** (12 days in mid-May, www.festival-cannes.com), and the **Grand Prix of Monaco** (4 days in late May, www.acm.mc). To accommodate the busy schedules of the rich and famous (and really mess up a lot of normal people), the film festival and car race often overlap.

Cruise-Ship Sightseeing: The French Riviera is a popular cruise destination. Arriving ships are divided about evenly between Nice, Villefranche-sur-Mer, and Monaco (for arrival help, see the "Connections" section at the end of each of those chapters). Because these three ports line up conveniently along a 10-mile stretch of coast—easily connected by train or bus—from any of them, those arriving by cruise have the Riviera by the tail. Hiring a local guide helps make the most of cruisers' limited time in port (see "Tours in the Riviera," later). For in-depth coverage, consider my guidebook, *Rick Steves Mediterranean Cruise Ports*.

GETTING AROUND THE RIVIERA

Trains and buses do a good job of connecting places along the coast, with bonus views along many routes. Buses also provide reasonable service to some inland hill towns. Nice makes the most convenient base for day trips, though public transport also works well from Riviera towns such as Antibes and Villefranche-sur-Mer. Driving can be challenging in this congested region (traffic, parking, etc.).

By Public Transportation

In the Riviera, buses are often less expensive and more convenient while trains are faster and more expensive. For an overview of the most useful train and bus connections, see the "Public Transportation in the French Riviera" chart later (confirm all connections and last train/bus times locally). You'll also find details under each destination's "Connections" section. For a scenic inland train ride, take the narrow-gauge train into the Alps (see page 54).

If taking the train or bus, have coins handy. Ticket machines don't take some US credit cards or any euro bills, smaller train stations may be unstaffed, and bus drivers can't make change for large bills.

Buses: Most of the area's top destinations are connected by bus, and tickets are cheap. This is an amazing deal in the Riviera. Any one-way bus or tram **ticket** costs €1.50 (€10 for 10 tickets) whether you're riding just within Nice or to Villefranche-sur-Mer, Monaco, Antibes, or even Grasse. This ticket is good for 74 minutes of travel in one direction anywhere within the bus system (but does not cover air-

port buses). Outside of the Inland Riviera, you can buy a single bus ticket from the driver or from machines at stops, and validate it in the machine on board (10-ride or all-day tickets must be purchased at machines or at Lignes d'Azur offices). At Inland Riviera destinations such as Vence and St.-Paul-de-Vence, buy bus tickets at a *tabac*. Your ticket allows transfers between the buses of the Lignes d'Azur (the region's main bus company, www.lignesdazur.com) and the TAM (Transports Alpes-Maritimes); if you board a TAM bus and need a transfer, ask for *un ticket correspondance*. A €5 all-day ticket is good on Nice's city buses, tramway, and selected buses serving nearby destinations (such as Villefranche, Cap Ferrat, and Eze-le-Village). The general rule of thumb: If the bus number has one or two digits, it's covered with the all-day ticket; with three digits it's not.

You'll be able to get around most of the Riviera on the following major bus routes:

- **Bus #100** runs eastbound from **Nice** along the Low Corniche (3-4/hour) stopping in **Villefranche-sur-Mer** (20 minutes), **Beaulieu-sur-Mer** (**Villa Kérylos**; 30 minutes), **Eze-Bord-de-Mer** (40 minutes, transfer to #83 to Eze-le-Village), **Monaco** (1 hour), and **Menton** (1.5 hours).
- **Bus #81** runs eastbound from **Nice** (2-3/hour) to **Villefranche-sur-Mer** (15 minutes), **Beaulieu-sur-Mer** (**Villa Kérylos**; 20 minutes), and all **Cap Ferrat** stops, ending at **St-Jean-Cap-Ferrat** (30 minutes).
- **Buses #82 and #112** run from **Nice** and upper **Villefranche-sur-Mer** to **Eze-le-Village** (together they depart about hourly; only #82 runs on Sunday; 30 minutes to reach Eze from Nice).

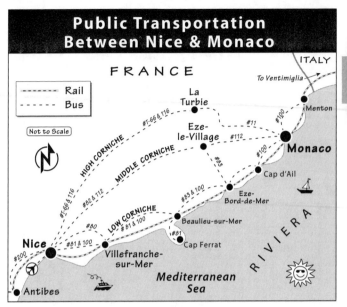

Public Transportation Between Nice & Monaco

Bus #112, which runs along the scenic Middle Corniche, continues from Eze-le-Village to **Monte Carlo** in Monaco (6/day, none on Sun, 20 minutes).

- **Bus #200** goes from **Nice** westbound (4/hour Mon-Sat, 2/hour Sun) to **Cagnes-sur-Mer** (1 hour), **Biot** (1.25 hours), **Antibes** (1.5 hours), and **Cannes** (2 hours).

- For the inland towns, **bus #400** runs from **Nice** (2/hour) to **St-Paul-de-Vence** (45 minutes) and **Vence** (50 minutes); **buses #500/510** run between **Vence** and **Grasse** (6/day, 50 minutes).

Trains: These are more expensive but much faster than the bus (Nice to Monaco by train is about €4), and there's no quicker way to move about the Riviera (http://en.voyages-sncf.com). Speedy trains link the Riviera's beachfront destinations—Cannes, Antibes, Nice, Villefranche-sur-Mer, Monaco, Menton, and the inland perfume town of Grasse. (Never board a train without a ticket or valid pass—fare inspectors accept no excuses. The minimum fine: €70.)

By Car

This is France's most challenging region to drive in. Beautifully distracting vistas (natural and human), loads of Sunday-driver tourists, and every hour being lush-hour in the summer make for a dangerous combination. Parking can be exasperating. Bring lots of coins and patience.

The Riviera is awash with scenic roads. To sample some of the Riviera's best scenery, connect Provence and the Riviera by driv-

FRENCH RIVIERA

Public Transportation in the French Riviera

From \ To		Cannes	Antibes	Nice
Cannes		N/A	**Train:** 2/hr, 15 min **Bus:** #200, 2-4/hr, 35 min	**Train:** 2/hr, 30 min **Bus:** #200, 2-4/hr, 2 hrs
Antibes		**Train:** 2/hr, 15 min **Bus:** #200, 2-4/hr, 35 min	N/A	**Train:** 2/hr, 20 min **Bus:** #200, 2-4/hr, 1.5 hrs
Nice		**Train:** 2/hr, 30 min **Bus:** #200, 2-4/hr, 2 hrs	**Train:** 2/hr, 20 min **Bus:** #200, 2-4/hr, 1.5 hrs	N/A
Villefranche-sur-Mer		**Train:** 2/hr, 50 min	**Train:** 2/hr, 40 min	**Train:** 2/hr, 10 min **Bus:** #100, 3-4/hr, 20 min; also #81, 2-3/hr, 15 min
Cap Ferrat		**Bus/Train:** #81 to Beaulieu-sur-Mer (2-3/hr, 10 min), then train to Cannes (2/hr, 1 hr)	**Bus/Train:** #81 to Beaulieu-sur-Mer (2-3/hr, 10 min), then train (2/hr, 40 min) Bus: #81 to Nice (2-3/hr, 30 min), then #200 (2-4/hr, 1.5 hrs)	**Bus:** #81, 2-3/hr, 30 min
Eze-le-Village		**Bus/Train:** #83 to Eze-Bord-de-Mer (8/day, 15 min), then train (2/hr, 1 hour)	**Bus/Train:** #83 to Eze-Bord-de-Mer (8/day, 15 min), then train (2/hr, 45 min)	**Bus/Train:** #83 to Eze-Bord-de-Mer (8/day, 15 min), then train (2/hr, 15 min) **Bus:** #82/#112, hourly, 30 min
Monaco		**Train:** 2/hr, 70 min	**Train:** 2/hr, 50 min	**Train:** 2/hr, 20 min **Bus:** #100, 3-4/hr, 1 hour

Note: Bus frequencies are given for Monday-Saturday (Sunday often has limited or no bus service).

Villefranche-sur-Mer	Cap Ferrat	Eze-le-Village	Monaco
Train: 2/hr, 50 min	**Train/Bus:** 2/hr, 1 hr to Beaulieu-sur-Mer, then bus #81 (2-3/hr, 10 min)	**Train/Bus:** 2/hr, 1 hr to Eze-Bord-de-Mer, then bus #83 (8/day, 15 min)	**Train:** 2/hr, 70 min
Train: 2/hr, 40 min	**Train/Bus:** 2/hr, 40 min to Beaulieu-sur-Mer, then bus #81 (2-3/hr, 10 min) **Bus:** #200 to Nice (2-4/hr, 1.5 hrs), then #81 (2-3/hr, 30 min)	**Train/Bus:** 2/hr, 45 min to Eze-Bord-de-Mer, then bus #83 (8/day, 15 min)	**Train:** 2/hr, 50 min
Train: 2/hr, 10 min **Bus:** #100, 3-4/hr, 20 min; also #81, 2-3/hr, 15 min	**Bus:** #81, 2-3/hr, 30 min	**Train/Bus:** 2/hr, 15 min to Eze-Bord-de-Mer, then bus #83 (8/day, 15 min) **Bus:** #82/#112, hourly, 30 min	**Train:** 2/hr, 20 min **Bus:** #100, 3-4/hr, 1 hour
N/A	**Bus:** #81, 2-3/hr, 15 min	**Train/Bus:** 2/hr, 5 min to Eze-Bord-de-Mer, then bus #83 (8/day, 15 min) **Bus:** #100 to Eze-Bord-de-Mer, then transfer to #83; also #82/#112 from upper Villefranche	**Train:** 2/hr, 10 min **Bus:** #100, 3-4/hr, 40 min
Bus: #81, 2-3/hr, 15 min	N/A	**Bus:** 30-min walk or bus #81 to Beaulieu-sur-Mer (3-4/hr, 10 min), then #83 to Eze-le-Village (8/day, 20 min)	**Bus:** 20-min walk or bus #81 to #100 (3-4/hr, 20 min)
Bus/Train: #83 to Eze-Bord-de-Mer (8/day, 15 min), then train (2/hr, 5 min) **Bus:** #83 to Eze-Bord-de-Mer, then transfer to #100; also #82/#112 to upper Villefranche	**Bus:** #83 to Beaulieu-sur-Mer (8/day, 20 min), then walk 30 min or transfer to #81)	N/A	**Bus:** #112, 6/day, 20 min
Train: 2/hr, 10 min **Bus:** #100, 3-4/hr, 40 min	**Bus:** #100, 3-4/hr, 20 min (plus 20-min walk or transfer to #81)	**Bus:** #112, 6/day, 20 min	N/A

ing the splendid coastal road between Cannes and Fréjus (D-6098 from Cannes/D-559 from Fréjus). Once in the Riviera, the most scenic and thrilling road trip is along the three coastal roads—called "corniches"—between Nice and Monaco (see page 84). Farther inland, take my recommended inland hill-towns drive (on page 161). Farther yet, explore the Grand Canyon du Verdon, with breathtaking gorges and alpine scenery. But for basic sightseeing between Monaco and Cannes, I'd ditch the car and use trains and buses.

By Boat

Trans Côte d'Azur offers seasonal boat service from Nice to Monaco or to St-Tropez, as well as between Cannes and St-Tropez (tel. 04 92 98 71 30, www.trans-cote-azur.com). For details, see the "By Boat" section under Nice Connections (page 69).

TOURS IN THE RIVIERA
Local Guides with Cars

These two energetic and delightful women adore educating people about this area's culture and history, and have comfortable minibuses: **Sylvie Di Cristo** (€600/day, €350/half-day for up to 8 people, mobile 06 09 88 83 83, http://frenchrivieraguides.com, dicristosylvie@gmail.com) and **Ingrid Schmucker** (€490/day for 2 people, €530/day for 3-4 people, €580 for 5-6, €200/half-day to explore old Nice on foot, mobile 06 14 83 03 33, https://kultours.fr, kultours06@gmail.com). Their websites explain their programs well, and they are happy to adapt to your interests.

Charming Fouad Zarrou runs **France Azur Excursions** and offers a fun experience. His tours are more about exploring the region's natural beauty, food, and wine than its cultural history. He provides comfortable transportation in his minivan (figure €300/half-day, mobile 06 20 68 10 70, http://franceazurexcursions.com, contact@franceazurexcursions.com).

Most hotels and TIs have information on economical shared minivan excursions from Nice (per person: roughly €50-70/half-day, €80-120/day).

Local Guides Without Cars

For a guided tour of Nice or the region using public transit or with a guide joining you in your rental car, consider **Pascale Rucker,** an art-loving guide with 25 years of experience who teaches with the joy and wonder of a flower child (€160/half-day, €260/day, mobile 06 16 24 29 52, pascalerucker@gmail.com). **Boba Vukadinovic-Millet** is an effective teacher, ideal for those wanting to dive more deeply into the region's history and art. She can arrange chauffeur-driven rental options (car, minivan, minibus, bus) for you if needed

Top Art Sights of the Riviera

These are listed in order of importance.

Chagall Museum (Nice)
Fondation Maeght (St-Paul-de-Vence)
Picasso Museum (Antibes)
Matisse Museum (Nice)
Museum of the Annonciade (St-Tropez)
Chapel of the Rosary (Vence)
Modern and Contemporary Art Museum (Nice)
Renoir Museum (Cagnes-sur-Mer)
Fine Arts Museum (Nice)

(from €250/half-day, from €350/day, mobile 06 27 45 68 39, www.yourguideboba.com, boba@yourguideboba.com).

Food Tours

For food and wine walking tours and cooking classes offered in Nice, see page 24.

THE RIVIERA'S ART SCENE

The list of artists who have painted the Riviera reads like a Who's Who of 20th-century art. Pierre-Auguste Renoir, Henri Matisse,

Marc Chagall, Georges Braque, Raoul Dufy, Fernand Léger, and Pablo Picasso all lived and worked here—and raved about the region's wonderful light. Their simple, semi-abstract, and—most importantly—colorful works reflect the pleasurable atmosphere of the Riviera. You'll experience the same landscapes they painted in this bright, sun-drenched region, punctuated with views of the "azure sea." Try to imagine the Riviera with a fraction of the people and development you see today.

But the artists were mostly drawn to the uncomplicated lifestyle of fishermen and farmers that has reigned here since time began. As the artists grew older, they retired in the sun, turned their backs on modern art's "isms," and painted with the wide-eyed wonder of children, using bright primary colors, basic outlines, and simple subjects.

A collection of modern- and contemporary-art museums (many described in this book) dot the Riviera, allowing art lovers to appreciate these masters' works while immersed in the same sun and culture that inspired them. Many of the museums were designed to blend pieces with the surrounding views, gardens, and fountains, thus highlighting that modern art is not only stimulating, but sometimes simply beautiful.

Entire books have been written about the modern-art galleries of the Riviera. If you're a fan, do some studying before your visit to be sure you know about that far-out museum of your dreams. If you've never enjoyed modern art, the two best places to give it a try here are the Fondation Maeght in St-Paul-de-Vence and the Chagall Museum in Nice.

THE RIVIERA'S CUISINE SCENE

The Riviera adds an Italian-Mediterranean flair to the food of Provence. While many of the same dishes served in Provence are available in the Riviera, there are differences, especially if you look for anything Italian or from the sea. Proximity to the water and historic ties to Italy are clear in this region's dishes.

That said, memorable restaurants that showcase the Riviera's cuisine can be difficult to find. Because most visitors come more for the sun than the food, and because the clientele is predominantly international, many restaurants aim for the middle and are hard to distinguish from one another. Trust my recommendations.

A fresh and colorful *salade niçoise* makes the perfect introduction to the Riviera's cuisine. Surprisingly, the authentic version contains no potatoes or green beans but consists of ripe tomatoes, plenty of raw vegetables (such as radishes, green peppers, celery, and perhaps artichoke or fava beans), as well as tuna (usually canned), anchovy, hard-boiled egg, and olives. This is my go-to salad for a tasty, healthy, cheap (€14), and fast lunch. I like to spend a couple of extra euros and eat it in a place with a nice ambience and view.

For lunch on the go, look for a *pan bagnat* (like a *salade niçoise* stuffed into a crusty roll drizzled with olive oil and wine vinegar). Other tasty bread treats include *pissaladière* (bread dough topped with caramelized onions, olives, and anchovies), *fougasse* (a spindly, lace-like bread sometimes flavored with nuts, herbs, olives, or ham), and *socca* (a thin chickpea-and-olive-oil crêpe, seasoned with pepper and often served in a paper cone by street vendors).

Said to have been invented in Nice, ravioli and potato gnocchi can be found on menus everywhere (ravioli can be stuffed with a variety of fillings, but the classic local version is made with beef and Swiss chard).

Bouillabaisse is the Riviera's most famous dish; you'll find it in seafront villages and cities. It's a spicy fish stew based on recipes handed down from sailors in Marseille. It must contain at least four types of fresh fish, though most have five to twelve kinds. A true bouillabaisse never has shellfish. The fish—cooked in a tomato-and-onion-based stock and flavored with saffron (and sometimes anise and orange)—is separated from the stock, and the two are served as separate courses. Diners then heighten the soup's flavor by adding toasted croutons slathered with *rouille* sauce (a thickened reddish mayonnaise heady with garlic and spicy peppers) and topped with grated parmesan or Emmental cheese. This dish often requires a minimum order of two and can cost up to €40-60 per person.

Far less pricey than bouillabaisse and worth trying is the local *soupe de poissons* (fish soup). It's a creamy soup flavored like bouillabaisse, with anise and orange, and served with croutons and *rouille* sauce (but has no chunks of fish). For a less colorful but still tasty soup, look for *bourride,* a creamy fish concoction thickened with an aioli sauce instead of the red *rouille.*

The Riviera specializes in all sorts of fish and shellfish. Options include *fruits de mer* (platters of seafood—including tiny shellfish, from which you get the edible part only by sucking really hard), herb-infused mussels, stuffed sardines, squid (slowly simmered with tomatoes and herbs), and tuna *(thon).* The popular *loup flambé au fenouil* is grilled sea bass, flavored with fennel and torched with *pastis* prior to serving.

For a truly local dessert, try the *Niçoise* specialty *tourte de blettes,* a sugar-dusted pie with a sweet filling of Swiss chard, rum-soaked raisins, pine nuts, and apple. In St-Tropez, the *tropézienne* is a brioche topped with sugar crystals and sandwiching with an airy vanilla cream. Desserts on the Riviera make use of the abundant local fruits, especially citrus in winter, and regional flavors such as orange flower water.

For details on dining in France's restaurants, cafés, and brasseries, getting takeout, and assembling a picnic—as well as a rundown of French cuisine—see the "Eating" section in the Practicalities chapter (page 176).

WINES OF THE RIVIERA

Do as everyone else does: Drink wines from Provence. Bandol (red) and cassis (white) are popular and from a region nearly on the Riviera. The only wines made in the Riviera are Bellet rosé and white, the latter often found in fish-shaped bottles.

NICE

Nice (sounds like "niece"), with its spectacular Alps-meets-Mediterranean surroundings, is the big-city highlight of the Riviera. Its traffic-free Vieux Nice—the old town—blends Italian and French flavors to create a spicy Mediterranean dressing, while its big squares, broad seaside walkways, and long beaches invite lounging and people-watching. Nice may be nice, but it's jammed in May, July, and August—reserve ahead and get a room with air-conditioning. Nice gets quiet and mild in April and October. Everything you'll want to see in Nice is either within walking distance, or a short bike, bus, or tram ride away.

Orientation to Nice

Focus your time on the area between the beach and the train tracks (about 15 blocks apart). The city revolves around its grand Place Masséna, where pedestrian-friendly Avenue Jean Médecin meets Vieux Nice and the Promenade du Paillon parkway (with quick access to the beaches). It's a 20-minute walk (or about €15 by taxi) from the train station to the beach, and a 20-minute stroll along the promenade from the fancy Hôtel Negresco to the heart of Vieux Nice.

A 10-minute ride on the smooth tram through the center of the city connects the train station, Place Masséna, Vieux Nice, and Place Garibaldi. A new, mostly underground tram line paralleling the Promenade des Anglais and running from the port to the airport may be in operation by the time you visit.

TOURIST INFORMATION

Nice has three helpful TIs (tel. 08 92 70 74 07, www.nicetourisme. com), including the main branches at the **train station** and at #5 **Promenade des Anglais** (both daily 9:00-18:00, July-Aug until 19:00), and by the fountains near **Place Masséna,** called "Pavillon" (May-mid-Sept only, daily 10:00-20:00). Ask for day-trip information (including maps of Monaco, Antibes, and Cannes) and details on boat excursions, bus stop locations, and schedules.

ARRIVAL IN NICE

By Train: All trains stop at Nice's main station, called Nice-Ville. With your back to the tracks, car rentals are to the right. Bag storage is to the left inside the station; you can also stash your bags a short block away at the recommended Hôtel Belle Meunière. The TI and bus stops (including #99 to the airport) are straight out the main doors.

A nearby tram line zips you to the center in a few minutes (several blocks to the left as you leave the station, departs every few minutes, direction: Hôpital Pasteur; see "Getting Around Nice," later). To walk to the beach, Promenade des Anglais, or many of my recommended hotels, cross Avenue Thiers in front of the station, go down the steps by Hôtel Interlaken, and continue down Avenue Durante.

By Bus: For arrival by bus, see "Nice Connections," at the end of this chapter. The region's primary bus company, Lignes d'Azur, has an information office across from the train station (see "Helpful Hints," later).

By Car: To reach the city center from the autoroute, take the *Nice Centre* exit and follow signs. Ask your hoteliers where to park (allow €20-30/day; some hotels offer deals but space is limited—arrange ahead). The parking garage at the Nice Etoile shopping center on Avenue Jean Médecin is near many recommended hotels (ticket booth on third floor, about €28/day, 18:00-8:00). Other centrally located garages have similar rates. On-street parking is strictly metered (usually a 2-hour limit) every day but Sunday, when it is typically free.

You can avoid driving in the center—and park for free during the day (no overnight parking)—by stashing your car at a parking lot at a remote tram or bus stop. Look for blue-on-white *Parcazur* signs (find locations at www.lignesdazur.com), and ride the bus or tram into town (10/hour, 15 minutes, buy round-trip tram or bus ticket and keep it with you—you'll need it later to exit the parking lot; for tram details, see "Getting Around Nice," later). The easiest

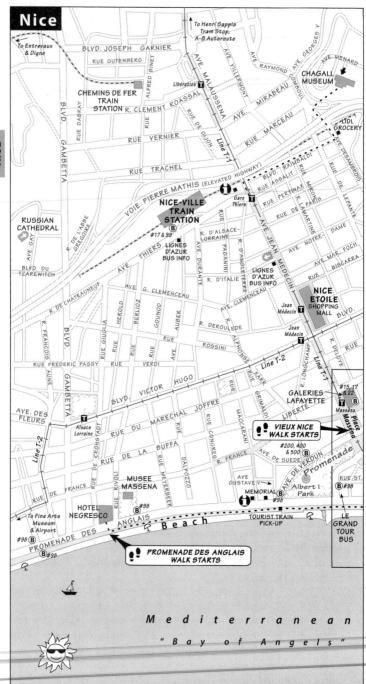

NICE

Nice

To Entrevaux
& Digne

To Henri Sappia
Tram Stop,
A-8 Autoroute

BLVD. JOSEPH GARNIER

RUE GUTENBERG

AVE. MALAUSSENA

AVE. VILLERMONT

AVE. RAYMOND

AVE. MIRABEAU

AVE. GEORGES V

AVE. MENARD

CHAGALL
MUSEUM

Libération

ALFRED BINET

R. CLEMENT ROASSAL

RUE DE DIJON

RUE MARCEAU

AVE. DESAMBROIS

LIDL
GROCERY

CHEMINS DE FER
TRAIN
STATION

RUE DABRAY

RUE VERNIER

RUE DE LEPANTE

BLVD. GAMBETTA

RUE TRACHEL

VOIE PIERRE MATHIS (ELEVATED HIGHWAY)

BLVD. RAIMBALDI

RUE ASSALIT

RUE PERTINAX

RUE PARIS

RUE MIRON

Gare
Thiers

NICE-VILLE
TRAIN
STATION

R. DE L'ABBE
GREGOIRE

#17 & 99

R. D'ALSACE-
LORRAINE

RUE PAGANINI

AVE. THIERS

RUE DURANTE

R. D'ANGLETERRE

RUE DES
MARTINE

AVE. NOTRE-
DAME

RUSSIAN
CATHEDRAL

AVE. GAY

LIGNES
D'AZUR
BUS INFO

AVE. JEAN MEDECIN

AVE. MAR. FOCH

BLVD DU
TZAREWITCH

R. D'ITALIE

AVE. CLEMENCEAU

LIGNES
D'AZUR
BUS INFO

BISCARRA

R. DE CHATEAUNEUF

AVE. G. CLEMENCEAU

AVE. DEROULEDE

Jean
Médecin

NICE
ETOILE
SHOPPING
MALL

BLVD.

R. FRANCOIS
AUNE

BLVD. GAMBETTA

RUE GIUGLIA

HEROLD

BERLIOZ

GOUNOD

AUBER

RUE
VERDI

ROSSINI

Jean
Médecin

Line T-2

R. DELOYE

RUE LONGCHAMP

Line T-1

RUE FREDERIC PASSY

BLVD. VICTOR HUGO

#15, 17
& 22

GALERIES
LAFAYETTE

AVE. DES
FLEURS

Alsace
Lorraine

RUE DU MARECHAL JOFFRE

RUE MACCARANI

GRIMALDI

LIBERTE

Masséna

Place
Masséna

VIEUX NICE
WALK STARTS

RUE DE CRONSTADT

RUE DE LA BUFFA

RUE MEYERBEER

RUE CONGRES

R. FRANCE

AVE. DE SUEDE

#200, 400
& 500

RUE DE
FRANCE

MUSEE
MASSENA

DALPOZZO

AVE
GUSTAVE

MEMORIAL

AVE. DE VERDUN

Promenade

RUE ST.

Albert I
Park

#98

Promenade

LE
GRAND
TOUR
BUS

To Fine Arts
Museum
& Airport

HOTEL
NEGRESCO

#98

RUE RIVOLI

ANGLAIS

Beach

TOURIST TRAIN
PICK-UP

#98

PROMENADE DES
ANGLAIS WALK STARTS

PROMENADE DES ANGLAIS
WALK STARTS

M e d i t e r r a n e a n

"B a y   o f   A n g e l s"

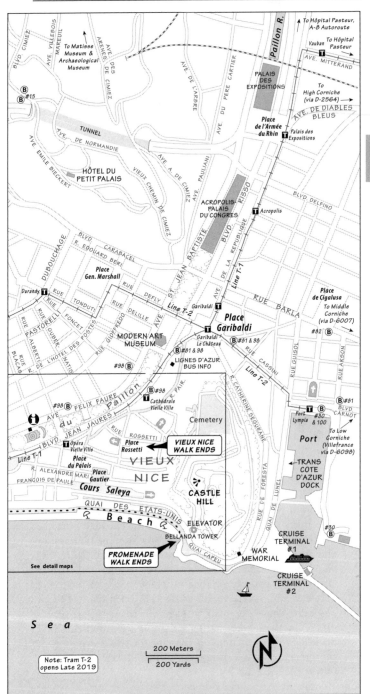

NICE

To Matisse Museum & Archaeological Museum

To Hôpital Pasteur, A-8 Autoroute

To Hôpital Pasteur

Vauban

AVE. MITTERAND

PALAIS DES EXPOSITIONS

To High Corniche (via D-2564)

AVE. DE DIABLES BLEUS

Place de l'Armée du Rhin

Palais des Expositions

BLVD. DELFINO

Acropolis

ACROPOLIS PALAIS DU CONGRES

Place de Cigalusa

To Middle Corniche (via D-6007)

RUE BARLA

Garibaldi

Place Garibaldi

Garibaldi Le Château

#81 & 98

#82

RUE CASSINI

RUE GUISOL

RUE AKSON

MODERN ART MUSEUM

LIGNES D'AZUR BUS INFO

Line T-2

#81

BLVD. CARNOT

#98

FELIX FAURE

#98

Cathédrale Vieille Ville

Cemetery

Port Lympia

#30 & 100

To Low Corniche (via D-6098)

Opéra Vieille Ville

Place Rossetti

VIEUX NICE WALK ENDS

Port

TRANS COTE D'AZUR DOCK

Place du Palais

Place Gautier

VIEUX NICE

CASTLE HILL

Cours Saleya

QUAI DES ETATS-UNIS

Beach

ELEVATOR

BELLANDA TOWER

PROMENADE WALK ENDS

#30

CRUISE TERMINAL #1

WAR MEMORIAL

See detail maps

CRUISE TERMINAL #2

Sea

200 Meters

200 Yards

Note: Tram T-2 opens Late 2019

HÔTEL DU PETIT PALAIS

TUNNEL

#15

Place Gen. Marshall

Durandy

Line T-2

Line T-1

lot to use is Parcazur Henri Sappia, right off the *Nice Nord* auto-route exit. It always has room and saves you from navigating city streets (daily until 2:30 in the morning). As lots are not guarded, don't leave anything of value in your car.

By Plane or Cruise Ship: For information on Nice's airport and cruise-ship port, see "Nice Connections" at the end of this chapter.

HELPFUL HINTS

Theft Alert: Nice has its share of pickpockets (especially at the train station, on the tram, and trolling the beach). Stick to main streets in Vieux Nice after dark.

Medical Help: Riviera Medical Services has a list of English-speaking physicians. They can help you make an appointment or call an ambulance (tel. 04 93 26 12 70, www.rivieramedical. com).

Sightseeing Tips: The Cours Saleya produce and flower market is closed Monday, and the Chagall and Matisse museums are closed Tuesday. All Nice museums—except the Chagall Museum—share the same €10 combo-ticket (valid 24 hours, €20/7 days, buy at any participating museum).

Baggage Storage: You can store your bags inside the train station (€5-10/bag per day), at the recommended **Hôtel Belle Meunière** (€5/bag per day), or at the **Bagguys** in Vieux Nice (€8/bag per day, daily 10:00-19:00, 22 Rue Centrale, info@ bagguys.fr).

Grocery Store: Small grocery shops are easy to find. The big **Monoprix** on Avenue Jean Médecin and Rue Biscarra has it all (open daily, see map on page 66).

Boutique Shopping: The chic streets where Rue Alphonse Karr meets Rue de la Liberté and then Rue de Paradis are known as the "Golden Square." If you need pricey stuff, shop here.

Renting a Bike (and Other Wheels): Bike-rental shops are a breeze to find in Nice, and several companies offer bike tours of the city. Bikes *(vélos)* can be taken on trains. **Holiday Bikes** has multiple locations, including one across from the train station, and they have electric bikes (www.loca-bike.fr). **Roller Station** is well situated near the sea and rents bikes, rollerblades, skateboards, and Razor-style scooters (bikes-€5/hour, €10/ half-day, €15/day, leave ID as deposit, open daily, 49 Quai des Etats-Unis—see map on page 60, tel. 04 93 62 99 05). The **Vélo Bleu** bike-sharing program has affordable bikes docked at many stations in the city for short-term use, but the French-only website makes it difficult for most travelers (www.velobleu.org).

Car Rental: Renting a car is easiest at Nice's airport, which has offices for all the major companies. Most companies are also represented at Nice's train station and near the southwest side of Albert I Park.

Lignes d'Azur Bus Tickets: Useful information offices are at 17 Rue Thiers (kitty-corner from the train station, information only), at 1 Rue d'Italie (sells tickets and passes), and at 4 Boulevard Jean Jaurès (the main office where you can buy tickets and passes). Office hours vary (generally Mon-Fri 9:00-18:00 or 19:00, Sat until 15:00, closed Sun). Ask for their helpful "Passenger Guide" with information on buses to all Riviera destinations in English.

English Radio: Tune in to Riviera-Radio at FM 106.5.

Views: For panoramic views, climb Castle Hill (see "Sights in Nice," later) or take a one-hour boat trip (see "Tours in Nice," later).

Beach Tips: To make life tolerable on the rocks, swimmers should buy a pair of the cheap plastic beach shoes sold at many shops. **Go Sport** at #13 on Place Masséna is a good bet (open daily, see map on page 60). Locals don't swim in July and August, as the warming sea brings swarms of stinging jellyfish. Ask before you dip.

GETTING AROUND NICE
By Public Transportation

Although you can walk to most attractions, smart travelers make good use of the buses and trams within Nice. For information on getting around the Riviera from Nice, see "Nice Connections" at the end of this chapter.

Tickets: Buses and trams are covered by the same €1.50 single-ride ticket, or you can pay €10 for a 10-ride ticket that can be shared (each use good for 74 minutes in one direction, including transfers between bus and tram). The €5 all-day pass is valid on city buses and trams, as well as buses to some nearby destinations (but not airport buses). You must validate your ticket in the machine on every trip—imitate how the locals do it. Buy single tickets from the bus driver or from the ticket machines on tram platforms (coins only—press the green button once to validate choice and twice at the end to get your ticket). Passes and 10-ride tickets are also available from machines at tram stops and from two Lignes d'Azur offices (see "Helpful Hints," above), but not from drivers. Info: www.lignesdazur.com.

Buses: The bus is handy for reaching the Chagall and Matisse museums and the Russian Cathedral (for specifics, see museum listings under "Sights in Nice"). Route diagrams in the buses identify each stop.

Trams: Nice has a modern and efficient L-shaped tram line

(T-1) that runs to the train station and a new line (T-2) that should connect the city center to the airport in late 2019 (http://tramway. nice.fr). Trams to the train station run every few minutes along Avenue Jean Médecin and Boulevard Jean Jaurès, and connect the main train station with Place Masséna and Vieux Nice (Opéra stop), the port (Place Garibaldi stop), and buses east along the coast (Vauban stop). These trams also stop near the Chemins de Fer de Provence train station (Libération stop)—the departure point for the scenic narrow-gauge rail journey.

Boarding the tram in the direction of Hôpital Pasteur takes you toward the beach and Vieux Nice (direction: Henri Sappia goes the other way). The new T-2 tramway goes from the airport through the city center to Nice's Port Lympia, paralleling the Promenade des Anglais a few blocks inland.

By Taxi or Uber

While pricey, **cabs** are useful for getting to Nice's less-central sights (figure €8 for shortest ride, €15 from Promenade des Anglais to the Chagall Museum). Cabbies normally pick up only at taxi stands *(tête de station),* or you can call 04 93 13 78 78. **Uber** works here like it does at home (including your US app and account), though there are fewer cars here, and the price is not much cheaper than a taxi. Still, drivers are often nicer and more flexible, and you usually get a car without much delay.

Tours in Nice

ON WHEELS
Hop-On, Hop-Off Bus
Le Grand Tour Bus provides a useful 14-stop, hop-on, hop-off service on an open-deck bus with good headphone commentary. The route includes the Promenade des Anglais, the old port, Cap de Nice, and the Chagall and Matisse museums. From April to October, it also runs to Villefranche-sur-Mer (1-day pass-€23, 2-day pass-€26, buy tickets on bus, 2/hour, daily 10:00-19:00, 1.75-hour loop with Villefranche-sur-Mer, main stop near where Promenade des Anglais and Quai des Etats-Unis meet—across from the Albert I Park, tel. 04 92 29 17 00, www.nice.opentour.com). While it's not the best way to get to the Chagall and Matisse museums, this bus is a good value if you're looking for a city overview and want to also visit these museums or spend time in Villefranche-sur-Mer (best seats are up top on the left as you face forward).

NICE

Nice at a Glance

▲▲▲**Promenade des Anglais** Nice's four-mile sun-struck seafront promenade. See page 38.

▲▲▲**Chagall Museum** The world's largest collection of Marc Chagall's work, popular even with people who don't like modern art. **Hours:** Wed-Mon 10:00-18:00, Nov-April until 17:00, closed Tue year-round. See page 39.

▲▲**Vieux Nice** Charming old city offering enjoyable atmosphere and a look at Nice's French-Italian cultural blend. See page 31.

▲**Matisse Museum** Modest collection of Henri Matisse's paintings, sketches, and paper cutouts. **Hours:** Wed-Mon 10:00-18:00, mid-Oct-mid-June from 11:00, closed Tue year-round. See page 47.

▲**Russian Cathedral** Finest Orthodox church outside Russia. **Hours:** Daily 9:30-17:30. See page 52.

▲**Castle Hill** Site of an ancient fort boasting great views. **Hours:** Park closes at 20:00 in summer, earlier off-season. See page 54.

Modern and Contemporary Art Museum Enjoyable collection from the 1960s and '70s, usually including Warhol and Lichtenstein. **Hours:** Tue-Sun 10:00-18:00, closed Mon. See page 51.

NICE

Tourist Train

For €10, you can spend 45 minutes on the tourist train tooting along the promenade, through the old city, and up to Castle Hill (2/hour, daily 10:00-18:00 or 19:00, recorded English commentary, meet train at the Monument du Centenaire statue at Albert I Park, across from the Promenade des Anglais, tel. 02 99 88 47 07).

Bike Tour

Tina Balter at **Lifesparkz Bike Tours** offers well-designed, customized bike tours for individuals or small groups of all abilities (mobile 06 40 52 94 39, www.lifesparkz.net).

BY BOAT

▲Trans Côte d'Azur Cruise

To see Nice from the water, hop on this one-hour tour run by Trans Côte d'Azur. You'll cruise in a comfortable yacht-size vessel to Cap

Ferrat and past Villefranche-sur-Mer, then return to Nice with a final lap along Promenade des Anglais.

Guides enjoy pointing out mansions owned by famous people, including Elton John and Sean Connery (€18; covered by French Riviera Pass—see page 6; April-Oct Tue-Sun 2/day, usually at 11:00 and 15:00, no boats Mon or during off-season; verify schedule, arrive 30 minutes early to get best seats). The boats leave from Nice's port, Bassin des Amiraux, just below Castle Hill—look for the ticket booth *(billeterie)* on Quai de Lunel. The same company also runs boats to Monaco and St-Tropez (see "Nice Connections," at the end of this chapter).

ON FOOT
Local Guides and Walking Tours
If interested in hiring a local guide for Nice and other regional destinations, see page 12 for suggestions.

The TI on Promenade des Anglais organizes weekly walking tours of Vieux Nice in French and English (€12, Sat morning at 9:30, 2.5 hours, reservations necessary, departs from TI, tel. 08 92 70 74 07).

Food Tours and Cooking Classes
Charming Canadian Francophile **Rosa Jackson**, a food journalist, Cordon Bleu-trained cook, and longtime resident of France, runs a cooking school—Les Petits Farcis—and offers a good food-market tour in Vieux Nice for small groups (€80-120/person based on group size). She also teaches cooking classes that include a morning shopping trip to the market on Cours Saleya and an afternoon cooking session for €195/person, and a pastry course for €80/person (12 Rue Saint Joseph, mobile 06 81 67 41 22, www.petitsfarcis. com).

A Taste of Nice Food Tours runs daily scratch-and-taste tours in Vieux Nice that combine cultural history with today's food scene. You'll stop for 10 different tastings of classic Niçois products. Tours meet daily except Monday at 10:00 on Quai des Etats-Unis at the Opéra Plage (€70/4 hours, tel. 09 86 65 75 17, www.atasteofnice. com, booking@atasteofnice.com).

Walks in Nice

These two self-guided walks take you down an iconic seaside promenade ("Promenade des Anglais Walk") and through the colorful old town blending French and Italian cultures ("Vieux Nice Walk").

PROMENADE DES ANGLAIS WALK

Welcome to the Riviera. There's something for everyone along this four-mile-long promenade, worth ▲▲▲. Stroll like the belle époque English aristocrats for whom the promenade was paved. Watch Europeans at play, admire the azure Mediterranean, anchor yourself on a blue seat, and prop your feet up on the made-to-order guardrail. Later, you can come back to join the evening parade of tans along the promenade.

The broad sidewalks of the Promenade des Anglais ("Walkway of the English") were financed by upper-crust English tour-

ists who wanted a clean and comfortable place to stroll and admire the view. The Brits originally came to Nice seeking relief from tuberculosis; both the warm climate and the salt air helped ease their suffering. It was an era when tanned bodies were frowned upon (aristocrats didn't want to resemble lower-class laborers who had to work outside). Most visitors wouldn't dare swim in the Mediterranean for another hundred years.

Length of This Walk: Allow one hour at a promenade pace for this leisurely, level walk. It's a straight one-mile line along this much-strolled beachfront, beginning near the landmark Hôtel Negresco and ending at the elevator to Castle Hill.

When to Go: While this walk is enjoyable at any time, the first half makes a great stroll before or after breakfast or dinner (meals served at some beach cafés). If you're doing the entire walk to Castle Hill, try to time it so you wind up on top of the hill at sunset.

Biking the Promenade: See page 38 for tips on cycling along the seafront.

○ Self-Guided Walk

• *Start at the pink-domed...*

❶ Hôtel Negresco

Built in 1913, Nice's finest hotel is also a historic monument, offering up the city's most expensive beds and a museum-like interior.

If you wonder why such a grand hotel has such an understated entry, it's because today's front door was originally

NICE

Promenade des Anglais Walk

1. Hôtel Negresco
2. Villa Masséna
3. Bay of Angels
4. Palais de la Méditerranée
5. Albert I Park
6. Steel Girders Sculpture
7. Metal Winch

the back door. In the 19th century, elegant people avoided the sun, and any posh hotel that cared about its clientele would design its entry on the shady north side. If you walk around to today's "back" you'll see a grand but unused front door.

The hotel is technically off-limits if you're not a guest, but if you're decently dressed and explain to the doorman that you'd like to get a drink at Negresco's classy-cozy Le Relais bar (see later), you'll be allowed past the registration desk. You can also explain that you want to shop at their store, which also might get you in—*bonne chance.*

If you get in, you can't miss a huge ballroom, the **Salon Royal.** The chandelier hanging from its dome is made of 16,000 pieces of crystal. It was built in France for the Russian czar's Moscow palace...but thanks to the Bolshevik Revolution in 1917, he couldn't take delivery. Bronze portrait busts of Czar Alexander III and his wife, Maria Feodorovna—who returned to her native Denmark after the Revolution—are to the right, facing the shops. Circle the interior of the ballroom and admire the soft light from the glass dome that Gustave Eiffel designed two decades after his more famous tower in Paris, then wander the perimeter to enjoy both historic and modern art. Fine portraits include Emperor Napoleon III and wife Empress Eugénie (who acquired Nice for France from Italy in 1860).

Touring the outer hall that rings the ballroom counter-clock-

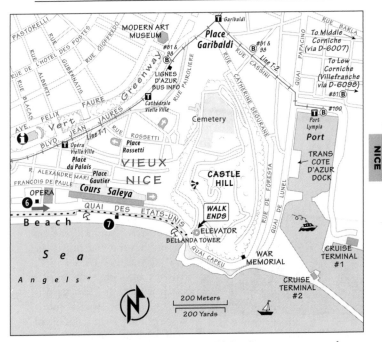

wise, you'll first pass **Le Relais Bar.** If the door is open, wander up the marble steps for a look into the wood-paneled interior (from 11:30 in high season, from 14:30 off-season). Next, nip into the toilets for either an early 20th-century powder room or a Battle of Waterloo experience. The chairs with the high, scooped backs were typical of the age (cones of silence for an afternoon nap sitting up). Further along, the hotel's **Chantecler** restaurant is one of the Riviera's best (allow €100 per person before drinks).

Over 6,000 works of art decorate the hotel, as art is a passion of the hotel's owner, Jeanne Augier. She's quite elderly now, lives up in the cupola, and has willed the Negresco to organizations that care for orphans and stray animals. Find the portrait of her as you leave the ballroom area on the right.

Peek into the **Salon Versailles** to the right of entry lobby as you leave, with a grand fireplace and France's Sun King, Louis XIV, on the wall (English descriptions explain the room).

• *Across the street from the Hôtel Negresco (to the east) is...*

❷ Villa Masséna

When Nice became part of France, France invested heavily in what it expected to be the country's new high society retreat—an elite resort akin to Russia's Sochi. This fine palace was built for Jean-Andre Masséna, a military hero of the Napoleonic age. Take a moment to stroll around the lovely garden. Immediately on your right, find a memorial to the 86 people who died in the 2016 terrorist attack on the Promenade des Anglais, with pictures, stuffed animals, and names engraved in granite (garden is free, open daily 10:00-18:00). The Masséna Museum inside the villa (described later in "Sights in Nice") offers an interesting look at belle-époque Nice.

• *From Villa Masséna, head for the beach and begin your Promenade des Anglais stroll. But first, grab a blue chair and gaze out to the...*

❸ Bay of Angels (Baie des Anges)

Face the water. The body of Nice's patron saint, Réparate, was supposedly escorted into this bay by angels in the fourth centu-

ry. To your right is where you might have been escorted into France—Nice's airport, built on a massive landfill. The tip of land beyond the runway is Cap d'Antibes. Until 1860, Antibes and Nice were in different countries—Antibes was French, but Nice was a protectorate of the Italian kingdom of Savoy-Piedmont, a.k.a. the Kingdom of Sardinia. During that period, the Var River—just west of Nice—was the geographic border between these two peoples (and to this day the river functions as a kind of cultural border). In 1850, the people here spoke Italian or Nissart (a local dialect) and ate pasta. As the story goes, the region was given a choice: Join newly united Italy or join France, which was enjoying prosperous times under the rule of Napoleon III. The majority voted in 1860 to go French...and *voilà!*

The lower green hill to your left is Castle Hill (where this walk ends). Farther left lie Villefranche-sur-Mer and Cap Ferrat (marked by the tower at land's end, and home to lots of millionaires), then Monaco (which you can't see, with more millionaires), then Italy. Behind you are the foothills of the Alps, which trap threatening clouds, ensuring that the Côte d'Azur enjoys sunshine more than 300 days each year. While 350,000 people live in Nice, pollution is carefully treated—the water is routinely tested and is very clean. But with climate change, the warmer water is attracting jellyfish in the summer, making swimming a stinging memory.

• *With the sea on your right, begin strolling.*

The Promenade

This area was the favorite haunt of 19th-century British tourists, who wanted a place to stroll in their finery while admiring the sea views (locals called it "Little London"). Before the promenade was built, they had to venture into Vieux Nice and climb to the two-

story gallery walkway that lines the southern edge of the Cours Saleya (you'll see it on the "Vieux Nice Walk"). When first built, this promenade was a dusty path about six feet wide and about 10 blocks long. It's been widened and lengthened over the years to keep up with tourist demand, including increased bicycle use. As you walk, be careful to avoid the bike lane.

NICE

Nearby sit two fine belle-époque establishments: the West End and Westminster hotels, both boasting English names to help those original guests feel at home. (The West End is now part of the Best Western group...to help American guests feel at home.) These hotels symbolize Nice's arrival as a tourist mecca in the 19th century, when the combination of leisure time and a stable economy allowed visitors to find the sun even in winter.

Find the easel showing a painting of La Jetée Promenade—Nice's elegant pier and first casino, built in 1883. Even a hundred years ago, there was sufficient tourism in Nice to justify constructing a palatial building to house this leisure activity imported from Venice. La Jetée Promenade stood east of those white-covered pilings just offshore, until the Germans dismantled it during World War II to salvage its copper and iron. When La Jetée was thriving, it took gamblers two full days to get to the Riviera by train from Paris. The painting shows what an event strolling the Promenade was—like going to the opera, it was all about dressing up, being seen, and looking good.

Although La Jetée Promenade is gone, you can still see the striking 1927 Art Nouveau facade of the ❹ **Palais de la Méditerranée,** once a magnificent complex housing a casino, luxury hotel, and theater. It became one of the most famous destinations in all of Europe until it was destroyed in the 1980s to make room for a new hotel (the Hyatt Regency). The facade of the grand, old building was spared the wrecking ball, but the classy interior was lost forever.

The modern Casino Ruhl (with the most detested facade on the strip) disfigures the next block. In the spirit of modern efficiency, a lovely old hotel that resembled the Negresco was destroyed in the 1980s to make room for this...thing.

Despite the lack of sand, the pebble beaches here are still a popular draw, and every year tons of rocks are trucked in to shore them up. France has a strong ethic of public access when it comes to its beaches, including a 1980 law guaranteeing free public access to beaches like these. All along the Riviera you'll find public beaches (and public showers).

You can go local and rent gear—about €15 for a *chaise longue* (long chair) and a *transat* (mattress), €5 for an umbrella, and €5 for a towel. You'll also pass several beach restaurants. Some of these eateries serve breakfast, all serve lunch, some do dinner, and a few have beachy bars...tailor-made for a break from this walk.

❺ **Albert I Park** is named after the Belgian king who defied a German ultimatum at the beginning of World War I. While the English came first, the Belgians and Russians were also big fans of 19th-century Nice. That tall statue at the edge of the park commemorates the 100-year anniversary of Nice's union with France. The happy statue features two beloved women embracing the idea of union (Marianne—Ms. Liberty, Equality, and Brotherhood, and the symbol of the Republic of France—and Catherine Ségurane, a 16th-century heroine who helped Nice against the Saracen pirates).

The park is part of a long, winding greenbelt called the Promenade du Paillon. The Paillon River flows under the park on its way to the sea. If it's been raining in the hills, you'll see the river flow into the sea on the beach opposite the statue. This is the historical divide between Vieux Nice and the new town. Before the river was covered, locals would do their laundry along its banks.

Continuing along the promenade you'll soon enter the **Quai des Etats-Unis** ("Quay of the United States"). This name was given as a tip-of-the-cap to the Americans for finally entering World War I in 1917. The big, blue chair statue celebrates the inviting symbol of this venerable walk and kicks off the best stretch of beach—quieter and with less traffic. Check out the laid-back couches at the **Plage Beau Rivage** lounge and consider a beachfront drink. The lovely hotel (not yet destroyed) that borders the beach was Henri Matisse's favorite when he first visited Nice. He loved it so much that he painted pictures of his hotel room at different times of day, creating masterpieces that are among his most recognized paintings.

Those tall, rusted ❻ **steel girders** reaching for the sky were erected in 2010 to celebrate the 150th anniversary of Nice's union with France. (The seven beams represent the seven valleys of the Nice region.) Done by the same artist who created the popular Arc of the Riviera sculpture in the parkway near Place Masséna, this "art" justifiably infuriates many locals as an ugly waste of money. But I know how to make it easier to appreciate the erection every local loves to hate: Stand directly under it, look straight up, and spin 720 degrees. Then look across the way to marvel at the 18th-century facades that line the Esplanade Georges Pompidou. Find the one that is entirely fake-painted on a flat stucco surface. Then, look down and notice the buried uplighting—a French forte. And then, give it another 720 degrees of spin and try to walk on.

At the next palm tree, some will enjoy looking left (at the impressive back side of Apollo, a couple of blocks away), while others head to the right for a view of the beach action. Topless bathing is now out of fashion. Locals say that the awareness of skin cancer and the proliferation of North African and tourist lookie-loos have made it less appealing. Some say the only people still bathing topless are older ladies who remember fondly the liberation of 1968... and tourists.

A block ahead on the left, the elegant back side of Nice's opera house faces the sea. The tiny bronze Statue of Liberty (right in front of you as you face the opera) reminds all that this stretch of seafront promenade is named for the USA.

The top level of the long, low galleries on the left was British tourists' preferred place for a stroll before the Promenade des Anglais was built. The ground floor served the city's fishermen, and the smell alone was motivation enough to find a new place to promenade. Behind the galleries bustles the **Cours Saleya Market**—long the heart and soul of Vieux Nice, with handy WCs under its arches.

Farther along, on the far-right side of the Quai des Etats-Unis (opposite Le Camboda restaurant), find the three-foot-tall white ❼ **metal winch** at the ramp to the beach. Long before tourism—and long before Nice dredged its harbor—hard-working fishing boats rather than vacationing tourists lined the beach. The boats were hauled in through the surf by winches like this and tied to the iron rings on either side.

• *You could end your walk here, but the view from the point just past the Hôtel la Pérouse is wonderful. Either way, you have several great options: Continue 10 minutes along the coast to the port, around the foot of Castle Hill (fine views of the entire promenade and a monumental war memorial carved into the hillside); hike or ride the elevator up to Castle Hill (catch the elevator next to Hôtel Suisse; see listing for Castle Hill in "Sights in Nice," later) head into Vieux Nice (you can follow my "Vieux Nice Walk"); or grab a blue chair or piece of beach and just be on vacation—Riviera style.*

VIEUX NICE WALK

This self-guided walk through Nice's old town, known as Vieux Nice and worth ▲▲, gives you a helpful introduction to the city's bicultural heritage and its most interesting neighborhoods.

Length of This Walk: Allow about one hour at a leisurely pace for this level walk from Place Masséna to Place Rossetti.

When to Go: It's best done in the morning (while the outdoor market thrives—consider coffee or breakfast at a café along the Cours Saleya), and preferably not on a Sunday, when things are

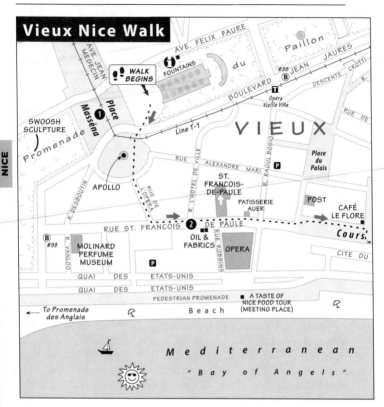

Vieux Nice Walk

quiet. This ramble is also a joy at night, when fountains glow and pedestrians control the streets.

❍ Self-Guided Walk

• *Start where Avenue Jean Médecin hits the people-friendly Place Mas-séna—the successful result of a long, expensive city upgrade and the new center of Nice.*

❶ Place Masséna

The grand Place Masséna is Nice's drawing room, where old meets new, and where the tramway bends between Vieux Nice and the train station. The square's black-and-white pavement feels like an elegant outdoor ballroom, with the sleek tram waltzing across its dance floor. While once congested with cars, the square today is crossed only by these

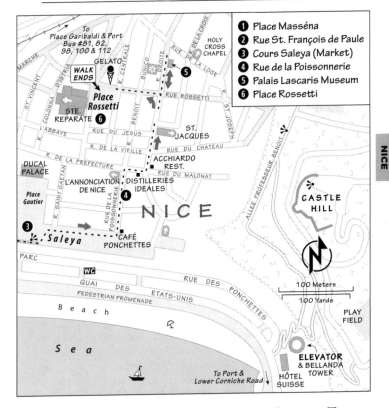

1 Place Masséna
2 Rue St. François de Paule
3 Cours Saleya (Market)
4 Rue de la Poissonnerie
5 Palais Lascaris Museum
6 Place Rossetti

trams, which swoosh silently by every couple of minutes. The men on pedestals sitting high above are modern-art additions that arrived with the tram. For a mood-altering experience, return after dark and watch the illuminated figures float yoga-like above. Place Masséna is at its sophisticated best after the sun goes down.

This vast square dates from 1848 and pays tribute to Jean-André Masséna, a French military leader during the Revolutionary and Napoleonic wars. Not just another pretty face in a long lineup of French military heroes, he's considered among the greatest commanders in history—anywhere, anytime. Napoleon called him "the greatest name of my military Empire." No wonder this city is proud of him.

Standing on the square with your back to the fountains, start a clockwise spin tour: Underneath, Nice's historic river, the Paillon, flows to the sea. For centuries this river was Nice's natural defense to the north and west (the sea protected the south, and Castle Hill defended the east). A fortified wall once ran along the river's length to the sea. It's been covered since the late 1800s.

The **modern swoosh sculpture** at palm-tree height in the

parkway is meant to represent the "curve of the French Riviera"—the arc of the bay. To the right stretches modern Nice, born with the arrival of tourism in the 1800s. **Avenue Jean Médecin,** Nice's Champs-Elysées, cuts from here through the new town to the train station. Looking up the avenue, you'll see the tracks, the freeway, and the Alps beyond. Once crammed with cars, buses, and delivery vehicles tangling with pedestrians, Avenue Jean Médecin was turned into a walking and cycling nirvana in 2007. I used to avoid this street. Now I can't get enough of it. Businesses along it flourish in the welcoming environment of generous sidewalks and no traffic.

Appreciate the city's Italian heritage—it feels more like Venice than Paris. The portico flanking Avenue Jean Médecin is Italian, not French. The rich colors of the buildings reflect the taste of previous Italian rulers.

Now turn to the fountains and look east to see Nice's ongoing effort to "put the human element into the heart of the town." An ugly concrete bus station and parking structures were demolished not long ago, and the **Promenade du Paillon** was created to fill the space. Today, this pedestrian-friendly parkway extends from the sea to the Museum of Modern Art—a modern-day Promenade des Anglais. Forming a key spine for biking, walking, and kids at play, the Promenade du Paillon is a delight any time of day. Notice the fountain—its surprise geysers delight children by day and its fine lighting enhances romance at night. Past the fountain stands a bronze statue of the square's namesake, Masséna. The hills beyond separate Nice from Villefranche-sur-Mer.

To the right of the Promenade du Paillon lies **Vieux Nice,** with its jumbled and colorful facades below Castle Hill. Looking closer and farther to the right, the **statue of Apollo** has horsy hair and holds a beach towel (in the fountain) as if to say, "It's beer o'clock, let's go."

• *Walk past Apollo into Vieux Nice (careful of those trams). A block down Rue de l'Opéra you'll see a grouping of rusted girders (described earlier). Turn left onto...*

❷ Rue St. François de Paule

This colorful street leads into the heart of Vieux Nice. On the left is the **Hôtel de Ville** (City Hall). Peer into the **Alziari olive oil shop** (at #14 on the right). Dating from 1868, the shop produces top-quality stone-ground olive oil. The proud and charming owner, Gilles Piot, claims that stone wheels create less acidity, since grinding with metal creates heat (see photo in back over the door). Locals fill their own containers from the huge vats.

A few awnings down, **La Couqueto** is a colorful shop filled with Provençal fabrics and crafts, including lovely folk characters *(santons).* Walk in for a lavender smell sensation—is madame working the sewing machine upstairs? The *boulangerie* next door is ideal for a cheap lunch and has good outdoor seating.

Next door is Nice's grand **opera house,** built by a student of Charles Garnier (architect of Monte Carlo's casino and opera house). Imagine this opulent jewel back in the 19th century, buried deep in Vieux Nice. With all the fancy big-city folks wintering here, this rough-edged town needed some high-class entertainment. And Victorians needed an alternative to those "devilish" gambling houses. (Queen Victoria, so disgusted by casinos, would actually close the drapes on her train window when passing Monte Carlo.) The four statues on top represent theater, dance, music, and party poopers.

Across the street, **Pâtisserie Auer**'s grand old storefront would love to tempt you with chocolates and candied fruits. It's changed little over the centuries. The writing on the window says, "Since 1820 from father to son." Wander in for a whiff of chocolate and a dazzling interior. The twin gold royal shields on the back mirrors remind shoppers that Queen Victoria indulged her sweet tooth here.

• *Continue on, sifting your way through a cluttered block of tacky souvenir shops to the big market square.*

❸ Cours Saleya

Named for its broad exposure to the sun *(soleil),* Cours Saleya (koor sah-lay-yuh)—a commotion of color, sights, smells, and people—

has been Nice's main market square since the Middle Ages (flower market all day Tue-Sun, produce market Tue-Sun until 13:00, antiques on Mon). While you're greeted by the ugly mouth of an underground parking lot, much of this square itself was a parking lot until 1980, when the mayor of Nice had this solution dug. If you're early enough for coffee, pause for a break at **Café le Flore**'s outdoor tables in the heart of the market (a block up on the left).

The first section is devoted to the Riviera's largest **flower market.** In operation since the 19th century, this market offers plants and flowers that grow effortlessly and ubiquitously in this climate, including the local favorites: carnations, roses, and jasmine. Locals know the season by what's on sale (mimosas in February, violets in March, and so on). Until the recent rise in imported flowers, this region supplied all of France with flowers. Still, fresh flowers are cheap here, the best value in this expensive city. The Riviera's three big industries are tourism, flowers, and perfume (made from these flowers...take a whiff).

The boisterous **produce section** trumpets the season with mushrooms, strawberries, white asparagus, zucchini flowers, and more—whatever's fresh gets top billing. What's in season today?

The market opens up at Place Pierre Gautier. It's also called Plassa dou Gouvernou—you'll see bilingual street signs here that include the old Niçois language, an Italian dialect. This is where farmers set up stalls to sell their produce and herbs directly. For a great **rooftop view** over the market, climb the steps by Le Grand Bleu restaurant (you may have to step past a few trash sacks, but it's allowed). Check out the top level of the two-story buildings nearby; this is where the Brits strolled before their exclusive Promenade des Anglais was built many blocks to the west.

Look up to the **hill** that dominates to the east. The city of Nice was first settled there by Greeks (circa 400 BC). In the Middle Ages, a massive castle stood there with soldiers at the ready. Over time, the city sprawled down to where you are now. With the river guarding one side (running under today's Promenade du Paillon parkway) and the sea the other, this mountain fortress seemed strong—until Louis XIV leveled it in 1706. Nice's medieval seawall ran along the line of two-story buildings where you're standing.

Now, look across Place Pierre Gautier to the large "palace." The **Ducal Palace** was where the kings of Sardinia, the city's Italian rulers until 1860, resided when in Nice. (For centuries, Nice was under the rule of the Italian capital of Turin.) Today, the palace is the local police headquarters. The land upon which the Cours Saleya sits was once the duke's gardens and didn't become a market until Nice's union with France.

• *Continue down Cours Saleya. The faded golden building that seals the end of the square is where Henri Matisse spent 17 years. I imagine he was inspired by his view. The Café les Ponchettes is perfectly positioned for you to enjoy the view too if you want a coffee break. At the café, turn onto...*

❹ Rue de la Poissonnerie

Look up at the first floor of the first building on your right. **Adam and Eve** are squaring off, each holding a zucchini-like gourd. This scene represents the annual rapprochement in Nice to make up for the sins of a too-much-fun Carnival (Mardi Gras, the pre-Lenten festival). Residents of Nice have partied hard during Carnival for more than 700 years. The **spice shop** below offers a fine selection of regional herbs.

As you continue down the street, look above the doors. The iron grills (like the one above #6) allow air to enter the buildings but keep out uninvited guests. You'll see lots of these open grills in Vieux Nice. They were part of a clever system that sucked in cool air from the sea, circulating it through homes and blowing it out through vents in the roof.

A few steps ahead, check out the small **Baroque church** (Notre-Dame de l'Annonciation, closed 12:00-14:30) dedicated to Ste. Rita, the patron saint of desperate causes and desperate people (see display in window). She holds a special place in locals' hearts, making this the most popular church in Nice. Drop in for a peek at the dazzling Baroque decor. The first chapel on the right is dedicated to St. Erasmus, protector of mariners.

• *Turn right on the next street, where you'll pass one of Vieux Nice's most happening bars (the recommended Distilleries Ideales), with a swash-buckling interior that buzzes until the wee hours. Pause at the next corner and study the classic Vieux Nice scene in all directions. Now turn left on Rue Droite and enter an area that feels like Little Naples.*

Rue Droite

In the Middle Ages, this straight, skinny street provided the most direct route from river to sea within the old walled town. Pass the recommended restaurant Acchiardo. Notice stepped lanes leading uphill to the castle. Pop into the Jesuit **Eglise St-Jacques** church (also called Eglise du Gésu) for an explosion of Baroque exuberance hidden behind that plain facade. At the wooden pulpit, notice the crucifix held by a sculpted arm. This clever support allowed the priest to focus on his sermon while reminding the congregation that Christ died for their sins.

We're turning left onto Rue Rossetti...but if you continued another block along Rue Droite you'd find the ❺ **Palais Lascaris** (c. 1647), home of one of Nice's most prestigious families. Today it's a museum and worth a quick look (peek in the entry for free or take a tour, covered by Nice museum €10 combo-ticket, Wed-Mon 10:00-18:00, from 11:00 off-season, closed Tue year-round). Inside you'll find a collection of antique musical instruments—harps, guitars, violins, and violas (good English explanations)—along with elaborate tapestries and a few well-furnished rooms. The palace has four levels—but only two are open to the public: The ground floor was used for storage, the first floor was devoted to reception rooms (and musical events), the owners lived a floor above that, and the servants lived at the top. Look up and make faces back at the guys under the balconies.

• *Shortly after making a left on Rue Rossetti, you'll cross Rue Benoit Bunico.*

In the 18th century, this street served as a **ghetto** for Nice's Jews. At sunset, gates would seal the street at either end, locking people in until daylight. To identify Jews as non-Christians, the

NICE

men were required to wear yellow stars and the women to wear yellow scarves. Wander a few steps up the street to find the white columns and archway across from #19 that mark what was the synagogue until 1848, when revolution ended the notion of ghettos in France.

• *Continue down Rue Rossetti to...*

❻ Place Rossetti

The most Italian of Nice's piazzas, Place Rossetti comes alive after dark—in part because of the **Fenocchio gelato shop,** popular for its many innovative flavors.

Check out the **Cathedral of St. Réparate**—an unassuming building for a big-city cathedral. It was relocated here in the 1500s, when Castle Hill was temporarily converted to military use. The name comes from Nice's patron saint, a teenage virgin named Réparate, whose martyred body floated to Nice in the fourth century accompanied by angels (remember the Bay of Angels?). The interior of the cathedral gushes Baroque, a response to the challenge of the Protestant Reformation in the 16th century. With the Catholic Church's Counter-Reformation, the theatrical energy of churches was cranked up with re-energized, high-powered saints and eye-popping decor.

• *This is the end of our walk. From here you can hike up Castle Hill (from Place Rossetti, take Rue Rossetti uphill; see Castle Hill listing under "Sights in Nice"). Or you can have an ice cream and browse the colorful lanes of Vieux Nice...or grab Apollo and hit the beach.*

Sights in Nice

▲▲▲PROMENADE DES ANGLAIS
Walking or Biking the Promenade

Enjoying Nice's four-mile seafront promenade on foot or by bike is an essential Riviera experience. Since the days when wealthy English tourists filled the grand seaside hotels, this stretch has been *the* place to be in Nice. (For a self-guided **walk,** see my "Promenade des Anglais Walk," earlier.)

To rev up the pace of your promenade saunter, rent a **bike** and glide along the coast in either or both directions (about 30 minutes each way; for rental info see "Helpful Hints," earlier). Both of the following paths start along Promenade des Anglais.

To the West: The path stops just before the airport at perhaps the most scenic *boules* courts in France. Pause here to watch the old-timers while away the afternoon tossing shiny metal balls.

To the East: The path rounds the hill—passing a scenic promontory and the town's memorial to both world wars—to the harbor of Nice, and gives you a chance to survey some fancy yachts. Walk or pedal around the harbor and follow the coast past the Corsica ferry terminal (you'll need to carry your bike up a flight of steps). From there the path leads to an appealing tree-lined residential district.

NICE

Beach
Beaches are free to the public (by law). Settle in on the smooth rocks, or get more comfortable by renting a lounge chair or mattress (*chaise longue* or *transat*-about €15, umbrella-€5, towel-€5). Have lunch in your bathing suit (€14 salads and pizzas in bars and

restaurants all along the beach). I enjoy stopping here first thing in the morning (before the crowds hit) for a peaceful breakfast or café au lait on the Mediterranean. *Plage Publique* signs (with English translations) explain the 10 beach no-nos.

MUSEUMS
A combo-ticket covers all of Nice's museums except the Chagall Museum (see details under "Helpful Hints," earlier). The Chagall Museum requires a separate admission (and is well worth it).

The first two museums (Chagall and Matisse) are a long walk northeast of Nice's city center. Because they're in the same direction and served by the same bus line (see "Getting There," next page), try to visit them on the same trip. From Place Masséna, the Chagall Museum is a 10-minute bus ride, and the Matisse Museum is a few stops beyond that.

▲▲▲Chagall Museum
(Musée National Marc Chagall)
Even if you don't get modern art, this museum—with the world's largest collection of Marc Chagall's work in captivity—is a delight. For fans of Chagall, it's a can't-miss treat.

After World War II, Chagall returned from the United States to settle first in Vence and later in St-Paul-de-Vence, both not far from Nice. Between 1954 and 1967, he painted a cycle of 17 large murals designed for, and donated to, this museum. These paintings, inspired by the biblical books of Genesis, Exodus, and the

NICE

Song of Songs, make up the "nave," or core, of what Chagall called the "House of Brotherhood." Combining his Russian and Jewish heritage with the Christian message, he hoped this would be a place where people of all faiths could come together and celebrate love.

Cost and Hours: €8, €2 more during frequent special exhibits; Wed-Mon 10:00-18:00, Nov-April until 17:00, closed Tue year-round; ticket includes helpful audioguide (though Chagall would suggest that you explore his art without guidance); must check daypacks, idyllic **$** garden café (salads and *plats*), tel. 04 93 53 87 20, http://en.musees-nationaux-alpesmaritimes.fr.

Getting There: The museum is located on Avenue Docteur Ménard. **Taxis** from the city center cost about €15. **Buses** connect the museum with downtown Nice. From downtown, catch bus #15 (Mon-Sat 6/hour, Sun 3/hour, 10 minutes). Catch the bus from the east end of the Galeries Lafayette department store, near the Masséna tram stop, on Rue Sacha Guitry (see map on page 57). Watch for a *Musée Chagall* sign on the bus shelter where you'll get off (on Boulevard de Cimiez).

You can **walk** from the train station to the museum in 20 minutes. Walk to the station's tram stop, turn left, then make a right on the last street before the overpass—Boulevard Raimbaldi. Follow Boulevard Raimbaldi for several blocks until you see a Lidl grocery store. Turn left on Avenue Raymond Comboul, walk under the freeway, and then follow the signs.

Overview

This small museum consists of six rooms: two rooms (the main hall and Song of Songs room) with the 17 murals, two rooms for special exhibits, an auditorium with stained-glass windows, and a mosaic-lined pond (viewed from inside). It takes about one hour to see the whole thing. In the main hall you'll find the core of the collection (Genesis and Exodus scenes). The adjacent octagonal Song of Songs room houses five more paintings.

At the end of this tour, in the auditorium, you can see a wonderful film about Chagall (52 minutes), which plays at the top of each hour (alternately in French and English—ask about showtimes when you arrive—you may want to see the movie first, then

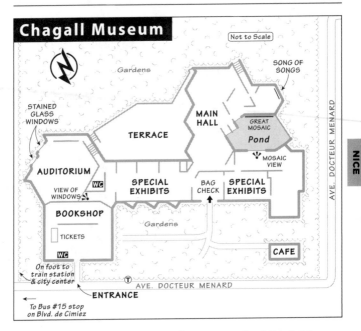

tour the museum; no showings during special exhibits). You can enter the auditorium at any point during the movie and find it worthwhile. Even the French version offers a fascinating look at old clips of the master and a chance to see the creative energy and charisma in his eyes.

◗ Self-Guided Tour

• *Buy your ticket, pass through the garden, and enter the museum at the baggage-check counter. Pick up your included audioguide and step into the main hall.*

Main Hall: Old Testament Scenes

Each painting is a lighter-than-air collage of images that draws from Chagall's Russian folk-village youth, his Jewish heritage, the Bible, and his feeling that he existed somewhere between heaven and earth. He believed that the Bible was a synonym for nature, and that both color and biblical themes were key for understanding God's love for his creation. Chagall's brilliant blues and reds celebrate nature, as do his spiritual and folk themes. Notice the focus on couples. To Chagall, humans loving each other mirrored God's love of creation.

The paintings are described in the order you should see them, going counterclockwise around the room.

Abraham and the Three Angels: In the heat of the day, Abraham looked up and saw three men. He said, "Let a little food and water be brought, so you can be refreshed..." (Genesis 18:1-5)

Abraham refreshes God's angels on this red-hot day and, in return, they promise Abraham a son (in the bubble, at right), thus making him the father of the future Israelite nation.

The Sacrifice of Isaac: Abraham bound his son Isaac and laid him on the altar. Then he took the knife to slay his son. But the angel of the Lord called out to him from heaven, "Abraham!" (Genesis 22:9-11)

Tested by God, Abraham prepares to kill his only son, but the angel stops him in time. Notice that Isaac is posed exactly as Adam is in *The Creation* (described next). Abraham's sacrifice echoes three others: the sacrifice all men must make (Adam, the everyman), the sacrifice of atonement (the goat tied to a tree at left), and even God's sacrifice of his own son (Christ carrying the cross, upper right).

The Creation: God said, "Let us make man in our image, in our likeness..." (Genesis 1:26)

A pure-white angel descends through the blue sky and carries a still-sleeping Adam from radiant red-yellow heaven to earth. Heaven is a whirling dervish of activity, spinning out all the events of future history, from the tablets of the Ten Commandments to the Crucifixion—an overture of many images that we'll see in later paintings. (Though not a Christian, Chagall saw the Crucifixion as a universal symbol of man's suffering.)

Moses Receives the Ten Commandments: The Lord gave him the two tablets of the Law, the tablets of stone inscribed by the finger of God... (Exodus 31:18)

An astonished Moses stretches toward heaven, where God reaches out from a cloud to hand him the Ten Commandments. While Moses tilts one way, Mount Sinai slants the other, leading our eye up to the left, where a golden calf is being worshipped by the wayward Children of Israel. But down to the right, Aaron and the menorah assure us that Moses will set things right. In this radiant final panel, the Jewish tradition—after a long struggle—is finally established.

• *Skip around the corner to...*

Driven from Paradise: So God banished him from the Garden of Eden...and placed cherubim and a flaming sword to guard the way... (Genesis 3:23-24)

An angel drives them out with a fire hose of blue (there's Adam still cradling his flaming-red *coq*), while a sparkling yellow, flower-filled tree stands like a wall preventing them from ever returning. Deep in the green colors, the painting offers us glimpses

Chagall's Style

Chagall uses a deceptively simple, almost childlike style to paint a world that's hidden to the eye—the magical, mystical world below the surface. Here are some of the characteristics of his paintings:

Deep, radiant colors, inspired by Expressionism and Fauvism (an art movement pioneered by Matisse and other French painters).

Personal imagery, particularly from his childhood in Russia—smiling barnyard animals, fiddlers on the roof, flower bouquets, huts, and blissful sweethearts.

A Hasidic Jewish perspective, the idea that God is everywhere, appearing in everyday things like nature, animals, and humdrum activities.

A fragmented Cubist style, multifaceted and multidimensional, a perfect style to mirror the complexity of God's creation.

Overlapping images, like double-exposure photography, with faint imagery that bleeds through, suggesting there's more to life under the surface.

Stained-glass-esque technique of dark, deep, earthy, "potent" colors, and simplified, iconic, symbolic figures.

Gravity-defying compositions, with lovers, animals, and angels twirling blissfully in midair.

Happy (not tragic) mood depicting a world of personal joy, despite the violence and turmoil of world wars and revolution.

Childlike simplicity, drawn with simple, heavy outlines, filled in with Crayola colors that often spill over the lines. Major characters in a scene are bigger than the lesser characters. The grinning barnyard animals, the bright colors, the magical events presented as literal truth...Was Chagall a lightweight? Or a lighter-than-air-weight?

of the future—Eve giving birth (lower-right corner) and the yellow sacrificial goat of atonement (top right).

Paradise: God put him in the Garden of Eden...and said, "You must not eat from the tree of the knowledge of good and evil..." (Genesis 2:15-17)

Paradise is a rich, earth-as-seen-from-space pool of blue, green, and white. On the left, amoebic, still-evolving animals float around Adam (celibately practicing yoga) and Eve (with lusty-red hair). On the right, an angel guards the tempting tree, but Eve

NICE

Marc Chagall (1887-1985)

1887-1910: Russia

Chagall is born in the small town of Vitebsk, Belarus. He's the oldest of nine children in a traditional Russian Hasidic Jewish family. He studies realistic art in his hometown. In St. Petersburg, he is first exposed to the Modernist work of Paul Cézanne and the Fauves.

1910-1914: Paris

A patron finances a four-year stay in Paris. Chagall hobnobs with the avant-garde and learns technique from the Cubists, but he never abandons painting recognizable figures or his own personal fantasies. (Some say his relative poverty forced him to paint over used canvases, which gave him the idea of overlapping images that bleed through. Hmm.)

1914-1922: Russia

Returning to his hometown, Chagall marries Bella Rosenfeld (1915), whose love will inspire him for decades. He paints happy scenes despite the turmoil of wars and the Communist Revolution. Moving to Moscow (1920), he paints his first large-scale works, sets for the New Jewish Theater. These would inspire many of his later large-scale works.

offers an apple and Adam reaches around to sample the forbidden fruit while the snake gawks knowingly.

The Rainbow: God said, "I have set my rainbow in the clouds as a sign of the covenant between me and the earth." (Genesis 9:13)

A flaming angel sets the rainbow in the sky, while Noah rests beneath it and his family offers a sacrifice of thanks. The pure-white rainbow's missing colors are found radiating from the features of the survivors.

Jacob's Ladder: He had a dream in which he saw a ladder resting on the earth with its top reaching to heaven, and the angels of God were ascending and descending on it... (Genesis 28:12)

In the left half, Jacob (Abraham's grandson, in red) slumps asleep and dreams of a ladder between heaven and earth. On the right, a lofty angel with a menorah represents how heaven and earth are bridged by the rituals of the Jewish tradition.

Jacob Wrestles with an Angel: So Jacob wrestled with him till daybreak. Jacob said, "I will not let you go unless you bless me..." (Genesis 32: 24, 26)

Jacob holds on while the angel blesses him with descendants (the Children of Israel) and sends out rays from his hands. On the

1923-1941: France and Palestine

Chagall returns to France. In 1931 he travels to Palestine, where the bright sun and his Jewish roots inspire a series of gouaches (opaque watercolor paintings). These gouaches would later inspire 105 etchings to illustrate the Bible (1931-1952), which would eventually influence the 17 large canvases of biblical scenes in the Chagall Museum (1954-1967).

1941-1947: United States/World War II

Fearing persecution for his Jewish faith, Chagall emigrates to New York, where he spends the war years. The Crucifixion starts to appear in his paintings—not as a Christian symbol, but as a representation of the violence mankind perpetrates on itself. In 1944 his beloved Bella dies, and he stops painting for months.

1947-1985: South of France

After the war, Chagall returns to France, eventually settling in St-Paul-de-Vence. In 1952 he remarries. His new love, Valentina Brodsky, plus the southern sunshine, brings Chagall a revived creativity—he is extremely prolific for the rest of his life. He experiments with new techniques and media—ceramics, sculpture, book illustrations, tapestry, and mosaic. In 1956 he's commissioned for his first stained-glass project. Eventually he does windows for cathedrals in Metz and Reims, and a synagogue in Jerusalem (1960). The Chagall Museum opens in 1973.

right are scenes from Jacob's life, including his son Joseph being stripped of his bright-red coat and sold into slavery by his brothers.

Noah's Ark: Then he sent out a dove to see if the water had receded... (Genesis 8:8)

Adam and Eve's descendants have become so wicked that God destroys the earth with a flood, engulfing the sad crowd on the right. Only righteous Noah (center), his family (lower right), and the animals (including our yellow goat) are spared inside an ark. Here Noah opens the ark's window and sends out a dove to test the waters.

Moses Brings Water from the Rock: The Lord said, "Strike the rock, and water will come out of it for the people to drink..." (Exodus 17:5-6)

In the brown desert, Moses nourishes his thirsty people with water miraculously spouting from a rock. From the (red-yellow) divine source, it rains down actual (blue) water, but also a gush of spiritual yellow light.

Moses and the Burning Bush: The angel of the Lord appeared to him in flames of fire from within a bush... (Exodus 3:2)

Horned Moses—Chagall depicts him according to a medieval

tradition—kneels awestruck before the burning bush, the event that calls him to God's service. On the left, we see Moses after the call, his face radiant, leading the Israelites out of captivity across the Red Sea, while Pharaoh's men drown (lower half of Moses' robe). The Ten Commandments loom ahead.

• *Return to Moses Receives the Ten Commandments, then walk past a window into a room with five red paintings.*

Song of Songs

NICE

Chagall wrote, "I've been fascinated by the Bible ever since my earliest childhood. I have always thought of it as the most extraordinary source of poetic inspiration imaginable. As far as I am concerned, perfection in art and in life has its source in the Bible, and exercises in the mechanics of the merely rational are fruitless. In art as well as in life, anything is possible, provided there is love."

The paintings in this room were inspired by the Old Testament Song of Songs. Chagall cherished verses such as: I sleep, but my heart is awake (5:2). Until the day breaks and the shadows flee, turn, my lover, and be like a gazelle or like a young stag on the rugged hills (2:17). Your stature is like that of the palm, and your breasts like clusters of fruit (7:7). Chagall, who dedicated this room to his wife Valentina (Vava), saw divine love and physical love as a natural mix.

Chagall enjoyed the love of two women in his long life—his first wife, Bella, then Valentina, who gave him a second wind as he was painting these late works. Chagall was one of the few "serious" 20th-century artists to portray unabashed love. Where the Bible uses the metaphor of earthly, physical, sexual love to describe God's love for humans, Chagall uses unearthly colors and a mystical ambience to celebrate human love. These red-toned canvases are hard to interpret literally, but they capture the rosy spirit of a man in love with life.

• *Head back toward the entry and turn left at The Sacrifice of Isaac to find the...*

Pond

The great mosaic (which no longer reflects in the filthy reflecting pond) evokes the prophet Elijah in his chariot of fire (from the Second Book of Kings)—with Chagall's addition of the 12 signs of the zodiac, which he used to symbolize Time.

• *Return to the main hall, veer left, and exit the hall to the right. Pass through the exhibition room with temporary displays. At the end, you'll find the...*

Auditorium

This room, where the Chagall documentary film shows (see "Overview," earlier), is worth a peaceful moment to enjoy three Chagall stained-glass windows depicting the seven days of creation (right to left): the creation of light, elements, and planets (a visual big bang that's four "days" wide); the creation of animals, plants, man and woman, and the ordering of the solar system (two "days" wide, complete with fish and birds still figuring out where they belong); and the day of rest (the narrowest—only one "day" wide, imagine angels singing to the glory of God).

• *Our tour is over. From here, you can return to downtown Nice or head to the Matisse Museum. Taxis usually wait in front of the museum. For the bus back to downtown Nice, turn right out of the museum, then make another right down Boulevard de Cimiez, and ride bus #15 heading downhill. To continue to the Matisse Museum, catch #15 using the uphill stop located across the street, or enjoy a 20-minute walk uphill passing belle-époque villas at every turn.*

To walk to the train station area from the museum (20 minutes), turn right out of the museum grounds and follow the first street to the right (hugging the museum). Drop down ramps and staircases, turn left at the bottom under the freeway and train tracks, then turn right on Boulevard Raimbaldi.

Nice's Other Museums

▲Matisse Museum (Musée Matisse)

This small, underachieving museum fills an old mansion in a park surrounded by scant Roman ruins, and houses a limited sampling of works from the various periods of Henri Matisse's artistic career. The museum offers an introduction to the artist's many styles and materials, both shaped by Mediterranean light and by fellow Côte d'Azur artists Picasso and Renoir.

Cost and Hours: Covered by €10 Nice museum combo-ticket; Wed-Mon 10:00-18:00, mid-Oct-mid-June from 11:00, closed Tue year-round, 164 Avenue des Arènes de Cimiez, tel. 04 93 81 08 08, www.musee-matisse-nice.org.

Getting There: Take a cab (€20 from Promenade des Anglais). Alternatively, hop bus #15, direction: Rimiez, from the east end of Galeries Lafayette (from train station, catch #17, direction: Cimiez Hôpital). Get off at the Arènes-Matisse bus stop (look for the crumbling Roman arena that once held 10,000 spectators), then walk 50 yards into the park to find the pink villa.

Background: Henri Matisse, the master of leaving things out, could suggest a woman's body with a single curvy line—letting the viewer's mind fill in the rest. Ignoring traditional 3-D perspective, he expressed his passion for life through simplified but recogniz-

Henri Matisse (1869-1954)

Here's an outline of Henri Matisse's busy life:

1880s and 1890s: At age 20, Matisse, a budding lawyer, is struck down with appendicitis. Bedridden for a year, he turns to painting as a healing escape from pain and boredom. After recovering, he studies art in Paris and produces dark-colored, realistic still lifes and landscapes. His work is exhibited at the Salons of 1896 and 1897.

1897-1905: Influenced by the Impressionists, he experiments with sunnier scenes and brighter colors. He travels to southern France, including Collioure (on the coast near Spain), and seeks still more light-filled scenes to paint. His experiments are influenced by Vincent van Gogh's bright, surrealistic colors and thick outlines, and by Paul Gauguin's primitive visions of a Tahitian paradise. From Paul Cézanne, he learns how to simplify objects into their basic geometric shapes. He also experiments (like Cézanne) with creating the illusion of 3-D not by traditional means, but by using contrasting colors for the foreground and background.

1905: Back in Paris, Matisse and his colleagues (André Derain and Maurice de Vlaminck) shock the art world with an exhibition of their experimental paintings. The thick outlines, simple forms, flattened perspective, and—most of all—bright, clashing, unrealistic colors seem to be the work of "wild animals" (*fauves*). Fauvism is hot, and Matisse is instantly famous. (Though notorious as a "wild animal," Matisse himself was a gentle, introspective man.)

1906-1910: After just a year, Fauvism is out, and African masks are in. This "primitive" art form inspires Matisse to simplify and distort his figures further, making them less realistic but more expressive.

1910-1917: Matisse creates his masterpiece paintings. Cubism is the rage, pioneered by Matisse's friend and rival for the World's Best Painter award, Pablo Picasso. Matisse dabbles in Cubism,

able scenes in which dark outlines and saturated, bright blocks of color create an overall decorative pattern.

Matisse understood how colors and shapes affect us emotionally. He could create either shocking, clashing works (early Fauvism) or geometrical, balanced, harmonious ones (later cutouts). Whereas other modern artists reveled in purely abstract design, Matisse (almost) always kept the subject matter at least vaguely recognizable. He used unreal colors and distorted lines not just to portray what an object looks like, but to express its inner nature

simplifying forms, emphasizing outline, and muting his colors. But ultimately it proves to be too austere and analytical for his deeply sensory nature. The Cubist style is most evident in his sculpture.

1920s: Burned out from years of intense experimentation, Matisse moves to Nice (spending winters there from 1917, settling permanently in 1921). Luxuriating under the bright sun, he's reborn, and he paints colorful, sensual, highly decorative works. Harem concubines lounging in their sunny, flowery apartments epitomize the lush life.

1930s: A visit to Tahiti inspires more scenes of life as a sunny paradise. Matisse experiments with bolder lines, swirling arabesques, and decorative patterns.

1940s: Duodenal cancer (in 1941) requires Matisse to undergo two operations and confines him to a wheelchair for the rest of his life. Working at an easel becomes a struggle for him, and he largely stops painting in 1941. But as World War II ends, Matisse emerges with renewed energy. Now in his 70s, he explores a new medium: paper cutouts pasted onto a watercolored surface (découpage on gouache-prepared surface). The technique plays to his strengths—the cutouts are essentially blocks of bright color (mostly blue) with a strong outline. Scissors in hand, Matisse says, "I draw straight into the color." (His doctor advises him to wear dark glasses to protect his weak eyes against the bright colors he chooses.) In 1947, Matisse's book *Jazz* is published, featuring the artist's joyful cutouts of simple figures. Like jazz music, the book is a celebration of artistic spontaneity. And like music in general, Matisse's works balance different tones and colors to create a mood.

1947-1951: Matisse's nurse becomes a Dominican nun in Vence. To thank her for her care, he spends his later years designing a chapel there. He oversees every aspect of the Chapel of the Rosary (Chapelle du Rosaire) at Vence, from the stained glass to the altar to the colors of the priest's robe (see page 154). Though Matisse is not a strong Christian, the church exudes his spirit of celebrating life and sums up his work.

1954: Matisse dies.

(even inanimate objects). Meditating on his paintings helps you connect with life—or so Matisse hoped.

As you tour the museum, look for Matisse's favorite motifs—including fruit, flowers, wallpaper, and sunny rooms—often with a window opening onto a sunny landscape. Another favorite subject is the *odalisque* (harem concubine), usually shown sprawled in a seductive pose and with a simplified, masklike face. You'll also see a few souvenirs from his travels, which influenced much of his work.

Visiting the Museum: The museum is in a constant state of

flux, so expect changes from this description. Enter on the basement floor and find
Matisse's colorful paper cutout *Flowers and
Fruits* hanging from the wall. This piece
makes a fine introduction to his decorative
art, shouting "Riviera!" The basement also
has a room devoted to two 25-foot-long wa-
tery cutouts for an uncompleted pool project
(La Piscine) for the city of Nice, which shows
his abiding love of deep blue.

On the mezzanine above, leaf through
discarded cutouts from various papier-mâché
works and find black-and-white photos of
the artist at work and play.

Rooms on the street level usually contain paintings from
Matisse's formative years as a student (1890s) and are the highlight of the museum for me. Notice how quickly his work evolves:
from dark still lifes *(nature mortes)*, to colorful Impressionist scenes,
to more abstract works, all in the matter of a few years. Find the
translation of his "Découverte de la Lumière" (discovery of light),
which the Riviera (and his various travels to sun-soaked places like
Corsica, Collioure, and Tahiti) brought to his art. To appreciate
the speed of change in his painting, notice the dramatic differences
in his portraits of Madame Matisse, painted just a few years apart.

Other rooms on this floor (or nearby) highlight Matisse's fascination with dance and the female body. You'll see pencil and charcoal drawings, and a handful of bronze busts; he was fascinated
by sculpture. *The Acrobat*—painted only two years before Matisse's
death—shows the artist at his minimalist best.

The floor above features sketches and models of Matisse's famous Chapel of the Rosary in nearby Vence (see page 154) and
related religious works. On the same floor, you might find paper
cutouts from his *Jazz* or *Dance* series, more bronze sculptures, various personal objects, and linen embroideries inspired by his travels
to Polynesia.

Leaving the Museum: Turn left from the museum into the
park, exiting at the Archaeological Museum, and turn right at the
street. The bus stop across the street is for bus #17, which goes to
the train station, and #20, which heads to the port. For bus #15
(frequent service to downtown and the Chagall Museum), continue walking—with the Roman ruins on your right—to the small
roundabout, and find the shelter (facing downhill).

Modern and Contemporary Art Museum
(Musée d'Art Moderne et d'Art Contemporain)

This ultramodern museum features an explosively colorful, far-out, yet manageable collection focused on American and European-American artists from the 1960s and 1970s (Pop Art and New Realism are highlighted; see page 13 for an overview of modern art on the Riviera). The exhibits cover three floors, one of which is devoted to temporary shows. The permanent collection usually includes a few works by Andy Warhol, Roy Lichtenstein, and Jean Tinguely. You should also find rooms dedicated to Yves Klein and Niki de Saint Phalle. English explanations are posted in some rooms, and there's a good timeline of Riviera artists from 1947 to 1977. The temporary exhibits can be as appealing to modern-art lovers as the permanent collection: Check the museum website for what's playing. Don't leave without exploring the views from the rooftop terrace.

Cost and Hours: Covered by €10 Nice museum combo-ticket, Tue-Sun 10:00-18:00, mid-Oct-mid-June from 11:00, closed Mon year-round, near Vieux Nice on Promenade des Arts, tel. 04 93 62 61 62, www.mamac-nice.org.

Fine Arts Museum (Musée des Beaux-Arts)

Housed in a sumptuous Riviera villa with lovely gardens, this museum lacks a compelling collection but holds 6,000 artworks from the 17th to 20th centuries. Start on the first floor and work your way up to enjoy paintings by Monet, Sisley, Bonnard, and Raoul Dufy, as well as a few sculptures by Rodin and Carpeaux.

Cost and Hours: Covered by €10 Nice museum combo-ticket, Tue-Sun 10:00-18:00, mid-Oct-mid-June from 11:00, closed Mon year-round, inconveniently located at the western end of Nice, take bus #12 from train station to Rosa Bonheur stop and walk to 3 Avenue des Baumettes; tel. 04 92 15 28 28, www.musee-beaux-arts-nice.org.

Archaeological Museum (Musée Archéologique)

This museum displays various objects from the Romans' occupation of this region. It's convenient—just below the Matisse Museum—but is of little interest except to ancient Rome aficionados (scant information in English). Entry includes access to the poorly maintained Roman bath ruins (ask for the English handout).

Cost and Hours: Covered by €10 Nice museum combo-ticket, Wed-Mon 11:00-18:00, closed Tue, near Matisse Museum at 160 Avenue des Arènes de Cimiez, tel. 04 93 81 59 57.

Masséna Museum (Musée Masséna)

Like Nice's main square, this museum was named in honor of Jean-André Masséna (born in Antibes), a highly regarded commander during France's Revolutionary and Napoleonic wars. The beach-front mansion is worth a look for its lavish decor and lovely gardens alone (few English labels in museum, but a €3 booklet in English may be available).

Cost and Hours: Covered by €10 Nice museum combo-ticket, always free to enter gardens, Wed-Mon 10:00-18:00, mid-Oct-mid-June from 11:00, closed Tue year-round, 35 Promenade des Anglais, tel. 04 93 91 19 10.

Visiting the Museum: There are three levels. The elaborate reception rooms on the ground floor host occasional exhibits and give the best feeling for aristocratic Nice from 1860, when it joined France, until World War I (find Masséna's portrait to the right).

The first floor up, offering a folk-museum-like look at Nice through the years, deserves most of your time. Start in a small room dedicated to the museum's namesake, Jean-André Masséna, then find Napoleonic paraphernalia, including the emperor's vest and sword, and Josephine's impressive cape and tiara. Moving counterclockwise around the floor, find bric-a-brac of the aristocracy and antique posters promoting vacations in Nice—look for the model and photos of the long-gone La Jetée Promenade and its casino, Nice's first. You'll see paintings of some of the Russian and British nobility who appreciated Nice's climate (including imperious Queen Victoria, who is most responsible for igniting tourism in Nice). You'll eventually see a dashing painting honoring Italian patriot and Nice favorite Giuseppe Garibaldi, then find a room with images of Nice before the Promenade des Anglais was built and before the town's river was covered over by Place Masséna. The top floor is a painting gallery with temporary exhibits.

The gardens on the seaward side of the museum house a memorial to the 86 people who died in the terrorist attack on the Promenade des Anglais in 2016.

OTHER SIGHTS IN NICE
▲Russian Cathedral (Cathédrale Russe)

Nice's Russian Orthodox church—claimed by some to be the finest outside Russia—is worth a visit. Five hundred rich Russian families wintered in Nice in the late 19th century, and they needed a worthy Orthodox house of worship. Dowager Czarina Maria Feodorovna and her son, Nicholas II, offered the land for the construction, which began in 1903. Nicholas underwrote much of the project and gave this church to the Russian community in 1912. (A few years later, Russian comrades who *didn't* winter on the Riviera assassinated him.) Here in the land of olives and anchovies, these proud onion domes seem odd. But, I imagine, so did those old Russians.

Cost and Hours: Free; daily 9:30-17:30 except during services, chanted services Sat at 18:00, Sun at 10:00; no tourist visits during services, no shorts, Avenue Nicolas II, tel. 04 93 96 88 02, www.sobor.fr.

Getting There: It's a 15-minute walk from the train station. Head west on Avenue Thiers for 10 minutes, then turn right on Avenue Gambetta, go under the tracks then look for signs. Or take any bus heading

west from the station on Avenue Thiers and get off as close to Avenue Gambetta as you can.

Visiting the Cathedral: Before entering, enjoy the exterior done in the "old Russian" style, inspired by the 16th- and 17th-century Russian religious architecture. Russian President Vladimir Putin funded the fine restoration of the facade. The park around the church stays open at lunch and makes a nice setting for picnics. There's also clean (pay) WC.

Step inside. The one-room interior is filled with icons and candles, and traditional Russian music adds to the ambience. The wall of icons (iconostasis) divides the spiritual realm from the temporal world of the worshippers. Only the priest can walk between the two worlds, by using the "Royal Door."

Get close to the altar and take a look at items lining the front. In the left corner, look for the icon of St. Nicholas, the most venerated one in the cathedral. On the right, find a striking icon of Our Lady of Kazan, painted on wood and set in an array of silver and precious stones. The archangel Michael with red boots and wings—the protector of the Romanov family—stands over a symbolic tomb of Christ a little right of center (on the doors used only by the priests).

The tall, black, hammered-copper cross commemorates the massacre of Nicholas II and his family in 1918. Notice the Jesus icon to the right of the Royal Door. According to a priest here, as worshippers meditate, staring deep into the eyes of Jesus, they enter a lake where they find their souls. Surrounded by incense, chanting, and your entire community...it could happen. Closer in on the right on the easel, the icon of the Virgin and Child is decorated with semiprecious stones from the Ural Mountains. Artists worked a triangle into each iconic face—symbolic of the Trinity.

NICE

▲Castle Hill (Colline du Château)

This hill—in an otherwise flat city center—offers sensational views over Nice, the port (to the east, created for trade and military use in the 15th century), the foothills of the Alps, and the Mediterranean. The views are best early, at sunset, or whenever the weather's clear.

Nice was founded on this hill. Its residents were crammed onto the hilltop until the 12th century, as it was too risky to live in the flatlands below. Today you'll find a playground, a café, and a cemetery—but no castle—on Castle Hill.

Cost and Hours: Park is free and closes at 20:00 in summer, earlier off-season.

Getting There: You can get to the top by foot, by elevator (free, daily April-Sept 9:00-19:00, until 20:00 in summer, Oct-March 10:00-18:00, next to beachfront Hôtel Suisse), or by pricey tourist train (see "Tours in Nice," earlier).

See the "Promenade des Anglais Walk" for a pleasant stroll that ends near Castle Hill.

Leaving Castle Hill: After enjoying the views and hilltop fun, you can walk via the cemetery directly down into Vieux Nice (just follow the signs), descend to the beach (via the elevator or a stepped lane next to it), or hike down the back side to Nice's port (departure point for boat trips and buses to Monaco and Ville-franche-sur-Mer).

EXCURSION FROM NICE

Narrow-Gauge Train into the Alps (Chemins de Fer de Provence)

Leave the tourists behind and take the scenic train-bus-train combination that runs between Nice and Digne through canyons,

along whitewater rivers, and through tempting villages (4/day, departs Nice from Chemins de Fer de Provence Station, two blocks from the Libération tram stop, 4 Rue Alfred Binet, tel. 04 97 03 80 80, www.trainprovence.com).

An appealing stop on the scenic railway is little **Entrevaux,** a good destination that feels forgotten and still stuck in its medieval shell (about €25 round-trip, 1.5 scenic hours from

Nice). Cross the bridge, meet someone friendly, and consider the steep hike up to the citadel (€3, TI tel. 04 93 05 45 73).

Nightlife in Nice

The city is a walker's delight after dark. Promenade des Anglais, Cours Saleya, Vieux Nice, Promenade du Paillon, and Place Masséna are all worth an evening wander. I can't get enough of the night scene on Place Masséna and around the adjacent fountains.

Nice's bars play host to a happening late-night scene, filled with jazz, rock, and trolling singles. Most activity focuses on Vieux Nice. Rue de la Préfecture and Place du Palais are ground zero for bar life, though Place Rossetti and Rue Droite are also good targets. **Distilleries Ideales** is a good place to start or end your evening, with a lively international crowd, a Pirates of the Caribbean interior, and a *Cheers* vibe (lots of beers on tap, where Rue de la Poissonnerie and Rue Barillerie meet, happy hour 18:00-21:00). **Wayne's Bar** and others nearby are happening spots for the younger, Franco-Anglo backpacker crowd (15 Rue Préfecture; see "Vieux Nice Hotels & Restaurants" map). Along the Promenade des Anglais, the classy Le Relais bar at **Hôtel Negresco** is fancy-cigar old English with frequent live jazz. To savor fine views over Nice, find the **Hotel Aston La Scala**'s seventh-floor bar/terrace, which is a good spot for a drink any night but offers jazz and blues on Thursdays and Fridays and a DJ on Saturdays (daily 17:00 to late, on the Promenade du Paillon at 12 Avenue Félix Faure, tel. 04 92 17 53 00).

Sleeping in Nice

Don't look for charm in Nice. Seek out a good location and modern, reliable amenities (like air-conditioning). The price rankings given here are for April through October. Prices generally drop considerably November through March and sometimes in April, but go sky-high during the Nice Carnival (in February), the Cannes Film Festival (May), and Monaco's Grand Prix (late May). Between the film festival and the Grand Prix, the second half of May is slammed. Nice is also one of Europe's top convention cities, and June is convention month here.

I've divided my sleeping recommendations into three areas: city center, Vieux Nice, and near the Promenade des Anglais. Those in the city center are between the train station and Place Masséna (easy access to the train station and Vieux Nice via the T-1 tram, 15-minute walk to Promenade des Anglais). Those in Vieux Nice are between Place Masséna and the sea (east of the parkway, good access to the sea at Quai des Etats-Unis). And those near the

Promenade des Anglais are farther west, between Boulevard Victor Hugo and the sea (a classier and quieter area easily reached by tram T-2, offering better access to the sea but longer walks to the train station and Vieux Nice). For parking, ask your hotelier, or see "Arrival in Nice—By Car" on page 17.

IN THE CITY CENTER

The train station area offers Nice's cheapest sleeps, but the neighborhood feels sketchy after dark. The cheapest places are older, well worn, and come with some street noise. Places closer to Avenue Jean Médecin are more expensive and in a more comfortable area.

$$$$ Hôtel du Petit Palais** is a little belle-époque jewel with 25 handsome rooms tucked neatly into a residential area on the hill several blocks from the Chagall Museum. It's bird-chirping peaceful and plush, with tastefully designed rooms, a garden terrace, and small pool. You'll walk 15 minutes down to Vieux Nice (or use bus #15); free street parking is usually easy to find (17 Avenue Emile Bieckert, tel. 04 93 62 19 11, wwww.petitpalaisnice.com, reservation@petitpalaisnice.com).

$$ Hôtel Vendôme** gives you a whiff of the belle époque, with pink pastels, high ceilings, and grand staircases in a mansion set off the street. The modern rooms come in all sizes; many have balconies (limited pay parking—book ahead, 26 Rue Pastorelli at the corner of Rue Alberti, tel. 04 93 62 00 77, www.hotel-vendome-nice.com, contact@vendome-hotel-nice.com).

$$ Hôtel St. Georges,** five blocks from the station toward the sea, offers a practical location, a pleasant backyard patio, and friendly Houssein at the reception. Rooms are dark and basic but adequate and fairly priced (family rooms, limited parking—book ahead, 7 Avenue Georges Clemenceau, tel. 04 93 88 79 21, www.hotelsaintgeorges.fr, contact@hotelsaintgeorges.fr).

$ Hôtel Durante** rents quiet rooms in a happy, orange building with rooms wrapped around a flowery courtyard. All but two of rooms overlook the well-maintained patio. The rooms have adequate comfort (mostly modern decor), the price is right, and the parking is free on a first-come, first-served basis (family rooms, 16 Avenue Durante, tel. 04 93 88 84 40, www.hotel-durante.com, info@hotel-durante.com).

$ Hôtel Ibis Nice Centre Gare,** 100 yards to the right as you leave the station, provides a secure refuge in this seedy area. It's big (200 rooms), modern, has well-configured rooms and a pool, and is next to a handy parking garage (bar, café, 14 Avenue Thiers, tel. 04 93 88 85 85, www.ibishotel.com, h1396@accor.com).

$ Hôtel Belle Meunière,** in an old mansion built for Napoleon III's mistress, attracts budget-minded travelers with cheap rates a block below the train station. Simple but well kept, the place

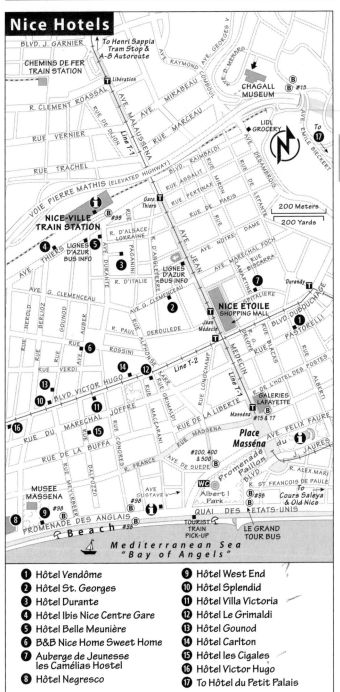

Nice Hotels

CHEMINS DE FER TRAIN STATION

BLVD. J. GARNIER

To Henri Sappia Tram Stop & A-8 Autoroute

Libération

R. CLEMENT ROASSAL

AVE. RAYMOND COMBOUL

AVE. GEORGES V

AVE. D. MÉHARD

CHAGALL MUSEUM

B #15

RUE VERNIER

RUE DE DIJON

AVE. MALAUSSÉNA

AVE. MIRABEAU

AVE. MARCEAU

LIDL GROCERY

AVE. EMILE BIECKERT

To 17

NICE

RUE TRACHEL

Line T-1

RUE DE PARIS

RUE DE LEPANTE

AVE. DESAMBROIS

VOIE PIERRE MATHIS (ELEVATED HIGHWAY)

BLVD RAIMBALDI

RUE ASSALIT

RUE PERTINAX

Gare Thiers

B #99

NICE-VILLE TRAIN STATION

R. D'ALSACE LORRAINE

RUE D'ANGLETERRE

PAGANINI

RUE DE PARIS

RUE NOTRE DAME

200 Meters

200 Yards

4

LIGNES D'AZUR BUS INFO

5

3

RUE DURANTE

RUE D'ITALIE

LIGNES D'AZUR BUS INFO

AVE. JEAN

AVE. NOTRE DAME

AVE. MARÉCHAL FOCH

RUE BISCARRA

7

Durandy

T

AVE. THIERS

AVE. G. CLEMENCEAU

AVE. G. CLEMENCEAU

2

HÔPITALIÈRE

NICE ETOILE SHOPPING MALL

BLVD. DUBOUCHAGE

1

PASTORELLI

HÉROLD

BERLIOZ

GOUNOD

AUBER

R. PAUL DÉROULÈDE

RUE ALPHONSE

Jean Médecin

T

RUE BLACAS

RUE G. PÈDRE

6

RUE VERDI

RUE

RUE

ROSSINI

14

12

Line T-2

RUE LONGCHAMP

T

MÉDECIN

Line T-1

RUE DE L'HÔTEL DES POSTES

ALBERTI

13

BLVD. VICTOR HUGO

10

11

JOFFRE

RUE GRIMALDI

RUE MACCARANI

RUE DE LA LIBERTE

GALERIES LAFAYETTE

Masséna

B #15 & 17

16

RUE DU MARECHAL

15

RUE DE LA BUFFA

RUE CONGRÈS

RUE DALPOZZO

AVE. FRANCE

RUE MASSENA

RUE DE MASSENA

Place Masséna

AVE. FELIX FAURE

du

J. JAURÈS

MUSEE MASSENA

RUE MEYERBEER

AVE GUSTAVE V

#98

AVE. DE SUEDE

#200, 400 & 500

B

WC

Albert I Park

Promenade Paillon BLVD.

R. ALEX.MARI

R. ST. FRANÇOIS DE PAULE

B #98

To Cours Saleya & Old Nice

8

9

#98

PROMENADE DES ANGLAIS

Beach

#98

QUAI DES ÉTATS-UNIS

TOURIST TRAIN PICK-UP

LE GRAND TOUR BUS

Mediterranean Sea "Bay of Angels"

1 Hôtel Vendôme
2 Hôtel St. Georges
3 Hôtel Durante
4 Hôtel Ibis Nice Centre Gare
5 Hôtel Belle Meunière
6 B&B Nice Home Sweet Home
7 Auberge de Jeunesse les Camélias Hostel
8 Hôtel Negresco

9 Hôtel West End
10 Hôtel Splendid
11 Hôtel Villa Victoria
12 Hôtel Le Grimaldi
13 Hôtel Gounod
14 Hôtel Carlton
15 Hôtel les Cigales
16 Hôtel Victor Hugo
17 To Hôtel du Petit Palais

has adequate rooms and charismatic Mademoiselle Marie-Pierre presiding with her perfect English (family rooms, air-con, no elevator but just 3 floors, laundry service, limited pay parking, 21 Avenue Durante, tel. 04 93 88 66 15, www.bellemeuniere.com, hotel. belle.meuniere@cegetel.net).

¢ **B&B Nice Home Sweet Home** is a good budget value. Laid-back Genevieve (a.k.a. Jennifer) Levert rents out four large rooms and one small single in her home. Her cavernous rooms are artfully decorated, with high ceilings, big windows, and space to spread out (cheaper rooms with shared bath, no air-conditioning, elevator, one floor up, laundry services, kitchen access, 35 Rue Rossini at intersection with Rue Auber, mobile 06 50 83 25 85, glevert@free.fr).

Hostel: The fun, good-value ¢ **Auberge de Jeunesse les Camélias** has a handy location, modern facilities, and lively evening atmosphere. Rooms accommodate four to eight people and come with showers and sinks—WCs are down the hall (includes breakfast, rooms closed 11:00-15:00 but can leave bags, laundry, kitchen, safes, bar, 3 Rue Spitalieri, tel. 04 93 62 15 54, www.hihostels.com, accueil.nice@hifrance.org).

NEAR THE PROMENADE DES ANGLAIS

These hotels are close to the beach. The Negresco and West End are big, vintage Nice hotels that open onto the sea from the heart of the Promenade des Anglais.

$$$$ Hôtel Negresco***** owns Nice's most prestigious address on the Promenade des Anglais and knows it. Still, it's the kind of place that if you were to splurge just once in your life... Rooms are opulent (see my "Promenade des Anglais Walk" for more description), tips are expected, and it seems the women staying here have cosmetically augmented lips (some view rooms, *très* classy bar, 37 Promenade des Anglais, tel. 04 93 16 64 00, www. hotel-negresco-nice.com, reservations@hotel-negresco.com).

$$$$ Hôtel West End**** opens onto the Promenade des Anglais with formal service and decor, classy public spaces, and high prices (some view rooms, 31 Promenade des Anglais, tel. 04 92 14 44 00, www.hotel-westend.com, reservation@westendnice. com).

$$$ Hôtel Splendid**** is a worthwhile splurge if you miss your Marriott. The panoramic rooftop pool, bar/restaurant, and breakfast room almost justify the cost...but throw in plush rooms, a free gym, and spa services, and you're as good as at home (pay parking, 50 Boulevard Victor Hugo, tel. 04 93 16 41 00, www. splendid-nice.com, info@splendid-nice.com).

$$$ Hôtel Villa Victoria**** is a service-oriented place managed by cheery and efficient Marlena and her staff, who welcome travelers into a classy old building with a spacious lobby overlooking a sprawling and wonderful rear garden-courtyard. Rooms are comfortable and well kept, but those facing the street come with some noise (pay parking, 33 Boulevard Victor Hugo, tel. 04 93 88 39 60, www.villa-victoria.com, contact@villa-victoria.com).

$$$ Le Grimaldi** is a lovely place with a beautiful lobby and 48 spacious rooms with high ceilings and tasteful decor (big breakfast extra, a few suites and connecting rooms ideal for families, 15 Rue Grimaldi, tel. 04 93 16 00 24, www.le-grimaldi.com, info@le-grimaldi.com).

$$ Hôtel Gounod** is a fine value behind Hôtel Splendid. Because the two share the same owners, Gounod's guests are allowed free access to Splendid's pool, hot tub, and other amenities. Most rooms are quiet, with high ceilings and traditional decor (family rooms, pay parking, 3 Rue Gounod, tel. 04 93 16 42 00, www.gounod-nice.com, info@gounod-nice.com).

$$ Hôtel Carlton** is a good deal. It's a well-run, unpretentious, and comfortable place with spacious, simply decorated rooms, many with decks (26 Boulevard Victor Hugo, tel. 04 93 88 87 83, www.hotel-carlton-nice.com, info@hotel-carlton-nice.com, helpful Lionel at reception).

$$ Hôtel les Cigales,** a few blocks from the Promenade des Anglais, is a sweet little place with 19 sharp and richly colored rooms and a cool upstairs terrace, all well managed by friendly Veronique and Elaine (RS%, 16 Rue Dalpozzo, tel. 04 97 03 10 70, www.hotel-lescigales.com, info@hotel-lescigales.com).

$ Hôtel Victor Hugo, a traditional and spotless seven-room hotel, is an adorable time-warp place where Gilles warmly welcomes guests. All rooms are on the ground floor and come with kitchenettes and air-conditioning. While it's a short walk from the Promenade des Anglais, it's a hefty walk from Vieux Nice (RS%, includes breakfast, 59 Boulevard Victor Hugo, tel. 04 93 88 12 39, www.hotel-victor-hugo-nice.com).

IN OR NEAR VIEUX NICE

Most of these hotels are either on the sea or within an easy walk of it. (Hôtel Lafayette and the Villa Saint Exupéry Beach hostel are more central).

$$$$ Hôtel la Perouse,** built into the rock of Castle Hill at the east end of the bay, is a fine splurge. This refuge-hotel is top-to-bottom flawless in every detail—from its elegant rooms (satin curtains, velour headboards) and attentive staff to its rooftop terrace with hot tub, sleek pool, and lovely **$$$$** garden restaurant. Sleep here to be spoiled and escape the big city (good family options, 11 Quai Rauba Capeu, tel. 04 93 62 34 63, www.hotel-la-perouse.com, lp@hotel-la-perouse.com).

NICE

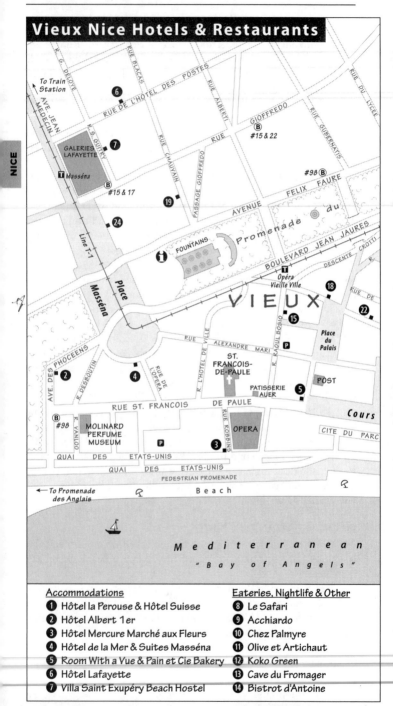

Vieux Nice Hotels & Restaurants

Accommodations
1. Hôtel la Perouse & Hôtel Suisse
2. Hôtel Albert 1er
3. Hôtel Mercure Marché aux Fleurs
4. Hôtel de la Mer & Suites Masséna
5. Room With a Vue & Pain et Cie Bakery
6. Hôtel Lafayette
7. Villa Saint Exupéry Beach Hostel

Eateries, Nightlife & Other
8. Le Safari
9. Acchiardo
10. Chez Palmyre
11. Olive et Artichaut
12. Koko Green
13. Cave du Fromager
14. Bistrot d'Antoine

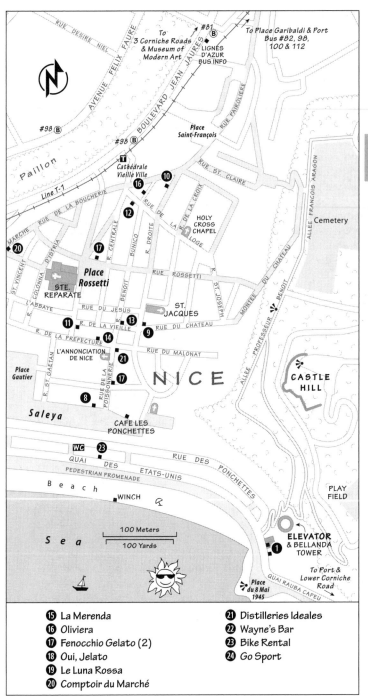

NICE

15 La Merenda
16 Oliviera
17 Fenocchio Gelato (2)
18 Oui, Jelato
19 Le Luna Rossa
20 Comptoir du Marché

21 Distilleries Ideales
22 Wayne's Bar
23 Bike Rental
24 Go Sport

NICE

$$$$ Hôtel Suisse,** below Castle Hill, has brilliant sea and city views for a price—sleep elsewhere if you don't land a view. It's surprisingly quiet given the busy street below (most view rooms have balconies, 15 Quai Rauba Capeu, tel. 04 92 17 39 00, www.hotels-ocre-azur.com, hotel.suisse@hotels-ocre-azur.com).

$$$ Hôtel Albert 1er* is a fair deal in a central, busy location on Albert I Park, two blocks from the beach and Place Masséna. The staff is formal and the rooms are well appointed and spotless, with heavy brown tones. Some have views of the bay, while others overlook the park or a quiet interior courtyard (4 Avenue des Phocéens, tel. 04 93 85 74 01, www.hotel-albert-1er.com, info@hotel-albert1er.com).

$$$ Hôtel Mercure Marché aux Fleurs** is ideally situated near the sea and Cours Saleya. Rooms are sharp, standard doubles are tight, and prices can be either reasonable or exorbitant (superior rooms worth the extra euros—especially those with views, 91 Quai des Etats-Unis, tel. 04 93 85 74 19, www.hotelmercure.com, h0962@accor.com).

$$ Hôtel de la Mer is an intimate, 12-room place with an enviable position overlooking Place Masséna, just steps from Vieux Nice and the beach. Rooms are modern, comfortable, and well priced (4 Place Masséna, tel. 04 93 92 09 10, www.hoteldelamernice.com, hotel.mer@wanadoo.fr). They also run the **$$$$ Suites Masséna** in the same building, with seven huge, modern, high-ceilinged rooms—designed for two but with room for three (tel. 04 93 13 48 11, www.lessuitesmassena.com).

$$ Room With a Vue rents four well-designed rooms (several with small balconies) right on Cours Saleya above the Pain et Cie bakery/café (3 Louis Gassin, tel. 04 93 62 94 32, roomwithavue@gmail.com, enthusiastic manager Fred).

$$ Hôtel Lafayette,* located a block behind the Galeries Lafayette department store, is a modest, homey place with 17 mostly spacious, well-designed and good-value rooms. All rooms are one floor up from the street—some traffic noise sneaks in (RS%, 32 Rue de l'Hôtel des Postes—see "Vieux Nice Hotels & Restaurants" map, tel. 04 93 85 17 84, www.hotellafayettenice.com, info@hotellafayettenice.com).

Hostel: ¢ Villa Saint Exupéry Beach is a sprawling place with more than 200 beds, split between a building with private rooms (figure **$**) and the hostel next door (dorms with 4-8 beds). The owners and many staff are English so communication is easy. The vibe is young and fun, with a bar, cheap restaurant, community kitchen, air-con, elevator, and *beaucoup* services including laundry, yoga classes, free walking tour of Vieux Nice, and scuba diving (no curfew, 6 Rue Sacha Guitry, tel. 04 93 16 13 45, www.villahostels.com, beach@villahostels.com).

NEAR THE AIRPORT

Several airport hotels offer a handy and cheap port-in-the-storm for those with early flights or who are just stopping in for a single night: **$$ Hôtel Campanile** (www.campanile.fr) and **$$$ Hôtel Nouvel** (www.novotel.com) are closest; **$$ Hôtel Ibis Budget Nice Aéroport** (www.ibis.com) is cheap and a few minutes away, though two other Ibis hotels are closer and a bit pricier. Free shuttles connect these hotels with both airport terminals.

Eating in Nice

You'll find plenty of regional dishes and lots of Italian influence blended with classic French cuisine in this Franco-Italian city. Just because you're in a resort, don't lower your standards. Locals expect to eat well and so should you. Sundays are tricky as many places are closed—check the hours before you get your heart set on a place and always be ready to book a day ahead. Think about booking in person while you take my "Vieux Nice Walk."

My favorite dining spots are in Vieux Nice. It's well worth booking ahead for these places. If Vieux Nice is too far, I've listed some great places handier to your hotel. Promenade des Anglais is ideal for picnic dinners on warm, languid evenings or a meal at a beachside restaurant. For a more romantic and peaceful meal, head for nearby Villefranche-sur-Mer (see next chapter). Avoid the fun-to-peruse but terribly touristy eateries lining Rue Masséna.

IN VIEUX NICE

Nice's dinner scene converges on Cours Saleya, which is entertaining enough in itself to make the generally mediocre food a fair deal. It's a fun, festive spot to compare tans and mussels. Most of my recommendations are on side lanes inland from here. Even if you're eating elsewhere, wander through here in the evening. For locations, see the "Vieux Nice Hotels & Restaurants" map.

On Cours Saleya

While local foodies would avoid Cours Saleya like a McDonalds, the energy of wall-to-wall restaurants taking over Vieux Nice's market square each evening is enticing. **$$$ Le Safari** is a fair option for Niçois cuisine, pasta, pizza, and outdoor dining. This sprawling café-restaurant, convivial and rustic with the coolest interior on the Cours, is packed with locals and tourists, and staffed with hurried waiters (daily noon to late, 1 Cours Saleya, tel. 04 93 80 18 44, www.restaurantsafari.fr).

Characteristic Places in Vieux Nice

$$ Acchiardo is a homey-but-lively eatery that mixes loyal clientele with hungry tourists. As soon as you sit down you know this is a treat. It's a family affair overseen by Monsieur Acchiardo and his good-looking sons, Jean-François and Raphael. A small plaque under the menu outside says the restaurant has been run by father and son since 1927. The food is delicious and copious, and the house wine is good and reasonable (Mon-Fri 19:00 until late, closed Sat-Sun and Aug, often a line out the door, reservations smart, indoor seating only, 38 Rue Droite, tel. 04 93 85 51 16).

$ Chez Palmyre, your best budget bet in Vieux Nice, is tiny and popular, so book ahead (a week is advised). The ambience is rustic and fun, with people squeezed onto shared tables to enjoy the homestyle cooking. Philippe serves everyone the same three-course, €17 *menu,* which changes every two weeks (closed Sat-Sun, 5 Rue Droite, tel. 04 93 85 72 32).

$$$ Olive et Artichaut is a sharp bistro-diner with a small counter, black-meets-white floor tiles, and a foodie vibe. It's a good choice to dine on carefully prepared Mediterranean dishes with creative twists (closed Mon-Tue, 6 Rue Ste. Réparate, tel. 04 89 14 97 51).

$$ Koko Green is a sweet little haven for vegan and raw-food types and is run by a delightful Franco-Kiwi couple (open Thu-Sun for lunch, Sat for lunch and dinner, 1 Rue de la Loge, tel. 07 81 63 14 88).

$$$ Cave du Fromager is run by young owners Maeva and Mattieu, who are crazy about cheese and wine. Come here to escape the heat and dine in cozy, cool, vaulted cellars surrounded by shelves of wine and cheery lights. You'll be treated to delicious dishes featuring fresh fish, pasta, and ham—most with cheese as a key ingredient. This is a good choice for vegetarians, and for singles who enjoy eating at the small counter and watching the chef work. Book ahead (closed Tue, just off Place du Jésus at 29 Rue Benoît Bunico, tel. 04 93 13 07 83, www.lacavedufromager.com).

$$ Bistrot d'Antoine has street appeal inside and out. It's a warm, vine-draped place whose menu emphasizes affordable Niçois cuisine and good grilled selections. It's popular, so call a day or two ahead to reserve a table. The upstairs room is quieter than the outdoor tables and ground-floor room (closed Sun-Mon, 27 Rue de la Préfecture, tel. 04 93 85 29 57).

$$ La Merenda is a shoebox where you'll sit on small stools and dine on simple, homestyle dishes in a communal environment. The menu changes with the season, but the hardworking owner, Dominique, does not. This place fills fast, so arrive early, or better yet, drop by during lunch to reserve for dinner—seatings are at 19:00 and 21:00 (closed Sat-Sun, cash only, 4 Rue Raoul Bosio, no telephone).

$$ Oliviera venerates the French olive. This fun shop/restaurant offers olive oil tastings and a menu of Mediterranean dishes paired with specific oils (like a wine pairing). Adorable owner Nadim speaks excellent English, knows all of his producers, and provides animated "Olive Oil 101" explanations with your meal. It's a good place for vegetarians—try his guacamole-and-apple dish; the pesto is also excellent (lunch only, closed Sun-Mon, cash only, 8 bis Rue du Collet, tel. 04 93 13 06 45).

And for Dessert...

Gelato lovers should save room for the tempting ice-cream stands in Vieux Nice (open daily until late). **Fenocchio** is the city's favorite, with mouthwatering displays of dozens of flavors ranging from lavender to avocado (two locations: 2 Place Rossetti and 6 Rue de la Poissonnerie). Gelato connoisseurs should head for **Oui, Jelato,** where quality is the priority rather than selection (5 Rue de la Préfecture, on the Place du Palais).

IN THE CITY CENTER
Near Nice Etoile, on Rue Biscarra

An appealing lineup of bistros overflowing with outdoor tables stretches along the broad sidewalk on Rue Biscarra (just east of Avenue Jean Médecin behind Nice Etoile, all closed Sun). Come here to dine with area residents away from most tourists. Peruse the choices—all five places are different and reservations are normally not needed.

Near Place Masséna

$$ Le Luna Rossa is a small neighborhood place serving delicious French-Italian dishes. Owner Christine and her staff welcome diners with enthusiastic service and reasonable prices. Pasta dishes are copious and served in cast-iron pans, and the *assortiment* main course is a great sampler dish. Dine inside or outside on a sidewalk terrace (closed Sun-Mon, just north of parkway at 3 Rue Chauvain, tel. 04 93 85 55 66).

$ L'Ovale takes its name from the shape of a rugby ball. Come here for an unpretentious and local café-bistro experience. Owner David serves traditional dishes from southwestern France (rich and meaty). Dining is inside only. Consider the *cassoulet,* the hearty *salade de manchons* with duck and walnuts, or the €18-23 three-course *menus* (daily, 29 Rue Pastorelli, tel. 04 93 80 31 65).

$$$ Les 5 Sens ("The Five Senses") is a lively and dressy restaurant serving classic French fare at higher-end prices that justify the cost for discerning diners (daily, 37 Rue Pastorelli, tel. 09 81 06 57 00).

$$ La Maison de Marie is a surprisingly high-quality refuge off Nice's touristy restaurant row. The interior tables are candlelit,

NICE

NICE

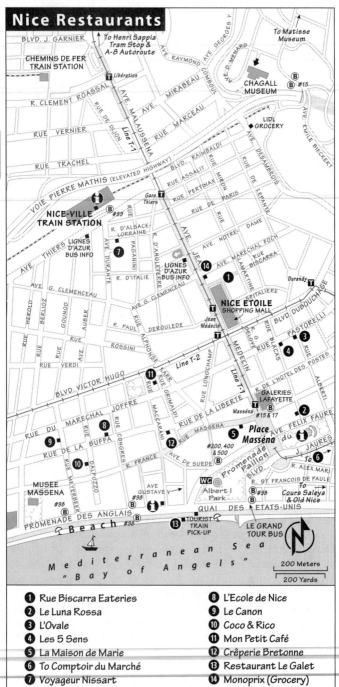

Nice Restaurants

To Henri Sappia Tram Stop & A-8 Autoroute

To Matisse Museum

BLVD. J. GARNIER

CHEMINS DE FER TRAIN STATION

Libération

CHAGALL MUSEUM

B #15

LIDL GROCERY

NICE-VILLE TRAIN STATION

B #99

Gare Thiers

LIGNES D'AZUR BUS INFO

NICE ETOILE SHOPPING MALL

Durandy

LIGNES D'AZUR BUS INFO

Jean Médecin

GALERIES LAFAYETTE

B #15 & 17

Masséna

Place Masséna

#200, 400 & 500

Promenade Paillon BLVD.

To

MUSEE MASSENA

#98

WC
Albert I Park

B #98

Cours Saleya & Old Nice

PROMENADE DES ANGLAIS

B #98

QUAI DES ETATS-UNIS

Beach #98

TOURIST TRAIN PICK-UP

LE GRAND TOUR BUS

N

Mediterranean Sea
"Bay of Angels"

200 Meters

200 Yards

❶ Rue Biscarra Eateries	❽ L'Ecole de Nice
❷ Le Luna Rossa	❾ Le Canon
❸ L'Ovale	❿ Coco & Rico
❹ Les 5 Sens	⓫ Mon Petit Café
❺ La Maison de Marie	⓬ Crêperie Bretonne
❻ To Comptoir du Marché	⓭ Restaurant Le Galet
❼ Voyageur Nissart	⓮ Monoprix (Grocery)

white-tablecloth classy, while the tables in the courtyard enjoy a relaxed bistro feel. Expect some smokers outside. The *menu* is a good value (daily, 5 Rue Masséna, tel. 04 93 82 15 93).

$$ Comptoir du Marché, named for its red, wood counter, feels like a wine shop-meets-bistro-meets-bakery with cozy ambience in and out. It's at a busy pedestrian corner and serves traditional French cuisine with a smile (closed Sun-Mon, 8 Rue du Marché, tel. 04 93 13 45 01).

Near the Train Station

$ Voyageur Nissart has blended good-value cuisine with friendly service since 1908. Kind owner Max and his able assistant Cédric are great hosts, and the quality of their food makes this place both very popular and a good choice for travelers on a budget (book ahead, leave a message in English). Try anything *à la niçoise,* including the fine *salade niçoise* (good €18 three-course *menus,* inexpensive wines, indoor and outdoor seating, closed Mon, a block below the train station at 19 Rue d'Alsace-Lorraine, tel. 04 93 82 19 60, www.voyageurnissart.com).

Near the Promenade des Anglais

These restaurants are handy for those sleeping in hotels near the Promenade des Anglais.

$$ L'Ecole de Nice brings wine-shop decor to a cozy-but-modern restaurant, and serves a limited selection of delicious dishes complemented by a vast selection of wines. The set-price *menu*—less than €30 for three courses—is a swinging deal (closed Sun, 16 Rue de la Buffa, tel. 04 93 81 39 30).

$$$ Le Canon is a fine-if-trendy choice, run by two friends intent on serving top-quality and inventive dishes that emphasize the region's local, fresh, and in-season ingredients (closed Sat-Sun, 23 Rue Meyerbeer, tel. 04 93 79 09 24).

$$$ Coco & Rico is a good place away from the tourist fray. Kind Isabelle welcomes you to her fun bistro with creative homemade dishes. The cuisine and wine list represent many regions of France, with a focus on what's fresh (closed Sun-Mon, indoor and outdoor seating, 3 Rue Dalpozzo, tel. 04 83 50 09 60).

$$$ Mon Petit Café delivers fine, traditional cuisine to appreciative diners in a warm, candlelit setting with rich colors and fine glassware, or on a pleasant front terrace. Book ahead for this dressy place and expect top service and mouth-watering cuisine (closed Sun-Mon, 11 bis Rue Grimaldi, tel. 04 97 20 55 36, www. monpetitcafe-nice.com).

$ Crêperie Bretonne is the only *crêperie* I list in Nice. Dine on the broad terrace or inside, with relaxed service and jukebox-meets-gramophone ambience. Their top-end, house-special crêpes are creative and enticing. Split a salad to start—try the goat cheese salad with honey (closed Sun, on Place Grimaldi, tel. 04 93 82 28 47).

Dining on the Beach
$$$ **Restaurant Le Galet** is your best eat-on-the-beach option. The city vanishes as you step down to the beach. The food is nicely presented, and the tables feel elegant, even at the edge of the sand. Arrive for the sunset and you'll have an unforgettable meal (open for dinner May-mid-Sept, 3 Promenade des Anglais—see "Nice Restaurants" map, tel. 04 93 88 17 23). Sunbathers can rent beach chairs and have drinks and meals served literally on the beach (lounge chairs-€16/half-day, €19/day).

Nice Connections

GETTING AROUND THE RIVIERA
Nice is perfectly situated for exploring the Riviera by public transport. Monaco, Eze-le-Village, Villefranche-sur-Mer, Antibes, Vence, and St-Paul-de-Vence are all within about a one-hour bus or train ride. With a little planning, you can link key destinations in an all-day circuit (for example: Nice, Monaco, and Eze-le-Village or La Turbie, then loop back to Nice). For a comparison of train and bus connections from Nice to nearby coastal towns, see the "Public Transportation in the French Riviera" sidebar on page 10. It's also possible to take a boat to several destinations in the Riviera.

By Train
From Nice-Ville Station to: Cannes (2/hour, 30 minutes), **Antibes** (2/hour, 20 minutes), **Villefranche-sur-Mer** (2/hour, 10 minutes), **Eze-le-Village** (2/hour, 15 minutes to Eze-Bord-de-Mer, then infrequent bus #83 to Eze, 8/day, 15 minutes), **Monaco** (2/hour, 20 minutes), **Menton** (2/hour, 35 minutes), **Grasse** (15/day, 1 hour).

By Bus
Regardless of length, most one-way rides on regional buses (except express airport buses) cost €1.50. Tickets are good for up to 74 minutes of travel in one direction, including transfers. For more info on buses in the Riviera, see page 8. To connect to regional destinations, use the following bus lines and stops (see "Nice Hotels" and "Vieux Nice Hotels & Restaurants" maps for stop locations; www.lignesdazur.com).

Eastbound Buses: Due to the new T-2 tram that will end at the port, expect some changes to stop locations for these buses.

Trams T-1 and/or T-2 will get you close to these stops, and transfers are free from tram to bus for all lines but #100.

Bus #100 runs from Nice's port through **Villefranche-sur-Mer** (3-4/hour, 20 minutes), **Monaco** (1 hour), and **Menton** (1.5 hours). Bus #81 runs from the Promenade des Arts stop to **Villefranche-sur-Mer** (2-3/hour, 15 minutes) and around **Cap Ferrat** (30 minutes to **St-Jean-Cap-Ferrat**). Buses #82 and #112 to **Eze-le-Village** leave from the Vauban tram stop (about hourly; only #82 runs on Sundays; 30 minutes). For **La Turbie,** buses run 6/day and take 45 minutes (Mon-Sat take #116 from Vauban tram stop; on Sun catch #T-66 from Pont St. Michel tram stop).

Westbound Buses: Bus #200 goes to **Antibes** (4/hour Mon-Sat, 2/hour Sun, 1.5 hours) and **Cannes** (2 hours). Bus #400 heads to **St-Paul-de-Vence** (2/hour, 45 minutes) and **Vence** (1 hour). Bus #94 also serves Vence (1-2/hour, 1 hour). Bus #500 goes to **Grasse** (2/hour, 1 hour). All use the Albert I/Verdun stop on Avenue de Verdun, a 10-minute walk along the parkway west of Place Masséna. You must buy tickets before boarding these buses.

By Boat

In summer, Trans Côte d'Azur offers scenic trips several days a week from Nice to Monaco and Nice to St-Tropez. Boats leave in the morning and return in the evening, giving you all day to explore your destination. Drinks and WCs are available on board.

Boats to **Monaco** depart at 9:30 and 16:00, and return at 11:00 and 17:00. The morning departure can be combined with the late-afternoon return from Monaco, allowing you a full day with Prince Albert II (€39 round-trip, €32 if you don't get off in Monaco, 45 minutes each way, June-Sept Tue, Thu, and Sat only).

Boats to **St-Tropez** depart at 9:00 and return from St-Tropez at 16:30 (€65 round-trip, 2.5 hours each way; early-July-Aug daily; late May-early-July and Sept Tue, Thu, and Sat-Sun only).

Reservations are required for both boats, and tickets for St-Tropez should be booked in advance (tel. 04 92 00 42 30, www.trans-cote-azur.com). The same company also runs one-hour round-trip cruises along the coast to Cap Ferrat (see listing under "Tours in Nice," earlier).

GETTING TO DESTINATIONS BEYOND THE RIVIERA
By Long-Distance Bus and Train

Ouibus and Flixbus run long-distance bus service from Nice; see "Transportation" in the Practicalities chapter. Compare schedules and fares with trains.

Most long-distance train connections from Nice to other French cities require a change in Marseille. The Intercité train to

Bordeaux (serving Antibes, Cannes, Toulon, and Marseille—and connecting from there to Arles, Nîmes, and Carcassonne) requires a reservation.

From Nice by Train to: Marseille (18/day, 2.5 hours), **Cassis** (hourly, 3 hours, transfer in Toulon and/or Marseille), **Arles** (11/day, 4 hours, most require transfer in Marseille or Avignon), **Avignon** (10/day, most by TGV, 4 hours, many require transfer in Marseille), **Lyon** (hourly, 4.5 hours, may require change), **Paris'** Gare de Lyon (hourly, 6 hours, may require change), **Aix-en-Provence** TGV Station (10/day, 2-3 hours, usually changes in Marseille), **Chamonix** (4/day, 10 hours, requires multiple changes), **Beaune** (7/day, 7 hours, 1-2 transfers), **Florence** (6/day, 8 hours, 1-3 transfers), **Milan** (3 Thello trains/day, 4 hours, www.thello.com; or 4/day, 5 hours, most with transfers), **Venice** (5/day, 9 hours, 1-3 transfers), **Barcelona** (2/day via Montpellier or Valence, 9 hours, more with multiple changes).

By Plane

Nice's easy-to-navigate airport (Aéroport de Nice Côte d'Azur, airport code: NCE) is literally on the Mediterranean—with landfill runways, a 30-minute drive west of the city center. The two terminals are connected by shuttle buses *(navettes)*. Both terminals have TIs, banks, ATMs, trams, and buses to Nice (tel. 04 89 88 98 28, www.nice.aeroport.fr). Planes leave roughly hourly for Paris (one-hour flight, about the same price as a train ticket, check www.easyjet.com for the cheapest flights to Paris' Orly airport).

Linking the Airport and City Center

By Taxi: A taxi into the center is expensive considering the short distance (figure €35 to Nice hotels, €60 to Villefranche-sur-Mer, €70 to Antibes, about €5 more at night and on weekends, small fee for bags). Nice's airport taxis are notorious for overcharging. Before riding, confirm your fare. It's always a good idea to ask for a receipt *(reçu)*.

By Tram: The T-2 tramway, scheduled to open in late 2019, will serve both airport terminals and will run frequently into Nice, paralleling the Promenade des Anglais and ending at Nice's Port Lympia. The tram will be handy for those sleeping at hotels near the Promenade des Anglais and Place Masséna.

By Bus: Two bus lines connect the airport with the city center, offering good alternatives to high-priced taxis. Note that these routes may be influenced by the new tram line; check routes before riding. **Bus #99** (airport express) runs to Nice's main train station (€6, 2/hour, 8:00-21:00, 30 minutes, drops you within a 10-minute walk of many recommended hotels). To take this bus to the airport, catch it right in front of the train station (departs on the half-hour).

If your hotel is within walking distance of the station, #99 is your best budget bet.

Bus #98 runs along Promenade des Anglais and along the edge of Vieux Nice (€6, 3-4/hour, from the airport 6:00-23:00, to the airport until 21:00, 30 minutes, see the "Nice" map at the beginning of this chapter for stops).

For all buses, buy tickets from the driver. To reach the bus information office and stops at Terminal 1, turn left after passing customs and exit the doors at the far end. Buses serving Terminal 2 stop across the street from the airport exit (information kiosk and ticket sales to the right as you exit).

By Airport Shuttle: These services vary in reliability but can be cost-effective for families or small groups. Airport shuttles are better for trips from your hotel to the airport, since they require you to book a precise pickup time in advance. Shuttle vans offer a fixed price (about €30 for one person, a little more for additional people or to Villefranche-sur-Mer). Your hotel can arrange this, and I would trust their choice of company.

Linking the Airport and Nearby Destinations

To get to **Villefranche-sur-Mer** from the airport, take bus #98 (described above) to Place Garibaldi. From there, use the same ticket to transfer to bus #81. If the new T-2 tram is running, take it to the last stop (Port Lympia). At the port, you can use the same ticket to transfer to bus #81 or buy a separate ticket for bus #100 (see the "Nice" map at the beginning of this chapter for bus-stop locations). Allow €60 for a taxi.

To reach **Antibes,** take bus #250 from either terminal (about 2/hour, 40 minutes, €11). For **Cannes,** take bus #210 from either terminal (1-2/hour, 50 minutes on freeway, €22). Express bus #110 runs from the airport directly to **Monaco** (2/hour, 50 minutes, €22).

By Cruise Ship

Nice's port is at the eastern edge of the town center, below Castle Hill; the main promenade and Vieux Nice are on the other side of the hill. Cruise ships dock at either side of the mouth of this port: Terminal 1 to the east or Terminal 2 to the west.

Getting into the City Center: The new T-2 tram will connect the port to the city center and airport. Until it opens, to reach Vieux Nice or the T-1 tram, head to Place Garibaldi by walking or riding the shuttle bus to the top of the port, then angling up Rue Cassini to the square (20-minute walk from either cruise terminal). From here it's a short **walk** to Vieux Nice or to the T-1 tram stop. You can ride the T-1 tram to Place Masséna for the start of my "Vieux Nice

Walk" or to catch a bus to the Chagall or Matisse museums (#15).

If arriving at Terminal 2 and heading to Vieux Nice, you can skip the walk to Place Garibaldi and stroll directly there by heading around the base of the castle-topped hill, with the sea on your left (10-15 minutes).

Other options to get into town include a **taxi** from the terminals (about €20 to points within Nice) or the **hop-on, hop-off bus,** which has a stop at the top of the port (see page 22).

Getting to Nearby Destinations: To visit Villefranche-sur-Mer or Monaco, it's best to take **bus #100** (the train is faster, but the bus stop is much closer to Nice's port). The bus stops along the top of the port, near the right end of Place de l'Ile de Beauté (see "Nice" map at the beginning of this chapter).

To take the **train** to Villefranche-sur-Mer, Monaco, Antibes, Cannes, or elsewhere, hop on the T-1 tram (stop near Place Garibaldi, described earlier), then ride to the Gare Thiers stop and walk one long block to the main train station. After the T-2 tram opens, you can ride it to the Jean Médecin stop and transfer to the T-1 tram. For bus and train connections to nearby destinations, see page 68.

Taxis at the terminals charge about €40 one-way to Villefranche-sur-Mer, or €95 one-way to Monaco.

EAST OF NICE

Villefranche-sur-Mer •
The Three Corniches • Cap Ferrat
• Eze-le-Village

Between Nice and Monaco lies the Riviera's richest stretch of real estate, paved with famously scenic roads (called the Three Corniches) and dotted with cliff-hanging villages, million-dollar vistas, and sea-splashed walking trails connecting beach towns. Fifteen minutes east of Nice, little Villefranche-sur-Mer stares across the bay to woodsy and exclusive Cap Ferrat. The eagle's-nest Eze-le-Village and the Corniche-topping Le Trophée des Alpes survey the scene from high above.

PLANNING YOUR TIME

Ideally, spend one day in Villefranche-sur-Mer and Cap Ferrat, and a second day in Monaco and either Eze-le-Village or La Turbie (or both if you're efficient).

If you only have one day, spend it in Villefranche-sur-Mer and Monaco: Those using Nice or Villefranche-sur-Mer as a home base can take the bus and follow my self-guided bus tour to Monaco (see the end of this chapter), arriving in Monaco in time to tour the casino when it's quieter, then witness the changing of the guard at 11:55. If you're returning to Nice, take the train or bus back to Villefranche-sur-Mer and follow my self-guided walk (then consider having an early dinner there before returning to Nice). If you're sleeping in Villefranche-sur-Mer, return from Monaco by bus via Eze-le-Village, spend the late afternoon there, then take a bus or taxi back to Villefranche.

Drivers can connect these destinations with some scenic driving along the Corniche roads.

Villefranche-sur-Mer

In the glitzy world of the Riviera, Villefranche-sur-Mer offers travelers an easygoing slice of small-town Mediterranean life. From here, convenient day trips let you gamble in Monaco, saunter the Promenade des Anglais in Nice, indulge in seaside walks and glorious gardens in Cap Ferrat, and enjoy views from Eze-le-Village and the Grande Corniche.

Villefranche-sur-Mer feels more Italian than French, with pastel-orange buildings; steep, narrow lanes spilling into the sea; and pasta on menus. Luxury yachts glisten in the bay. Cruise ships make regular calls to Villefranche-sur-Mer's deep harbor, creating periodic rush hours of frenetic shoppers and bucket-listers. Sand-pebble beaches, a handful of interesting sights, and quick access to Cap Ferrat keep other visitors just busy enough.

Originally a Roman port, Villefranche-sur-Mer was overtaken by fifth-century barbarians. Villagers fled into the hills, where they stayed and farmed their olives. In 1295 the Duke of Provence—like many in coastal Europe—needed to stand up to the Saracen Turks. He asked the olive farmers to move from the hills down to the water and establish a front line against the invaders, thus denying the enemy a base from which to attack Nice. In return for tax-free status, they stopped farming, took up fishing, and established a *Ville-* (town) *franche* (without taxes). Since there were many such towns, this one was specifically "Tax-free town on the sea" *(sur Mer)*. In about 1560, the Duke of Savoy built an immense, sprawling citadel in the town. And today, while the town has an international following, two-thirds of its 8,000 people call it their primary residence. That makes Villefranche-sur-Mer feel more like a real community than neighboring Riviera towns.

Orientation to Villefranche-sur-Mer

TOURIST INFORMATION

The TI is just off the road that runs between Nice and Monaco, located in a park (Jardin François Binon) below the Nice/Monaco bus stop, labeled *Octroi* (daily 9:00-18:30; mid-Sept-mid-June Mon-Sat 9:00-12:30 & 14:00-17:30, closed Sun; tel. 04 93 01 73 68, www.villefranche-sur-mer.com). Pick up regional bus schedules and information on seasonal sightseeing boat rides. The TI has an excellent brochure-map showing seaside walks around neigh-

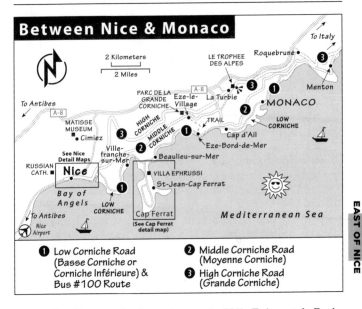

Between Nice & Monaco

2 Kilometers / 2 Miles

To Italy

LE TROPHEE DES ALPES · Roquebrune · ❸ · Menton

To Antibes · A-8

PARC DE LA GRANDE CORNICHE · Eze-le-Village · La Turbie · A-8 · ❸ · MONACO

MATISSE MUSEUM · Cimiez · ❸ · HIGH CORNICHE · MIDDLE CORNICHE · ❶ · TRAIL · ❷ · LOW CORNICHE · Cap d'Ail · Eze-Bord-de-Mer

See Nice Detail Maps

RUSSIAN CATH. · **Nice** · Villefranche-sur-Mer · ❷ · · Beaulieu-sur-Mer

Bay of Angels · ❶ · LOW CORNICHE · ■ VILLA EPHRUSSI · St-Jean-Cap Ferrat

To Antibes · Nice Airport · Cap Ferrat (See Cap Ferrat detail map) · *Mediterranean Sea*

❶ Low Corniche Road (Basse Corniche or Corniche Inférieure) & Bus #100 Route

❷ Middle Corniche Road (Moyenne Corniche)

❸ High Corniche Road (Grande Corniche)

EAST OF NICE

boring Cap Ferrat and information on the Villa Ephrussi de Rothschild's gardens.

ARRIVAL IN VILLEFRANCHE-SUR-MER

By Bus: Get off at the Octroi stop. To reach the old town, walk past the TI along Avenue Général de Gaulle, take the first stairway on the left, then make a right at the street's end. The hop-on, hop-off bus from Nice stops at the citadel (see page 22).

By Train: Not all trains stop in Villefranche-sur-Mer (you may need to transfer to a local train in Nice or Monaco). Villefranche-sur-Mer's train station is just above the beach, a short stroll from the old town and most of my recommended hotels (taxis won't take such a short trip).

By Car: From Nice's port, follow signs for *Menton, Monaco,* and *Basse Corniche.* In Villefranche-sur-Mer, turn right at the TI (first signal after Hôtel la Flore) for parking and hotels. For a quick visit to the TI, park at the pay lot just below the TI. You'll pay to park in all public parking areas except from 19:00 to 9:00. Parking around the citadel is reasonable (about €2/hour) but the most central lot at the harbor is pricey (Parking Wilson, €26/day). Parking is free near Port de la Darse. Some hotels have their own parking.

By Plane: Allow an hour to connect from Nice's airport to Villefranche-sur-Mer (for details, see page 71).

By Cruise Ship: For arrival by cruise ship, see page 84.

HELPFUL HINTS

Market Day: A fun bric-a-brac market enlivens Villefranche-sur-Mer on Sundays (on Place Amélie Pollonnais by Hôtel Welcome, and in Jardin François Binon by the TI). On Saturday and Wednesday mornings, a market sets up in Jardin François Binon. A small trinket market springs to action on Place Amélie Pollonnais whenever cruise ships grace the harbor.

Wi-Fi: There's free Wi-Fi near the TI in the Jardin François Binon, at the port, and in cafés on Place Amélie Pollonnais.

Electric Bike Rental: The adventurous can try **Eco-Loc** electric bikes as an alternative to taking the bus to Cap Ferrat, Eze-le-Village, or even Nice. You get about 25 miles on a fully charged battery (after that you're pedaling; €20/half-day, €30/day, mid-April-Sept daily 9:00-17:00, deposit and ID required, best to reserve 24 hours in advance; helmets, locks, and baskets available; pick up bike by the cruise terminal entrance at the port, mobile 06 66 92 72 41, www.ecoloc06.fr).

Spectator Sports: Lively *boules* action takes place each evening just below the TI and the huge soccer field.

GETTING AROUND VILLEFRANCHE-SUR-MER

By Bus: Little **minibus #80** saves you the sweat of walking uphill (and gets you within a 15-minute walk of Mont-Alban Fort, described later), but runs only about once per hour from the old port to the top of the hill, stopping at Place Amélie Pollonnais (by the cruise terminal), Hôtel la Fiancée du Pirate, and the Col de Villefranche stop (for buses to Eze-le-Village), before continuing to the outlying suburban Nice Riquier train station (€1.50, runs daily 7:00-19:00, see the "Villefranche-sur-Mer" map for stop locations, schedule posted at stops and available at TI). Also, consider the **hop-on, hop-off bus** that makes a loop trip from the citadel to Nice (see page 22).

By Taxi: Taxis wait between the cruise terminal and Place Amélie Pollonnais. Beware of taxi drivers who overcharge. Normal weekday, daytime rates to outside destinations should be about €25 to Cap Ferrat, €40 to central Nice or Eze-le-Village, and €70 to the airport or Monaco. For a reliable taxi, call **Didier** (mobile 06 15 15 39 15). General taxi tel. 04 93 55 55 55.

Villefranche-sur-Mer Town Walk

For tourists, Villefranche is a tiny, easy-to-cover town that snuggles around its harbor under its citadel. This quick self-guided walk laces together everything of importance, starting at the waterfront near where cruise-ship tenders land and finishing at the citadel.

• *If arriving by bus or train, you'll walk five minutes to the starting point. Go to the end of the short pier directly in front of Hôtel Welcome, where we'll start with a spin tour (spin to the right) to get oriented.*

The Harbor: Look out to sea. Cap Ferrat, across the bay, is a landscaped paradise where the 1 percent of the 1 percent compete

for the best view. The Rothschild's pink mansion, Villa Ephrussi (about dead center, hugging the top) is the most worthwhile sight to visit in the area. To its right, in the saddle of the hill, the next big home, with the red-tiled roof, belonged to the late Paul Allen. Geologically, Cap Ferrat is the southern tip of the Alps. The range emerges from the sea here and arcs all across Europe, over 700 miles, to Vienna.

Today, ships bring tourists rather than pirates. The bay is generally filled with beautiful yachts. (In the evenings, you might see well-coiffed captains being ferried in by dutiful mates to pick up statuesque call girls.) Local guides keep a list of the world's 100 biggest yachts and talk about some of them as if they're part of the neighborhood.

At 2,000 feet, this is the deepest natural harbor on the Riviera and was the region's most important port until Nice built its own in the 18th century. Greek, Roman, and American naval ships appreciated the setting. In fact, the United States Sixth Fleet called Villefranche-sur-Mer's port home for almost 20 years. The biggest cruise ships drop their hooks here rather than in Nice or Monaco. The tiny jetty is the landing point for the cruise-ship tenders that come ashore each morning in season.

Up on the hill, the 16th-century citadel (where this walk ends) is marked by flags. The yellow fisherman's chapel (with the little-toe bell tower) has an interior painted by Jean Cocteau. Hôtel Welcome offers the balconies of dreams. Up the skinny lane just right of the hotel stands the baroque facade of St. Michael's Church. The waterfront, lined by fancy fish restaurants, curves to the town beach. Fifty yards above the beach stands the train station and above that, supported by arches, is the Low Corniche road, which leads to Monaco. Until that road was built in the 1860s, those hills were free of any development all the way to Monaco. The big yellow building just above can be rented for €300,000 a month (as Madonna did once for a birthday).

• *Leave the pier and walk left 30 yards past the last couple of fishing boats surviving from the town's once-prominent fishing community to find a small bronze bust of Jean Cocteau, the artist who said, "When I look at Villefranche, I see my youth." A few more steps take you to the little chapel he painted.*

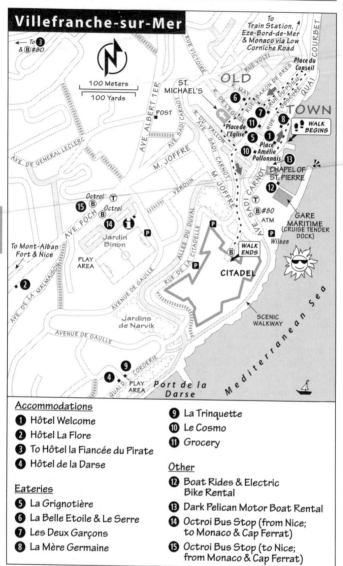

Villefranche-sur-Mer

To ❸ & ⓑ #80

To Train Station, Eze-Bord-de-Mer & Monaco via Low Corniche Road

OLD TOWN

ST. MICHAEL'S

POST

Place de l'Eglise

Place Amélie Pollonnais

WALK BEGINS

CHAPEL OF ST. PIERRE

Octroi

Jardin Binon

PLAY AREA

To Mont-Alban Fort & Nice

WALK ENDS

CITADEL

GARE MARITIME (CRUISE TENDER DOCK)

ATM

Wilson

Jardins de Narvik

SCENIC WALKWAY

Port de la Darse

PLAY AREA

Mediterranean Sea

100 Meters
100 Yards

AVE. ALBERT 1ER · AVE. SADI CARNOT · RUE VICTOIRE · RUE VOLTI · QUAI COURBET · RUE DE L'EGLISE · R. DU YALLON · M. JOFFRE · VERDUN · AVE. DE GENERAL LECLERC · AVE. FOCH · ALLEE DU DUVAL · RUE DE LA CITADELLE · AVENUE DE GAULLE · QUAI CORDERIE · AVE. DE LA MALMAISON

EAST OF NICE

Accommodations
- ❶ Hôtel Welcome
- ❷ Hôtel La Flore
- ❸ To Hôtel la Fiancée du Pirate
- ❹ Hôtel de la Darse

Eateries
- ❺ La Grignotière
- ❻ La Belle Etoile & Le Serre
- ❼ Les Deux Garçons
- ❽ La Mère Germaine
- ❾ La Trinquette
- ❿ Le Cosmo
- ⓫ Grocery

Other
- ⓬ Boat Rides & Electric Bike Rental
- ⓭ Dark Pelican Motor Boat Rental
- ⓮ Octroi Bus Stop (from Nice; to Monaco & Cap Ferrat)
- ⓯ Octroi Bus Stop (to Nice; from Monaco & Cap Ferrat)

Chapel of St. Pierre (Chapelle Cocteau): This chapel is the town's cultural highlight. Cocteau, who decorated the place, was a Parisian transplant who adored little Villefranche-sur-Mer and whose career was distinguished by his work as an artist, poet, novelist, playwright, and filmmaker. Influenced by his pals Marcel Proust, André Gide, Edith Piaf, and Pablo Picasso, Cocteau was a leader among 20th-century avant-garde intellectuals. At the door,

Marie-France—who is passionate about Cocteau's art—collects a €3 donation for a fishermen's charity. She then sets you free to enjoy the chapel's small but intriguing interior. She's delighted to give you a small tour if you ask (Wed-Sun 9:30-12:30 & 14:00-18:00, usually closed Mon-Tue, hours vary with cruise-ship traffic and season).

In 1955 Cocteau tattooed the barrel-vaulted chapel with heavy black lines and pastels. Each of Cocteau's Surrealist works—the Roma (Gypsies) of Stes-Maries-de-la-Mer who dance and sing to honor the Virgin, girls wearing traditional outfits, and three scenes from the life of St. Peter—is explained in English. Is that Villefranche-sur-Mer's citadel in the scene above the altar?

• *From the chapel, turn right and stroll the harbor promenade 100 yards past romantic harborside tables.* **Restaurant La Mère Germaine** *is named for Mother Germaine, who famously took care of US Navy troops in World War II (step inside to see sketches and old photos on the wall). Immediately after the restaurant, a lane leads up into the old town. Walk up a few steps until you reach a long tunnel-like street.*

Rue Obscure, the Old Town, and St. Michael's Church: Here, under these 13th-century vaults, you're in another age. Turn right and walk to the end of Rue Obscure (which means "dark street"). At the end, wind up to the sunlight past a tiny fountain at Place du Conseil, and a few steps beyond that to a viewpoint overlooking the harbor.

Turn around and stroll back past the fountain, straight down the lane, and gently downhill. Notice the homes built under the heavy arches. At Place des Deux Garçons (the square with a namesake restaurant), turn right on Rue May and climb the stepped lane. Take your first left at the restaurant to find St. Michael's Church, facing a delightful square with a single magnolia tree (Place de l'Eglise). The deceptively large church features an 18th-century organ, a particularly engaging crucifix at the high altar, and (to the left) a fine statue of a recumbent Christ—carved, they say, from a fig tree by a galley slave in the 1600s.

• *Leaving St. Michael's, go downhill halfway to the water, where you hit the main commercial street. Go right on Rue du Poilu (browsing a real-estate window if you'd like to move here), then curve left, pass the square, and walk up to the...*

Citadel: The town's mammoth castle was built in the 1500s by the Duke of Savoy to defend against the French. When the region joined France in 1860, the castle became just a barracks. Since the 20th century, it's housed the police station, City Hall, a summer outdoor theater, and art galleries. The single fortified entry—originally a drawbridge over a dry moat (a.k.a. kill zone)—still leads into this huge complex.

The exterior walls slope thickly at the base, indicating that they were built in the "Age of Black Powder"—the 16th century—when the advent of gunpowder made thicker, cannonball-deflecting walls a necessity for any effective fortification. The bastions are designed for smarter crossfire during an attack. The inside feels vast and empty. If you wander around, you'll find a memorial garden for victims of World War II, five free and empty museums and galleries, a garden in the bastion, and the City Hall (which offers a free WC, as all City Halls in France are required to by law).

• *And that concludes our introductory walk. For a brilliant seaside stroll (described next), drop back down below the citadel to the harbor parking lot (Parking Wilson) and find the stone path that leads to the right.*

Activities in Villefranche-sur-Mer

▲Seafront Walks

A seaside walkway originally used by customs agents to patrol the harbor leads under the citadel and connects the old town with the workaday harbor (Port de la Darse). At the port you'll find a few cafés, France's Institute of Oceanography (an outpost for the University of Paris oceanographic studies), and an 18th-century dry dock. This scenic walk turns downright romantic after dark. You can also wander the other direction along Villefranche-sur-Mer's waterfront and continue beyond the train station for postcard-perfect views back to Villefranche-sur-Mer (ideal in the morning—go before breakfast). You can even extend your walk to Cap Ferrat (see "Getting to Cap Ferrat," later).

Hike to Mont-Alban Fort

This fort, with a remarkable setting on the high ridge that separates Nice and Villefranche-sur-Mer, is a good destination for hikers (also accessible by car and bus; info at TI). From the TI, walk on the main road toward Nice about 500 yards past Hôtel La Flore. Look for wooden trail signs labeled *Escalier de Verre* and climb about 45 minutes as the trail makes long switchbacks through the woods up to the ridge. Find your way to Mont-Alban Fort (interior closed to tourists) and its sensational view terrace over Villefranche-sur-Mer and Cap Ferrat. To visit with a much shorter hike, minibus #80 drops you a 15-minute walk away (by the recommended Hôtel Fiancée du Pirate). Bus #14 from Nice drops you just five minutes away (catch it at the Masséna/Guitry stop by Galeries Lafayette department store).

Boat Rides (Promenades en Mer)

To view this beautiful coastline from the sea, consider taking a quick **sightseeing cruise** with AMV (€12-22, some stay in the bay, others go as far as Monaco, select days June-Sept, departs across from Hôtel Welcome, tel. 04 93 76 65 65, www.amv-sirenes.com).

You can also rent your own **motorboat** through Dark Pelican (€110/half-day, €175/day, deposit required, on the harbor at the Gare Maritime, tel. 04 93 01 76 54, www.darkpelican.com).

Sleeping in Villefranche-sur-Mer

You have a handful of great hotels in all price ranges to choose from in Villefranche-sur-Mer. The ones I list have sea views from at least half of their rooms—well worth paying extra for.

$$$$ **Hôtel Welcome****** has the best location in Ville-franche-sur-Mer, and charges for it. Anchored seaside in the old town, with all of its 35 plush, balconied rooms overlooking the harbor and a lounge/wine bar that opens to the water, this place lowers my pulse and empties my wallet (pricey garage—must reserve, 3 Quai Amiral Courbet, tel. 04 93 76 27 62, www.welcomehotel.com, resa@welcomehotel.com).

$$ **Hôtel La Flore***** is a fine value—particularly if your idea of sightseeing is to enjoy a panoramic view from your spacious bed-room balcony (even street-facing rooms have nice decks). The hotel is warmly run and good for families. Several rooms in the annex sleep four and come with kitchenettes, views, and private hot tubs. It's a 15-minute uphill hike from the old town, but the parking is free, and the bus stops for Nice and Monaco are close by (on main road at 5 Boulevard Princesse Grace de Monaco, tel. 04 93 76 30 30, www.hotel-la-flore.fr, infos@hotel-la-flore.fr).

$$ **Hôtel la Fiancée du Pirate***** is a family-friendly view ref-uge high above Villefranche-sur-Mer on the Middle Corniche (best for drivers, although it is on bus lines #80, #82, and #112 to Eze-le-Village and Nice). Don't be fooled by the modest facade—Eric and Laurence offer 15 lovely and comfortable rooms, a large pool, a hot tub, a nice garden, and a terrific view lounge area. The big breakfast features homemade crêpes (RS%, laundry service, free parking, 8 Boulevard de la Corne d'Or, Moyenne Corniche/N-7, tel. 04 93 76 67 40, www.fianceedupirate.com, info@fianceedupirate.com).

$ **Hôtel de la Darse**** is a shy little hotel burrowed in the shadow of its highbrow neighbors and the only budget option in Villefranche. It's a great value with handsome rooms, but isn't cen-tral—figure 10 scenic minutes of level walking to the harbor and a steep 15-minute walk up to the main road (hourly minibus #80 stops in front; handy for drivers, free parking usually available close by). Seaview rooms are easily worth the extra euros (no elevator, tel. 04 93 01 72 54, www.hoteldeladarse.com, info@hoteldeladarse.com). From the TI, walk or drive down Avenue Général de Gaulle (walkers should turn left on Allée du Colonel Duval into the Jar-dins de Narvik and follow steps to the bottom).

Eating in Villefranche-sur-Mer

Locals don't come here in search of refined cuisine and nor should you. For me, dining in Villefranche-sur-Mer is about comfort food, attitude, and ambience. Compari-son-shopping is half the fun—make an event out of a predinner stroll through the old city. Saunter past the string of pricey candlelit places lining the waterfront and consider the smaller, less expensive eateries embedded in the old town. For dessert, pop into a *gelateria,* and then enjoy a floodlit, postdinner walk along the sea.

$$$ La Grignotière, hiding in the back lanes, features Mediterranean comfort food. Servings are generous and tasty. Consider the giant helping of spaghetti and *gambas* (prawns) or the chef's personal-recipe bouillabaisse, all served by gregarious Brigitte and gentle Chantal (cozy seating inside, a few tables outside, daily, 3 Rue du Poilu, tel. 04 93 76 79 83).

$$ La Belle Etoile is the romantic's choice, with a charming interior filled with white tablecloths and soft lighting. This intimate place, serving fine Mediterranean cuisine, is a few blocks above the harbor on a small lane (closed Tue-Wed, 1 Rue Baron de Bres, tel. 04 97 08 09 41).

$$$ Les Deux Garçons offers candlelit tables on a quiet square and a refined cuisine that attracts locals in search of a special dinner (closed Wed, 18 Rue du Poilu, tel. 04 93 76 62 40).

$ Le Serre, nestled in the old town near St. Michael's Church, is a simple, cozy place that opens at 18:00 for early diners. Hard-working owner Sylvie serves well-priced dinners to a loyal local clientele and greets all clients with equal enthusiasm. Choose from the many thin crust pizzas (named after US states), salads, and meats. Try the *daube niçoise* meat stew or the great-value, three-course *menu* (open evenings only, cheap house wine, 16 Rue de May, tel. 04 93 76 79 91).

$$$$ La Mère Germaine, right on the harbor, is the only place in town classy enough to lure a yachter ashore. It's dressy, with formal service and high prices. The name commemorates the current owner's grandmother, who fed hungry GIs during World War II. Try the bouillabaisse, served with panache (daily, reserve for harborfront table, 9 Quai de l'Amiral Courbet, tel. 04 93 01 71 39, www.meregermaine.com).

$ La Trinquette is a relaxed, low-key place away from the fray on the "other port," next to the recommended Hôtel de la Darse (a lovely 10-minute walk from the other recommended restaurants).

Gentle Jean-Charles runs the place with charm, delivering reliable cuisine, friendly vibes at good prices, and a cool live-music scene on weekends (daily in summer, closed Wed off-season, 30 Avenue Général de Gaulle, tel. 04 93 16 92 48).

$$ Le Cosmo serves brasserie fare on the town's appealing main square (daily, Place Amélie Pollonnais, tel. 04 93 01 84 05).

Grocery Store: A handy **Casino** is a few blocks above Hôtel Welcome at 12 Rue du Poilu (Thu-Tue 8:00-12:30 & 15:30-19:30 except closed Sun afternoon and all day Wed).

Dinner Options for Drivers: If you have a car and are staying a few nights, take a short drive to Eze-le-Village or La Turbie for a late stroll, an early dinner, or a sunset drink (dining suggestions later in this chapter). If it's summer (June-Sept), the best option of all is to go across to a restaurant on one of Cap Ferrat's beaches, such as **$$$ Restaurant de la Plage de Passable**, for a before-dinner drink or a dinner you won't soon forget (see "Sights on Cap Ferrat," later).

Villefranche-sur-Mer Connections

For a comparison of connections by train and bus, see the "Public Transportation in the French Riviera" sidebar on page 10. If you're going to Nice's airport, take a cab or an airport shuttle van (see "Nice Connections," on page 71).

BY TRAIN

Trains are faster and run later than buses (until 24:00). It's a level, 10-minute walk from the port to the train station.

From Villefranche-sur-Mer by Train to: Monaco (2/hour, 10 minutes), **Nice** (2/hour, 10 minutes), **Antibes** (2/hour, 40 minutes), **Eze-Bord-de-Mer** (2/hour, 5 minutes) then transfer to bus #83 for Eze-le-Village (see "Getting to Eze-le-Village," later).

BY BUS

In Villefranche-sur-Mer, the most convenient bus stop is Octroi, just above the TI.

Bus #81 runs from Villefranche-sur-Mer in one direction to **Nice** (15 minutes) and in the other direction through **Beaulieu-sur-Mer** (5 minutes) to **Cap Ferrat,** ending at the port in the village of **St-Jean** (15 minutes; for other transportation options, see "Getting to Cap Ferrat," later). The last bus departs from Nice around 20:15, and from St-Jean around 20:50.

Bus #100 runs along the coastal road from Villefranche-sur-Mer westbound to **Nice** (3-4/hour, 20 minutes) and eastbound to **Beaulieu-sur-Mer** (10 minutes), **Monaco** (40 minutes), and **Men-**

ton (1.25 hours). The last bus from Nice to Villefranche leaves at about 21:00 and from Villefranche to Nice at about 22:00.

To reach **Eze-le-Village** by bus you have two choices: Walk or take bus #80 to upper Villefranche-sur-Mer, then catch bus #82 or #112, which together provide about hourly service to Eze-le-Village (only #82 runs on Sun). You can also take bus #100 or #81 to the Plage Beaulieu stop in nearby Beaulieu-sur-Mer, then catch bus #83 to Eze-le-Village, 8/day).

For more on these buses, including ticket info, routes, and frequencies, see page 8.

BY CRUISE SHIP

Tenders deposit passengers at a slick terminal building (Gare Maritime) at the Port de la Santé, right in front of Villefranche-sur-Mer's old town.

Getting into Town: It's easy to **walk** to various points in Villefranche-sur-Mer. The town's charming, restaurant-lined square is a straight walk ahead from the terminal, the main road (with the TI and bus stop) is a steep hike above, and the train station is a short stroll along the beach. **Minibus #80,** which departs from in front of the cruise terminal, saves you some hiking up to the main road and bus stop (described earlier).

Getting to Nearby Towns: To connect to other towns, choose between the **bus** or **train**. Leaving the terminal, you'll see directional sights pointing left, to *Town center/bus* (a 10- to 15-minute, steeply uphill walk to the Octroi bus stop with connections west to Nice or east to Monaco); and right, to *Gare SNCF/train station* (a 10-minute, level stroll with some stairs at the end). See train and bus connections earlier.

Taxis wait in front of the cruise terminal and charge exorbitant rates (minimum €15 charge to train station, though most will refuse such a short ride). For farther-flung trips, see the price estimates on page 76. For an all-day trip, you can try negotiating a flat fee (e.g., €300 for a 4-hour tour).

The Three Corniches

Nice, Villefranche-sur-Mer, and Monaco are linked by three coastal routes: the Low, Middle, and High Corniches. The roads are nicknamed after the decorative frieze that runs along the top of a building (cornice). Each Corniche (kor-neesh) offers sensational views and a different perspective. The villages and sights in this section are listed from west to east in the order you'll reach them when traveling from Villefranche-sur-Mer to Monaco.

The corniches are peppered with impressive villas such as La Leopolda, a sprawling estate with a particularly grand entry that's named for its 1930s owner, King Leopold II of Belgium (who owned the entire peninsula of Cap Ferrat in addition to this estate). Those driving up to the Middle Corniche from Villefranche-sur-Mer can look down on this yellow mansion and its lush garden, which fill an entire hilltop. The property was later owned by the Agnelli family (of Fiat fame and fortune), and then by the Safra family (Brazilian bankers). Its current value is more than a half-billion dollars.

THE CORNICHE ROADS

For an overview of these three roads, see the "Between Nice & Monaco" map.

Low Corniche: The Basse Corniche (also called "Corniche Inférieure") strings ports, beaches, and seaside villages together for a traffic-filled ground-floor view. It was built in the 1860s (along with the train line) to bring people to the casino in Monte Carlo. When this Low Corniche was finished, many hill-town villagers descended to the shore and started the communities that now line the sea. Before 1860, the population of the coast between Villefranche-sur-Mer and Monte Carlo was zero. Think about that as you make the congested trip today.

Middle Corniche: The Moyenne Corniche is higher, quieter, and far more impressive. It runs through Eze-le-Village and provides breathtaking views over the Mediterranean, with several scenic pullouts.

High Corniche: Napoleon's crowning road-construction achievement, the Grande Corniche caps the cliffs with staggering views from almost 1,600 feet above the sea. Two thousand years ago, this was called the Via Aurelia, used by the Romans to conquer the West.

By Car

Drivers can find the three routes from Nice by driving up Boulevard Jean Jaurès, past Vieux Nice and the port. For the Low Corniche (to Villefranche-sur-Mer and Cap Ferrat), follow signs to N-98 *(Monaco par la Basse Corniche),* which leads past Nice's port. Signs for N-7 and the Middle Corniche *(Moyenne Corniche)* appear shortly after the turnoff to the Low Corniche. Signs for the High *(Grande)* Corniche appear a bit after that; follow D-2564 to *Col des 4 Chemins* and the *Grande Corniche.*

The Best Route from Nice to Monaco: This breathtaking drive, worth ▲▲▲, takes the Middle Corniche from Nice or Villefranche-sur-Mer to Eze-le-Village, then uphill following signs to the *Grande Corniche* and *La Turbie.* For cloud piercing, 360-degree views, take Boulevard Maréchal Leclerc uphill from Eze-le-Village's western edge and follow signs for *Parc de la Grande Corniche*. The road becomes the winding Route de la Revère, which has viewpoints galore with views north to the Alps, straight down to the village, and along the Riviera from Naples to Barcelona (well, almost). Bring a picnic, as benches and tables are plentiful. Continue east from here along the Grande Corniche to La Turbie, keeping an eye out for brilliant views back over Eze-le-Village, then finish by dropping down into Monaco.

By Bus

Buses travel along each Corniche; the higher the route, the less frequent the buses (see the "Between Nice & Monaco" map). **Bus #100** runs along the **Low Corniche** from Nice to Monaco (3-4/hour). **Bus #112** provides the single best route to enjoy this area as it connects Monaco and Nice via Eze-le-Village along the **Middle Corniche** (6/day, none on Sun). **Bus #T-66** connects Nice with La Turbie along the **High Corniche** (3-6/day), and **bus #11** does the same from Monaco (6/day). There are no buses between Eze-le-Village and La Turbie (45-minute walk), though buses do connect Nice and Monaco with La Turbie.

If traveling by bus, follow my self-guided bus tour to Monaco (at the end of this chapter), then consider returning to Nice or Villefranche-sur-Mer by bus via Eze-le-Village, or to Nice via La Turbie (see "Monaco Connections" on page 116).

Cap Ferrat

This exclusive peninsula, rated ▲▲, decorates Villefranche-sur-Mer's views. Cap Ferrat is a peaceful eddy off the busy Nice-Monaco route (Low Corniche). You could spend a leisurely day on this peninsula, wandering the sleepy port village of St-Jean-Cap-Ferrat (usually called "St-Jean"), touring the Villa Ephrussi de Rothschild mansion and gardens, and walking on sections of the beautiful trails that follow the coast. If you owned a house here, some of the richest people on the planet would be your neighbors.

Tourist Information: The main TI is near the harbor in St-Jean (Mon-Sat 9:30-18:30, Sun 10:00-17:30; Oct-April Mon-Sat 9:00-17:00, closed Sun; 5 Avenue Denis Séméria, bus #81 stops here at the *office du tourisme*). A smaller TI is near the Villa Ephrussi (closed Sat off-season, closed Sun year-round, 59 Avenue Denis Séméria, tel. 04 93 76 08 90, office-tourisme@saintjeancapferrat.fr).

PLANNING YOUR TIME

Here's how I'd spend a day on the Cap: From Nice or Villefranche-sur-Mer, take bus #81 to the Villa Ephrussi de Rothschild stop (called Passable), then visit the villa. Walk 30 minutes, mostly downhill, to St-Jean for lunch (many options, including grocery shops for picnic supplies) and poke around the village. Take the 45-minute walk on the Plage de la Paloma trail (ideal for picnics). After lunch, take bus #81 or walk the beautiful 30-minute trail to the Villa Kérylos in Beaulieu-sur-Mer and maybe tour that villa. Return to Villefranche-sur-Mer, Nice, or points beyond by train or bus. (If you have a car, skip the loop drive around the peninsula; there's nothing to see from the road except the walls in front of homes owned by people whose challenge in life is keeping the public out.)

You can add Eze-le-Village to this day by taking bus #81 or walking the seaside trail from St-Jean-Cap-Ferrat to Beaulieu-sur-Mer (Plage Beaulieu stop), and transferring to bus #83 to Eze-le-Village (skip Villa Kérylos). Bus #83 only runs eight times day so check the schedule (www.lignedazur.com). If doing this, consider reversing it and starting in Eze-le-Village when it's quieter.

Here's an **alternative plan** for the star-gazing, nature-loving beach bum: Visit Villa Ephrussi then walk to St-Jean for lunch, hike six miles around the entirety of Cap Ferrat (2-3 hours), and enjoy the late afternoon on the beach at Plage de Passable. At sunset, have a drink or dinner at the recommended Restaurant de la Plage de Passable, then walk or catch a taxi back.

Warning: In high season, late-afternoon buses back to Villefranche-sur-Mer or Nice along the Low Corniche can be jammed (worse on weekends), potentially leaving passengers stranded at stops for long periods. To avoid this, either take the train or board bus #81 on the Cap itself (before it gets crowded).

GETTING TO CAP FERRAT

From Nice or Villefranche-sur-Mer: Bus #81 (direction: Port de St-Jean) runs to all Cap Ferrat stops (for info on tickets, route, and frequency, see page 8). For the Villa Ephrussi de Rothschild, get off at the Passable stop (allow 30 minutes from Nice and 10 minutes from Villefranche-sur-Mer's Octroi stop). Find schedules posted at stops, or get one from a TI. The times listed for *Direction Le Port/Cap Ferrat* are when buses depart from Nice—allow 15 minutes after that for Villefranche-sur-Mer. The return bus (direction: Nice) begins in St-Jean.

Cap Ferrat is quick by **car** (take the Low Corniche) or **taxi** (allow €30 one-way from Villefranche-sur-Mer, €65 from Nice). You'll pay for metered parking in summer, but it's free from mid-October through April.

EAST OF NICE

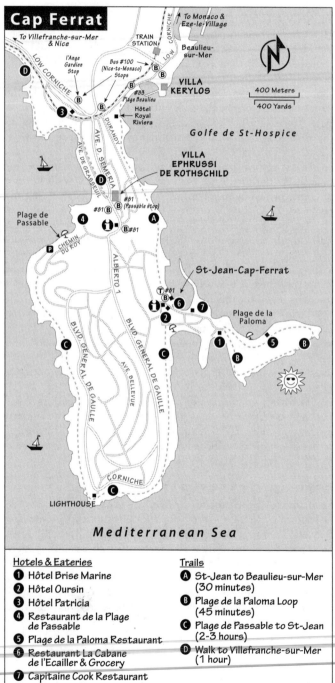

Cap Ferrat

To Villefranche-sur-Mer
& Nice

To Monaco &
Eze-le-Village

TRAIN
STATION

l'Ange
Gardien
Stop

Beaulieu-
sur-Mer

Bus #100
(Nice-to-Monaco)
Stops

LOW CORNICHE

VILLA
KERYLS

B

#93
Plage Beaulieu

400 Meters

400 Yards

Hôtel
Royal
Riviera

AVE. D. SEMERIA

Golfe de St-Hospice

VILLA
EPHRUSSI
DE ROTHSCHILD

#81
(Passable stop)

Plage de
Passable

B

A

CHEMIN
DU ROY

B #81

P

St-Jean-Cap-Ferrat

Plage de la
Paloma

ALBERTO 1

T #81

B

BLVD. GÉNÉRAL DE GAULLE

BLVD. GÉNÉRAL DE GAULLE

AVE. BELLEVUE

C

C

CORNICHE

C

LIGHTHOUSE

Mediterranean Sea

Hotels & Eateries
1 Hôtel Brise Marine
2 Hôtel Oursin
3 Hôtel Patricia
4 Restaurant de la Plage
   de Passable
5 Plage de la Paloma Restaurant
6 Restaurant La Cabane
   de l'Ecailler & Grocery
7 Capitaine Cook Restaurant

Trails
A St-Jean to Beaulieu-sur-Mer
   (30 minutes)
B Plage de la Paloma Loop
   (45 minutes)
C Plage de Passable to St-Jean
   (2-3 hours)
D Walk to Villefranche-sur-Mer
   (1 hour)

You can also **walk** an hour from Villefranche-sur-Mer to Cap Ferrat: Go past the train station along the small beach lane, then climb the steps at the far end of the beach and walk parallel to the tracks on Avenue Louise Bordes. Continue straight past the mansions, and take the first right on Avenue de Grasseuil. You'll see signs to *Villa Ephrussi de Rothschild,* then to Cap Ferrat's port.

Sights on Cap Ferrat

▲VILLA EPHRUSSI DE ROTHSCHILD

In what seems like the ultimate in Riviera extravagance, Venice, Versailles, and the Côte d'Azur come together in the pastel-pink Villa Ephrussi. Rising above Cap Ferrat, this 1905 mansion has views west to Villefranche-sur-Mer and east to Beaulieu-sur-Mer. As you enter the grounds, look back and see the villa's neighbor— the late Paul Allen's mansion—on an equally prominent high point surrounded by a private forest.

Cost and Hours: Palace and gardens-€14, includes audioguide; mid-Feb-Oct daily 10:00-18:00, July-Aug until 19:00; Nov-mid-Feb Mon-Fri 14:00-18:00, Sat-Sun 10:00-18:00; tel. 04 93 01 33 09, www.villa-ephrussi.com. Kids enjoy the free treasure-hunt booklet.

Getting There: With luck, drivers can find a free spot to park along the entry road just inside the gate. The nearest bus stop is Passable, just a few minutes after the bus turns onto Cap Ferrat (bus #81, 5-minute walk uphill to the villa). If returning to Nice or Villefranche-sur-Mer by bus, check the posted schedule, and keep in mind that you're only a minute from the time-point listed for Port de St-Jean.

Visiting the Villa: Buy your ticket at the side of the building with the gift shop and get the small map of the gardens, then walk to the main entrance and pick up an audioguide. Start with the well-furnished belle-époque ground floor (well described by the audioguide). Upstairs, an 18-minute film (with English subtitles) explains the gardens and villa and gives you good background on the life of rich and eccentric Béatrice, Baroness de Rothschild, the French banking heiress who built and furnished the place.

As you stroll through the upstairs rooms, you'll pass royal furnishings and personal possessions, including the baroness's porcelain collection and her bathroom case for cruises. Her bedroom, sensibly, has views to the sea on both the port and starboard sides, and toward the bow, stretching like the prow of a vast cruise ship, is her garden. Don't miss the view from her private terrace.

The gorgeous **gardens** are why most come here. (The audioguide does not cover the gardens.) The ship-shaped gardens were in-

EAST OF NICE

spired by Béatrice's many ocean-liner trips. She even dressed her small army of gardeners like sailors. Behind the mansion, stroll through the seven lush gardens re-created from locations all over the world—and with maximum sea views. Don't miss the Jardin Exotique's wild cactus, the rose garden at the far end, and the view back to the house from the "Temple of Love" gazebo. Cross the stepping-stone bridge by the playful fountains, if you dare.

An appropriately classy **$$ garden-tearoom** serves drinks and lunches with a view (12:00-17:30).

Walks from the Villa Ephrussi: It's a lovely 30-minute stroll, mostly downhill and east, from the Villa Ephrussi to the Villa Kérylos in Beaulieu-sur-Mer (described later) or to the port of St-Jean. To get to either, make a U-turn left at the stop sign below the Villa Ephrussi and follow signs along a small road toward the Hôtel Royal Riviera on Avenue Henri Honoré Sauvan (see "Cap Ferrat" map). Walk about 5 minutes down; when the road comes to a T, keep straight, passing a gate down a pedestrian path, which ends at the seafront trail (on Place David Niven)—go left to reach the Villa Kérylos, or head right to get to St-Jean. It's about 15 minutes to either destination once you join this path.

To get to Plage de Passable from the Villa Ephrussi, turn left on the main road just below the villa; after 50 yards you'll find signs leading down to the beach.

BEACHES
Plage de Passable

This pebbly little beach, located below the Villa Ephrussi, comes with great views of Villefranche-sur-Mer. It's a peaceful place, popular with families. One half is public (free, with snack bar, shower, and WC), and the other is run by a small restaurant (€30 includes changing locker, lounge chair, and shower; they have 260 "beds," but still reserve ahead in summer or on weekends as this is a prime spot, tel. 04 93 76 06 17). If you were ever to do the French Riviera rent-a-beach ritual, this would be the place.

To park near the beach (curbside or in a nearby lot), figure about €12/day in metered spots (free mid-Oct-April). Bus #81 stops a 10-minute walk uphill from the beach, near Villa Ephrussi.

For me, the best reason to come here is for dinner. Arrive before sunset, then watch as darkness descends and lights flicker over Villefranche-sur-Mer's heavenly setting. **$$$ Restaurant de la Plage de Passable** is your chance to dine on the beach with romance and class (with good-enough food) while enjoying terrific views and the sounds of children still at play (daily late May-early Sept, always make a reservation, tel. 04 93 76 06 17).

Plage de la Paloma

This half-private, half-public beach is a 10-minute walk from St-Jean-Cap-Ferrat (described below). For €26 you get a lounge chair and the freedom to relax on the elegant side. Or enjoy the pebbly free beach (with shower and WC).

$$$ Plage de la Paloma Restaurant is inviting for dining on the beach, with salads for lunch and elegant dinners (daily from 12:00 and from 20:00, closed late Sept-Easter, tel. 04 93 01 64 71, www.paloma-beach.com).

ST-JEAN-CAP-FERRAT

This quiet harbor town lies in Cap Ferrat's center, yet is off most tourist itineraries and feels overlooked. St-Jean houses yachts,

boardwalks, views, and boutiques packaged in a "take your time, darling" atmosphere. It's a few miles off the busy Nice-to-Monaco road—convenient for drivers. A string of restaurants lines the port, with just enough visitors and locals to keep them in business. St-Jean is especially peaceful at night. Sit on a whale-tail bench, enjoy the giant clam-shell flowerboxes, and work on your Cyrillic (as many signs come in Russian to cater to the needs of the town's wealthiest guests).

There's a small TI in the village center (described earlier). The stop for the bus back to Villefranche-sur-Mer is a half-block above the TI, and the taxi stand is next to the bus stop (tel. 04 93 76 86 00). The hiking trail to Beaulieu-sur-Mer (with access to the Villa Ephrussi and Villefranche-sur-Mer for hard-core walkers) begins past the beach, to the left of the port as you look out to the water (details follow). If it's lunchtime, you'll find plenty of good options.

Eating in St-Jean: For picnics, the short pedestrian street in St-Jean has all you need (grocery store, bakery, charcuterie, and pizza to go), and you'll have no trouble finding portside or seaside seating. There's a big **Casino grocery** on the port below the main drag. Plage de la Paloma, described earlier, is a 10-minute walk away. Easygoing cafés and pizza joints with views over the port are easy to find.

$$$ Restaurant La Cabane de l'Ecailler, right on the harbor, with fancy yachts for a view, is elegant and expensive but offers a reasonable two-course lunch on weekdays (Nouveau Port de Plaisance, tel. 04 93 87 39 31).

$$ Capitaine Cook is a sweet little mom-and-pop place that takes its fish seriously yet seems to turn its back on the harbor (no views). There's a small patio out back and a cozy interior (good three-course *menu*, tasty *soupe de poisons* and bouillabaisse, closed Wed, a block uphill from the port toward Plage de la Paloma at 11 Avenue Jean Mermoz, tel. 04 93 76 02 66).

▲▲WALKS AROUND CAP FERRAT

The Cap is perfect for a walk; you'll find well-maintained and well-marked foot trails covering most of its length. You have three easy, mostly level options of varying lengths. The TIs in Villefranche-sur-Mer and St-Jean have maps of Cap Ferrat with walking paths marked, or you can use the following itineraries with this book's map.

Between St-Jean and Beaulieu-sur-Mer (30 minutes)

A level walk takes you past sumptuous villas, great views, and fun swimming opportunities. From St-Jean's port, walk along the harbor and past the beach with the water on your right. Head up the steps to Promenade Maurice Rouvier and continue; before long you'll see smashing views of the whitewashed Villa Kérylos.

To get from Beaulieu-sur-Mer to St-Jean or the Villa Ephrussi, start at the Villa Kérylos (with the sea on your left), walk toward the Hôtel Royal Riviera, and find the trail. If going to St-Jean, stay left at the Villa Sonja Rello (about halfway down); if going to the Villa Ephrussi, after about 20 minutes look for signs leading uphill at Place David Niven (walk up the path to Avenue Henri Honoré Sauvan, then keep going). If you're walking from St-Jean to the Villa Ephrussi, turn left off the trail at Place David Niven.

Plage de la Paloma Loop Trail (45 minutes)

A few blocks east of St-Jean's port, a scenic trail offers an easy sampling of Cap Ferrat's beauty. From the port, walk or drive about a quarter-mile east (with the port on your left, passing Hôtel La Voile d'Or); parking is available at the port or on streets near Plage de la Paloma. You'll find the trailhead where the road comes to a T—look for a *Plage Paloma* sign pointing left, but don't walk left. Cross the small gravel park *(Jardin de la Paix)* to start the trail, and do the walk counterclockwise. The trail is level and paved, yet uneven enough that good shoes are helpful. Plunk your picnic on one of the benches along the trail, or eat at the restaurant on Plage de la Paloma at the end of the walk (described earlier).

Plage de Passable Around the Cape to St-Jean (2-3 hours)
For a longer hike that circles the cape, follow the signs below the
Villa Ephrussi marked *Plage Passable* (10 minutes downhill on foot
from the villa, parking available nearby). Walk down to the beach
(you'll pass the recommended Restaurant de la Plage de Passable—
ideal for lunch), turn left, and cross the beach. Go along a paved
road behind the apartment building, and after about 60 yards, take
the steps down to the trail *(Sentier Littoral)*. Walk as far as you
want and double back, or do the whole enchilada—it's about six
miles (10 kilometers) around the cape. Near the end of the trail,
you'll pass through the port of St-Jean, where you can take bus
#81 back to the Plage de Passable/Villa Ephrussi stop, or ride to
Villefranche-sur-Mer or to Nice.

Sleeping on Cap Ferrat

In St-Jean: While St-Jean is the main town serving the notoriously
wealthy community of Cap Ferrat, it does have some affordable
hotels.

$$$ Hôtel Brise Marine,*** graced with gardens and a
seaview terrace, is a peaceful retreat. Warmly run by Monsieur
Maître-Henri, this aged mansion—with Old World character—
feels lost in time. Most of its 16 comfortable rooms come with sim-
ple furnishings but fine views, and some have balconies—worth
requesting (secure pay parking with reservation, between the port
and Plage de la Paloma at 58 Avenue Jean Mermoz, tel. 04 93 76
04 36, www.hotel-brisemarine.com, info@hotel-brisemarine.com).

$ Hôtel Oursin** is central in the village, with 13 well-priced
rooms all on one floor. Run by quirky mother-and-son team Chan-
tal and Aubrey, it's a humble place with white walls that feels
more like a B&B than a hotel, though it does have air-con (1 Av-
enue Denis Séméria, tel. 04 93 76 04 65, www.hoteloursin.com,
reception@hoteloursin.com).

Between St-Jean and Villefranche-sur-Mer: Sitting across
from Villefranche, at the start of Cap Ferrat, **$ Hôtel Patricia***
is a 20-minute walk to Villefranche or the Villa Ephrussi, and 10
minutes to Beaulieu-sur-Mer. Helpful owners Joelle and Franck
provide 11 simple and homey rooms with eclectic decor (no eleva-
tor, air-con in some rooms, pay parking, near bus #100's l'Ange
Gardien stop at 310 Avenue de l'Ange Gardien, tel. 04 93 01 06
70, www.hotel-patricia.riviera.fr, hotel.lavillapatricia@gmail.com).

Villa Kérylos

The village of Beaulieu-sur-Mer, right on the Low Corniche road (just after Cap Ferrat), is busy with traffic and tourists. It's a good

place to pick up the hiking trail to Cap Ferrat sights and to visit the unusual Villa Kérylos. In 1902, an eccentric millionaire modeled his mansion after a Greek villa from the island of Delos from about 200 BC. No expense was spared in re-creating this Greek fantasy, from the floor mosaics to Carrara marble columns to exquisite wood furnishings modeled on discoveries made in Pompeii. The rain-powered shower is fun (but from a later time), and the included audioguide will increase your Greek IQ. The mosaic workshop—open only high season and weekend afternoons—offers a chance to test your talents.

Cost and Hours: €12, €14 combo-ticket with Le Trophée des Alpes, includes audioguide; daily 10:00-19:00, Oct-May until 17:00; tel. 04 93 01 47 29, www.villakerylos.fr.

Getting There: Drivers should park near the casino in Beaulieu-sur-Mer, not on the villa's access road. **Buses** #81 and #100 drop you at the Villa Kérylos stop at the villa's access road (for details on these buses, see page 8). **Trains** (2/hour, 10 minutes from Nice or Monaco) leave you a 10-minute walk away: Turn left out of the train station and left again down the main drag, then follow signs. The **walking trail** from Villa Kérylos to Cap Ferrat and the Villa Ephrussi de Rothschild begins on the other side of the bay, beneath Hôtel Royal Riviera.

Eze-le-Village

Capping a peak high above the sea, flowery and flawless Eze-le-

Village (pronounced "ehz"; don't confuse it with the seafront town of Eze-Bord-de-Mer) is entirely consumed by tourism. This *village d'art et de gastronomie* (as it calls itself) is home to perfume outlets, stylish boutiques, steep cobbled lanes, and magnificent views. Touristy as it Eze, its stony state of preservation and magnificent hilltop setting over the Mediterranean affords a fine memory. Day-tripping by bus to Eze-le-Village from Nice, Monaco, or Villefranche-sur-Mer works well. While Eze-le-Village can be tranquil early and late, during the day it is mobbed by cruise-ship and tour-bus groups. Come early or late in the day.

GETTING TO EZE-LE-VILLAGE

There are two Ezes: Eze-le-Village (the spectacular hill town on the Middle Corniche) and Eze-Bord-de-Mer (a modern beach resort far below the "village" of Eze). Parking in Eze-le-Village will be a headache in 2019 as construction is underway for a new underground garage.

From Nice and upper Villefranche-sur-Mer, buses #82 and #112 together provide about hourly service to Eze-le-Village (only #82 runs on Sun, 30 minutes from Nice).

From Nice, Villefranche-sur-Mer, or Monaco, you can also take the train or the Nice-Monaco bus (#100) to Eze-Bord-de-Mer, getting off at the Gare d'Eze stop. From there, take the infre-quent #83 shuttle bus straight up to Eze-le-Village (8/day, daily about 9:00-18:00, schedule posted at stop, 15 minutes). Those com-ing from Villefranche-sur-Mer can also take buses #81 or #100 and transfer to bus #83 at the Plage Beaulieu stop in Beaulieu-sur-Mer.

To connect Eze-le-Village directly with Monte Carlo in Mo-naco, take bus #112 (6/day Mon-Sat, none on Sun, 20 minutes).

There are no buses between La Turbie (Le Trophée d'Auguste) and Eze-le-Village (45-minute walk along the road's shoulder).

A taxi between the two Ezes or from Eze-le-Village to La Turbie will run you about €30; allow €65 to Nice's port (mobile 06 09 84 17 84 or 06 18 44 47 93).

Orientation to Eze-le-Village

Tourist Information: The helpful TI is adjacent to Eze-le-Vil-lage's main parking lot, just below the town's entry. Ask here for bus schedules. Call at least a week in advance to arrange a €12, one-hour English-language tour of the village that includes its gardens (TI open daily 9:00-18:00, July-Aug until 19:00, Nov-March until

16:00 and closed Sun, Place de Gaulle, tel. 04 93 41 26 00, www. eze-tourisme.com).

Helpful Hints: The stop for **buses** to Nice is across the road by the Avia gas station, and the stops for buses to Eze-Bord-de-Mer and Monaco are on the village side of the main road, near the Casino grocery. Public **WCs** are just behind the TI and in the village behind the church.

Eze-le-Village Walk

This self-guided walk gives you a quick orientation to the village.

• *From the TI, hike uphill into the town. You'll come to an exclusive hotel gate and the start of a steep trail down to the beach, marked* Eze/Mer. *For a panoramic view and an ideal picnic perch, side-trip 90 steps down this path (for details, see "Hike to Eze-Bord-de-Mer," later). Continuing up into the village, find the steps immediately after the ritzy hotel gate and climb to...*

Place du Centenaire: In this square, a stone plaque in the flower bed (behind the candy stand) celebrates the 100th anniversary of the 1860 plebiscite, the time when all 133 Eze residents voted to leave the Italian Duchy of Savoy and join France. A town map here helps you get oriented.

• *Now pass through the once-formidable town gate and climb into the 14th-century village.*

As you walk, stop to read the information plaques (in English) and contemplate the change this village has witnessed in the last 90 years. Eze-le-Village was off any traveler's radar until well after World War II (running water was made available only in the 1930s), yet today hotel rooms outnumber local residents two to one (66 to 33).

• *Wandering the narrow lanes, consider a detour to* **Château de la Chèvre d'Or** *for its elegant bar-lounge and sprawling view terrace (high prices but high views). Continue on, following signs to the...*

Château Eza: This was the winter getaway of the Swedish royal family from 1923 until 1953; today it's a 15-room hotel. The château's tearoom (Salon de Thé), on a cliff overlooking the jagged Riviera and sea, offers another scenic coffee or beer break—for a price. The view terrace is also home to an expensive-but-excellent **$$$$** restaurant (open daily, tel. 04 93 41 12 24).

• *Backtrack a bit and continue uphill (follow signs to* Jardin Exotique*). The lane ends at the hilltop castle ruins—now blanketed by the...*

Jardin d'Eze: You'll find this prickly festival of cactus and exotic plants suspended between the sea and sky at the top of Eze-le-Village. Since 1949, the ruins of an old château have been home to 400 different plants 1,400 feet above the sea (€6, usually daily 9:00-19:00, Oct-May until about 16:00, well described in English, tel. 04 93 41 10 30). At the top, you'll be treated to a commanding 360-degree view, with a helpful *table d'orientation.* On a clear day (they say...) you can see Corsica. The castle was demolished by Louis XIV in 1706. Louis destroyed castles like this all over Europe (most notably along the Rhine), because he didn't want to risk having to do battle with their owners at some future date.

• *As you descend, follow the pastel bell tower and drop by the...*

Eze Church: Though built during Napoleonic times, this church has an uncharacteristic Baroque fanciness—a reminder that 300 years of Savoy rule left the townsfolk with an Italian savoir faire and a sensibility for decor. Notice the pulpit with the arm holding a crucifix, reminding the faithful that Christ died for their sins.

Sights in Eze-le-Village

Fragonard Perfume Factory

This factory, with its huge tour-bus parking lot, lies on the Middle Corniche, 100 yards below Eze-le-Village. Designed for tour groups, it cranks them through all day long. If you've never seen mass tourism in action, this place will open your eyes. (The gravel is littered with the color-coded stickers each tourist wears so that salespeople know which guide gets the kickback.) Drop in for an informative and free tour (2/hour, 15 minutes). You'll see how the perfume and scented soaps are made before being herded into the gift shop.

Cost and Hours: Daily 8:30-18:30; best Mon-Fri 9:00-11:00 & 14:00-15:30, when people are actually working in the "factory," tel. 04 93 41 05 05.

Nearby: For a more intimate (but unguided) look at perfume, cross the main road in Eze-le-Village to visit the **Gallimard** shop. Explore the small museum (no English) and let the lovely ladies show you their scents (daily 9:00-18:00, across from Eze parking lot). They can give you a short tour if you ask.

Hike to Eze-Bord-de-Mer

A steep trail leaves Eze-le-Village from the foot of the hill-town entry, near the fancy hotel gate (100 yards up from the main road), and descends 1,300 feet to the sea along a no-shade, all-view trail. The trail is easy to follow but uneven in a few sections—allow 45 minutes (good walking shoes are essential; expect to be on all fours in certain sections). Once in Eze-Bord-de-Mer, you can catch a bus or train to all destinations between Nice and Monaco. While walking this trail in the late 1800s, Friedrich Nietzsche was moved to write his unconventionally spiritual novel, *Thus Spoke Zarathustra*.

Eating in Eze-le-Village

There's a handy **Casino** grocery at the foot of the village by the bus stop (daily 8:00-19:30) and an excellent bakery across the main road from that. Take your feast to the sensational picnic spot at the beginning of the trail to Eze-Bord-de-Mer or see my driving directions under "The Corniche Roads" (described earlier) to get to an eagle's-nest picnic site. **$ Le Cactus** serves crêpes, salads, and sandwiches at outdoor tables near the entry to the old town and inside their cozy, vaulted dining room (daily until about 19:30, tel. 04 93 41 19 02). For a real splurge, dine at **$$$$ Château de la Chèvre d'Or** (described earlier, on my "Eze-le-Village Walk").

Le Trophée des Alpes

High above Monaco, on the Grande Corniche in the overlooked village of La Turbie, lies the ancient Roman "Trophy of the Alps," one of this region's most evocative historical sights (with dramatic views over the entire country of Monaco as a bonus). Rising well above all other buildings, this massive monument, worth ▲, commemorates Augustus Caesar's conquest of the Alps and its 44 hostile tribes. It's exciting to think that, in a way, Le Trophée des Alpes (also called "Le Trophée d'Auguste" for the emperor who built it) celebrates a victory that kicked off the Pax Romana—joining Gaul and Germania, freeing up the main artery of the Roman Empire, and linking Spain and Italy.

GETTING THERE

By Car: Take the High Corniche to La Turbie, ideally from Eze-le-Village (La Turbie is 10 minutes east of, and above, Eze-le-Village), then look for signs to *Le Trophée d'Auguste*. Once in La Turbie, drive to the site by turning right in front of the La Régence café. Those coming from farther afield can take the efficient A-8 to the La Turbie exit. To reach Eze-le-Village from La Turbie, follow signs to *Nice*, and then look for signs to *Eze-le-Village*.

By Bus: From Nice, you can get here Monday through Saturday on **buses #116** or **#T-66** (6/day each from the Vauban tram stop); on Sunday take bus #T-66 (from the Pont St. Michel tram stop). From Monaco, bus #11 connects to La Turbie (8/day Mon-Sat, 5/day Sun, 30 minutes). La Turbie's bus stop is near the post office (La Poste) on Place Neuve.

On Foot: Eze-le-Village is a 45-minute roadside walk downhill from La Turbie (no buses). There's a bike lane for half of the trip, but the rest is along a fairly quiet road with no shoulder. Follow D-2564 from La Turbie to Eze-le-Village, and don't miss the turnoff for D-45. The views of Eze-le-Village are magnificent as you get close.

ORIENTATION TO LE TROPHEE DES ALPES

Cost and Hours: €6, €14 combo-ticket with Villa Kérylos, Tue-Sun 9:30-13:00 & 14:30-18:30, off-season 10:00-13:30 & 14:30-17:00, closed Mon year-round.

Tours and Information: The €3 audioguide may be overkill, as English explanations are posted throughout the site. Tel. 04 93 41 20 84, www.la-turbie.monuments-nationaux.fr.

VISITING THE MONUMENT

You'll enter through a small park that delivers grand views over Monaco and allows you to appreciate the remarkable setting selected by the Romans for this monument. Circumnavigate the hulking structure. Notice how the Romans built a fine stone exterior using 24 massive columns that held together a towering cylinder filled with rubble and coarse concrete. Find the huge inscription on the back side of the monument. Flanked by the vanquished in chains, the towering inscription (one of the longest such inscriptions surviving from ancient times) tells the story: It was erected "by the senate and the people to honor the emperor."

The structure served no military purpose when built except to intimidate local tribes. The monument was fortified a thousand years later in the Middle Ages (like the Roman Arena in Arles) as a safe haven for villagers. When Louis XIV ordered the destruction of the area's fortresses in the early 18th century, he sadly included this one. The monument later became a quarry for homes in La Turbie before being restored in the 1930s and 1940s with money from the Tuck family of New Hampshire.

A guardian will escort you halfway up the monument and give you a detailed explanation in English if you ask.

The good little one-room **museum** shows a model of the monument, a video, and information about its history and reconstruction. There's also a translation of the dramatic inscription, which lists all the feisty alpine tribes that put up such a fight.

NEAR THE MONUMENT: LA TURBIE

The sweet old village of La Turbie sees almost no tourists, but it has plenty of cafés and restaurants. To stroll the old village, walk behind the post office and find brick footpaths that lead through the peaceful back lanes of the village.

Eating in La Turbie: Your best bet is the welcoming **$$ Restaurant La Terrasse,** with tables under umbrellas and big views (daily for lunch and dinner, near the post office at the main parking lot, 17 Place Neuve, tel. 04 93 41 21 84). Charming owners Jacques and Helen speak flawless English.

Quickie Riviera Bus Tour

The Riviera from Nice to Monaco is so easy to tour by bus and train that those with a car should consider leaving it at their hotel. While the train laces together the charms of this dramatic stretch of Mediterranean coast as if on a scenic bracelet, the public bus affords a far better view of the crags, dreamy villas, and much-loved beaches that make it Europe's coast with the most.

Planning Your Ride

This tour is designed for those riding the bus from Nice to Monaco and back. You could also ride the entire route to Menton (1.5 hours), enjoy Menton (see the end of the next chapter), and then see Monaco on the way back to Nice. Get an early start. Keep in mind that afternoon buses back to Nice are often crammed and agonizingly slow after Villefranche-sur-Mer—at these times, take the train.

Bus Tips: Bus #100 runs frequently along the Low Corniche (3-4/hour). The first stop in Nice is at the city's port—see map on page 18). One €1.50 ticket is good for 74 minutes, no matter how far you go (one-way only). Pay the driver as you get on.

Riding from Nice toward Monaco, grab a seat on the right and start before 9:00. Stops are announced on most buses and shown on a screen at the front. The last bus leaves Monaco for Nice at about 21:30 (always verify last times).

Since bus fares are cheap, consider hopping on and off at great viewpoints (the next bus is always 15-20 minutes away). All stops have names that are usually posted on the shelter or bus stop sign— I'll use the bus stop names to orient you as we go.

Some bus drivers on this line are in training for the Grand Prix of Monaco—hold on tight.

From Nice to Monaco

This route along the Low Corniche was inaugurated with the opening of the Monte Carlo Casino in 1863. It was designed to provide easy and safe access from Nice (and the rest of France) to the gambling fun in Monaco. Here's what you'll see along the way:

Nice Harbor: This harbor—dredged by 400 convicts—was finished in the mid-1800s. Before then, boats littered Nice's beaches. You'll see some yachts, an occasional cruise ship, and maybe the ferry to Corsica. The one-hour boat tour along Cap Ferrat and Villefranche-sur-Mer leaves from the right side, about halfway down (see page 23). If you return by bus #100, it's a pleasant 30-minute walk around the distant point to or from the Promenade des Anglais and Nice's old town.

From Nice to Villefranche-sur-Mer: As you glide away from Nice, look back for views of the harbor, Castle Hill, and the sweeping Bay of Angels. Imagine the views from the homes below, and imagine 007 on his deck admiring a sunset (the soft, yellow, rounded tower straight ahead near the top of the hill was part of Sean Connery's property). Elton John's home is higher up the hill (and out of view). Imagine his neighbor, Tina Turner, dropping by for a glass of wine.

You'll soon pass the Palais Maeterlinck, one of several luxury hotels to go belly-up in recent years and be converted to luxury condos. Next, you'll come to the yacht-studded bay of Villefranche-sur-Mer and the peninsula called Cap Ferrat—retreat of the rich and famous, marked by its lighthouse on the point just across the bay. This bay is a rare natural harbor along the Riviera. Since it's deeper than Nice's, it hosts huge cruise ships, which drop anchor and tender passengers in.

Villefranche-sur-Mer: To see Villefranche-sur-Mer, get off at the stop labeled *Octroi*.

After passing through Villefranche-sur-Mer, look for sensational views back over the town (best from the Madonne-Noire stop). Spot the small point of land on the water with umbrella pine trees as the road arcs to the right—the Rolling Stones recorded 1972's *Exile on Main Street* in the basement of the Villa Nellcôte, the mansion below the l'Ange Gardien stop. The Baroness Rothschild's pink Villa Ephrussi, with its red-tiled roof, breaks the horizon on Cap Ferrat's peninsula.

Cap Ferrat: This peninsula is home to the Villa Ephrussi de Rothschild, the port town of St-Jean, and some lovely seaside paths. To visit Cap Ferrat, get off at l'Ange Gardien stop. As you leave Cap Ferrat, remember that this road was built in the 1860s to bring customers to Monaco. Before then, there was nothing along this route—no one even lived here—all the way to Monaco.

Beaulieu-sur-Mer: To take the seaside walk to St-Jean on Cap Ferrat get off at Plage Beaulieu. To visit the Villa Kérylos get off at the next stop for Kérylos.

Just after the town of Beaulieu-sur-Mer, the cliffs create a microclimate and a zone nick-named "Little Africa." (The bus stop is labeled *Petite Afrique*.) Exotic vegetation (including the only bananas on the Riviera) grows among private, elegant villas that made Beaulieu-sur-Mer *the* place to be in the 19th century.

Eze-Bord-de-Mer: Soon after leaving Beaulieu-sur-Mer, be ready for quickie views way up to the fortified town of Eze-le-Village. After passing through a rock arch, you'll swing around a big bend going left: Eze-le-Village crowns the ridge toward the right. To reach Eze-le-Village by bus, the #83 shuttle bus makes the climb from the Gare d'Eze stop in Eze-Bord-de-Mer—see page 95. U2's Bono owns a villa on the beach below.

Cap d'Ail: After passing through several short tunnels, you emerge at Cap d'Ail. Near the Deux Tunnels stop, you can't miss the huge, yellowish, hospital-like building below that once thrived as a luxury hotel popular with the Russian aristocracy. Now it's luxury condos. At the next stop (Cap d'Ail-Edmonds), try to look left and above at the switchbacks halfway up the barren hillside (visible from the left side of the bus). It was at the bend connecting these two switchbacks that Princess Grace Kelly (the American movie star who married into the royal family of Monaco) was killed in a car crash in 1982.

Monaco (three bus stops): Cap d'Ail borders Monaco—you're about to leave France. You'll pass by some junky development along this no-man's-land stretch. Eventually, to the right, just before the castle-topped hill (Monaco-Ville), is Monaco's Fontvieille district, featuring tall, modern apartments all built on land reclaimed from the Mediterranean. The first Monaco stop (Place d'Armes) is best for visiting the palace and other old-town sights in Monaco-Ville.

If you stay on the bus, you'll pass through the tunnel, then emerge to follow the road that Grand Prix racers speed along. In late May you'll see blue bleachers and barriers set up for the big race.

You'll pass the second Monaco stop (on the port, named Princesse Antoinette), then enjoy the harbor and city views as you climb to the last Monaco stop (Casino), near the TI. Get off here for the casino. For information on Monaco, see the next chapter. If you stay on the bus for a few more minutes, you'll be back in France, and in 15 more minutes you'll reach the end of the line, **Menton** (described in the following chapter).

Bonne route!

MONACO

Despite high prices, wall-to-wall daytime tourists, and a Disney-esque atmosphere, Monaco is a Riviera must. Monaco is on the go. Since 1929, cars have raced around the port and in front of the casino in one of the world's most famous auto races, the Grand Prix de Monaco. The modern breakwater—constructed elsewhere and towed in by sea—enables big cruise ships to dock here, and the district of Fontvieille, reclaimed from the sea, bristles with luxury high-rise condos. But don't look for anything too deep in this glittering tax haven. Many of its 36,000 residents live here because there's no income tax—there are only about 6,000 true Monegasques.

This minuscule principality (0.75 square mile) borders only France and the Mediterranean. The country has always been tiny, but it used to be...less tiny. In an 1860 plebiscite, Monaco lost two-thirds of its territory when the region of Menton voted to join France. To compensate, France suggested that Monaco build a fancy casino and promised to connect it to the world with a road (the Low Corniche) and a train line. This started a high-class tourist boom that has yet to let up.

Although "independent," Monaco is run as a part of France. A French civil servant appointed by the French president—with the blessing of Monaco's prince—serves as state minister and manages the place. Monaco's phone system, electricity, water, and so on, are all French.

The glamorous romance and marriage of the American actress Grace Kelly to Prince Rainier added to Monaco's fairy-tale mystique. Princess Grace first came to Monaco to star in the 1955 Alfred Hitchcock movie *To Catch a Thief*, in which she was filmed racing along the Corniches. She married the prince in 1956 and adopted the country, but tragically, the much-loved princess died in 1982 after suffering a stroke while driving on one of those same scenic roads. She was just 52 years old.

The death of Prince Rainier in 2005 ended his 56-year-long enlightened reign. Today, Monaco is ruled by Prince Albert Alexandre Louis Pierre, Marquis of Baux—son of Prince Rainier and Princess Grace. Prince Albert was long considered Europe's most eligible bachelor—until he finally married on July 2, 2011, at age 53. His bride, known as Princess Charlene, is a South African commoner 20 years his junior.

A graduate of Amherst College, Albert is a bobsled enthusiast who raced in several Olympics, and an avid environmentalist who seems determined to clean up Monaco's tarnished tax-haven, money-laundering image. (Monaco is infamously known as a "sunny place for shady people.") Monaco is big business, and Prince Albert is its CEO. Its famous casino contributes only 5 percent of the state's revenue, whereas its many banks—which offer a hard-to-resist way to hide your money—are hugely profitable. The prince also makes money for Monaco with a value-added tax (20 percent, same as in France), plus real estate and corporate taxes.

Monaco is a special place: There are more people in Monaco's philharmonic orchestra (about 100) than in its army (about 80). Yet the princedom is well guarded, with police and cameras on every corner. (They say you could win a million dollars at the casino and walk to the train station in the wee hours without a worry.) Stamps are printed in small quantities and increase in value almost as soon as they're available. And collectors snapped up the rare Monaco versions of euro coins (with Prince Rainier's portrait) so quickly that many Monegasques have never even seen one.

Orientation to Monaco

The principality of Monaco has three tourist areas: Monaco-Ville, Monte Carlo, and La Condamine. **Monaco-Ville** fills the rock high above everything else and is referred to by locals as Le Rocher ("The Rock"). This is the oldest part of Monaco, home to the Prince's Palace and all the key sights except the casino. **Monte Carlo** is the area around the casino. **La Condamine** is the port,

which lies between Monaco-Ville and Monte Carlo. From here it's a 20-minute walk up to the Prince's Palace or to the casino, or a few minutes by frequent bus to either (see "Getting Around Monaco," later).

Most travelers will want to organize their trip around the 11:55 Changing of the Guard at the palace and touring the casino. The surgical-strike plan is to start at Monaco-Ville (where you'll spend the most time and see the Changing of the Guard), wander down along the port area, and finish by gambling away whatever you have left in Monte Carlo (the casino's high-roller game rooms don't open until 14:00, but the rest of the joint opens at 9:00). If you don't care to gamble and can get started early, consider reversing this route: Tour the casino first, then visit Monaco-Ville in time to see the Changing of the Guard. You can walk the entire route in about 1.5 hours, or take three bus trips and do it in 15 minutes.

TOURIST INFORMATION

The main TI is at the top of the park above the casino (Mon-Sat 9:00-19:00, Sun 11:00-13:00, 2 Boulevard des Moulins, tel. 00-377/92 16 61 16 or 00-377/92 16 61 66, www.visitmonaco.com). Another TI is at the train station (daily mid-June-mid-Sept 9:00-18:00, off-season Tue-Sat until 17:00, closed 12:30-14:00, closed Sun-Mon).

ARRIVAL IN MONACO

By Bus #100 from Nice and Villefranche-sur-Mer: See my "Quickie Riviera Bus Tour" on page 100 to plan your route. Bus riders need to pay attention to the monitor showing the next stop. Cap d'Ail is the town before Monaco, so be on the lookout after that (the last stop before Monaco is called "Cimetière"). You'll enter Monaco through the modern cityscape of high-rises in the Fontvieille district. When you see the rocky outcrop of old Monaco, be ready to get off.

There are three stops in Monaco. In order from Nice, they are Place d'Armes (at the base of Monaco-Ville), Princesse Antoinette (on the port), and Monte Carlo-Casino (in front of the TI on Boulevard des Moulins).

Most riders will get off at **Place d'Armes** to visit Monaco-Ville first. Use the crosswalk in front of the tunnel, then keep right and find bus stops #1 and #2 and the ramp to the palace. Casino-first types wait for the *Monte Carlo-Casino* stop. There's no reason to exit at the port stop.

By Train from Nice: The long, entirely underground train station is in the center of Monaco. From here, it's a 15-minute walk to the casino or the port, and about 15 minutes to the base of the palace (and frequent local buses). The station has no baggage storage. The TI, train-ticket windows, and WCs are up the escalator

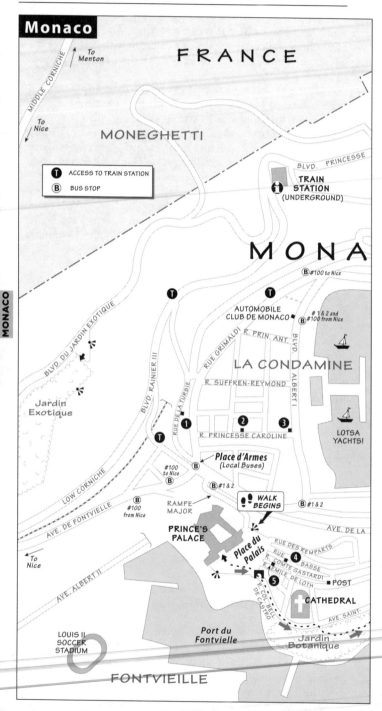

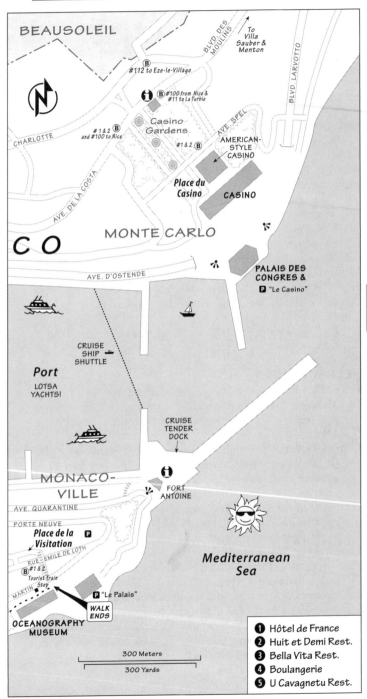

MONACO

BEAUSOLEIL

BLVD. DES MOULINS

To Villa Sauber & Menton

BLVD. LARVOTTO

(B) #112 to Eze-le-Village

(B) #100 from Nice & #11 to La Turbie

Casino Gardens

AVE. SPEL

#1 & 2 and #100 to Nice (B)

CHARLOTTE

#1 & 2 (B)

AMERICAN-STYLE CASINO

AVE. DE LA COSTA

Place du Casino

CASINO

CO

MONTE CARLO

AVE. D'OSTENDE

PALAIS DES CONGRES &
(P) "Le Casino"

CRUISE SHIP SHUTTLE

Port

LOTSA YACHTS!

CRUISE TENDER DOCK

MONACO-VILLE

FORT ANTOINE

AVE. QUARANTINE

PORTE NEUVE

Place de la Visitation (P)

Mediterranean Sea

RUE EMILE DE LOTH

(B) #1 & 2
Tourist Train Stop

MARTIN

(P) "Le Palais"

WALK ENDS

OCEANOGRAPHY MUSEUM

300 Meters

300 Yards

1	Hôtel de France
2	Huit et Demi Rest.
3	Bella Vita Rest.
4	Boulangerie
5	U Cavagnetu Rest.

at the Italy end of the station. There are three exits from the train platform level (one at each end and one in the middle).

To reach Monaco-Ville and the palace, take the exit at the Nice end of the tracks (signed *Sortie Fontvieille/Le Rocher*), which leads through a long tunnel and along a pedestrian plaza to the base of Monaco-Ville at Place d'Armes (turn left when you reach the busy street). From here, it's about a 15-minute hike up to the palace, or five minutes by bus (#1 or #2) plus a short walk.

To reach Monaco's port and the casino, take the middle exit, following *Sortie Port Hercule* signs down the steps and escalators, and then *Accès Port* signs until you pop out at the port, where you'll see the stop for buses #1 and #2 across the busy street. From here, it's a 20-minute walk to the casino (up Avenue d'Ostende to your left), or a short trip via bus #1 or #2.

If you plan to return to Nice by train in the evening (after ticket windows close), buy your return tickets on arrival or use the ticket machines (about €4 in coins or use a credit card with a chip).

By Car: Follow *Centre-Ville* signs into Monaco (warning: traffic can be heavy), then watch for the signs to parking garages at *Le Casino* (for Monte Carlo) or *Le Palais* (for Monaco-Ville). You'll pay about €12 for four hours.

By Cruise Ship: See "Monaco Connections," near the end of this chapter.

HELPFUL HINTS

Grand Prix Prep: If you come anytime from early April through May, you'll encounter construction detours as the country prepares for its largest event of the year, the Grand Prix de Monaco.

Combo-Tickets: If you plan to see both of Monaco's big sights (Prince's Palace and Oceanography Museum), buy the €20.50 combo-ticket. Another combo-ticket includes the Prince's private car collection in Fontvieille (not covered in this book).

Changing of the Guard: This popular event takes place daily (in good weather) at 11:55 at the Prince's Palace. Arrive by 11:30 to get a good viewing spot.

Loop Trip by Bus or Train: From Nice, you can get to Monaco by bus or train, then take a bus from Monaco to Eze-le-Village or La Turbie, and return to Nice from there by bus. For bus numbers, frequencies, and stop locations, see "Monaco Connections," near the end of this chapter.

Evening Events: Monaco's cultural highlights include its **Philharmonic Orchestra** (tel. 00-377/98 06 28 28, www.opmc. mc) and **Monte Carlo Ballet** (tel. 00-377/99 99 30 00, www. balletsdemontecarlo.com).

Passport Stamp: For an official memento of your visit, get your passport stamped at the TI.

Post Office: The handiest post office for local stamps is in Monaco-Ville (described on my self-guided walk; Mon-Fri 8:00-19:00, Sat until 13:00, closed Sun).

GETTING AROUND MONACO

By Local Bus: Buses #1 and #2 link all areas with frequent service (10/hour, fewer on Sun, buses run until 21:00). If you pay the driver, a single ticket is €2, 6 tickets-€11, a day pass-€5.50; save by using red curbside machines, where you get 12 tickets for €11. You can split a 6-or 12-ride ticket with your travel partners. Bus tickets are good for a free transfer if used within 30 minutes.

For a **cheap and scenic loop ride** through Monaco, ride bus #2 from one end to the other and back (25 minutes each way). You'll need two tickets and must get off the bus at the last stop and then get on again.

By Open Bus Tour: You could pay €23 for a hop-on, hop-off open-deck bus tour that makes 12 stops in Monaco, but I wouldn't. If you want a scenic tour of the principality that includes its best views, take local bus #2 for much less (see above).

By Tourist Train: An efficient way to enjoy a scenic blitz tour, **Monaco Tours** tourist trains begin at the Oceanography Museum and pass by the port, casino, and palace (€10, 2/hour, 30 minutes, recorded English commentary).

By Taxi: If you've lost all track of time at the casino, you can call the 24-hour taxi service (tel. 00-377/93 15 01 01)...assuming you still have enough money to pay for the cab home.

Monaco-Ville Walk

All of Monaco's major sights (except the casino) are in Monaco-Ville, packed within a few Disneyesque blocks. This self-guided walk connects these sights in a tight little loop, starting from the palace square.

• *To get from anywhere in Monaco to the palace square (Monaco-Ville's sightseeing center and home of the palace), take bus #1 or #2 to the end of the line at Place de la Visitation. Turn right as you step off the bus and walk five minutes down Rue Emile de Loth. You'll pass the post office, a worthwhile stop for its collection of valuable Monegasque stamps (we'll go there later—to visit it now, see the end of this walk).*

Palace Square (Place du Palais)

This square is the best place to get oriented to Monaco. Facing the palace, walk to the right and look out over the city (er...principality). This rock gave birth to the little pastel Hong Kong look-alike

in 1215, and it's managed to remain an independent country for most of its 800 years. Looking beyond the glitzy port, notice the faded green dome roof: It belongs to the casino that put Monaco on the map in the 1800s. The casino was located away from Monaco-Ville because Prince Charles III (r. 1856-1889) wanted to shield his people from low-life gamblers.

The modern buildings just past the casino mark the eastern limit of Monaco. The famous Grand Prix runs along the port and then up the ramp to the casino (at top speeds of 180 mph). Italy is so close, you can almost smell the pesto. Just beyond the casino is France again (it flanks Monaco on both sides)—you could walk one-way from France to France, passing through Monaco, in about 60 minutes.

The odd statue of a woman with a fishing net is dedicated to the glorious reign of **Prince Albert I** (1889-1922). The son of Charles III (who built the casino), Albert I was a true Renaissance Man. He had a Jacques Cousteau-like fascination with the sea (and built Monaco's famous aquarium, the Oceanography Museum) and was a determined pacifist who made many attempts to dissuade Germany's Kaiser Wilhelm II from becoming involved in World War I.

Escape the crowds for a moment with a short detour up the street, keeping the view on your left. Gawk at the houses lining the street and imagine waking up to that view every day.

• *Head toward the palace, passing electric car chargers (Prince Albert is an environmentalist), and find a statue of a monk grasping a sword.*

*Meet **François Grimaldi**, a renegade sword-carrying Italian dressed as a monk, who captured Monaco in 1297 and began the dynasty that still rules the principality. Prince Albert is his great-great-great... grandson, which gives Monaco's royal family the distinction of being the longest-lasting dynasty in Europe.*

Now walk to the...

Prince's Palace (Palais Princier)

A medieval castle once sat where the palace is today. Its strategic setting has had a lot to do with Monaco's ability to resist attackers. Today, Prince Albert and his wife live in the palace, while poor Princesses Stephanie and Caroline live down the street. The palace guards protect the prince 24/7 and still stage a **Changing of the Guard** ceremony with all the pageantry of an important nation (daily at 11:55 in good weather, fun to watch but jam-packed, arrive by 11:30). An audioguide takes you through part of the prince's lavish palace in 30 minutes. The rooms are well furnished and impressive, but interesting only if you haven't seen a château lately. Even if you don't tour the palace, get close enough to check out the photos of the last three princes in the palace entry.

Cost and Hours: €8, includes audioguide, €20.50 combo-ticket includes Oceanography Museum; hours vary but generally daily 10:00-18:00, July-Aug until 19:00, closed Nov-March; buy ticket at the *Billeterie* at the souvenir stand 75 yards opposite the palace entrance; tel. 00-377/93 25 18 31, www.palais.mc.

• *Head to the west end of the palace square. Below the cannonballs is the district known as...*

Fontvieille

Monaco's newest, reclaimed-from-the-sea area has seen much of Monaco's post-WWII growth (residential and commercial—notice the lushly planted building tops). Prince Rainier continued—some say, was obsessed with—Monaco's economic growth, creating landfills (topped with apartments, such as in Fontvieille), flashy ports, more beaches, a big sports stadium marked by tall arches, and a rail station. (An ambitious new landfill project is in the works and would add still more prime real estate to Monaco's portfolio.) Today, thanks to Prince Rainier's past efforts, tiny Monaco is a member of the United Nations. (If you have kids with you, check out the nifty play area just below.)

• *With your back to the palace, leave the square through the arch at the far right (onto Rue Colonel Bellando de Castro) and find the...*

Cathedral of Monaco (Cathédrale de Monaco)

The somber but beautifully lit cathedral, rebuilt in 1878, shows that Monaco cared for more than just its new casino. It's where centuries of Grimaldis are buried, and where Princess Grace and Prince Rainier were married. Inside, circle slowly behind the altar (counterclockwise). The second tomb is that of Albert I, who did much to put Monaco on the world stage. The second-to-last tomb—inscribed *"Gratia Patricia,*

MCMLXXXII" and displaying the 1956 wedding photo of Princess Grace and Prince Rainier—is where the princess was buried in 1982. Prince Rainier's tomb lies next to hers (cathedral open daily 8:30-19:15).

• *Leave the cathedral and dip into the immaculately maintained **Jardin Botanique**, with more fine views. In the gardens, turn left. Eventually you'll find the impressive building housing the...*

Oceanography Museum
(Musée Océanographique)

Prince Albert I had this cliff-hanging museum built in 1910 as a monument to his enthusiasm for things from the sea. The museum's aquarium, which Jacques Cousteau captained for 32 years, has 2,000 different specimens, representing 250 species. You'll find Mediterranean fish and colorful tropical species (all well described in English). Rotating exhibits occupy the entry floor. Upstairs, the fancy Albert I Hall is filled with ship models, whale skeletons, oceanographic instruments and tools, and scenes of Albert and his beachcombers hard at work—but sadly, only scant English information. Don't miss the elevator to the rooftop terrace view café.

Cost and Hours: €11-16, kids-€7-12 (price depends on season), €20.50 combo-ticket includes Prince's Palace; daily 10:00-19:00, longer hours July-Aug, Oct-March until 18:00; down the steps from Monaco-Ville bus stop, at the opposite end of Monaco-Ville from the palace; tel. 00-377/93 15 36 00, www.oceano.mc.

• *The red-brick steps across from the Oceanography Museum lead up to stops for buses #1 and #2, both of which run to the port, the casino, and the train station. To walk back to the palace and through the old city, turn left at the top of the brick steps. If you're into stamps, walk down Rue Emile de Loth to find the **post office**, where philatelists and postcard writers with panache can buy—or just gaze in awe at—the impressive collection of Monegasque stamps.*

Sights in Monaco

Jardin Exotique

This cliffside municipal garden, located above Monaco-Ville, has eye-popping views from France to Italy. It's home to more than a thousand species of cacti (some giant) and other succulent plants, but worth the entry only for view-loving botanists (some posted English explanations provided). Your ticket includes entry to a skippable natural cave, an anthropological museum, and a view snack bar/café. You can get similar views over Monaco for free from behind the souvenir stand at the Jardin's bus stop; or, for even grander vistas, cross the street and hike toward La Turbie.

Cost and Hours: €7.20, daily 9:00-19:00, Oct-April until about dusk, take bus #2 from any stop in Monaco or take the elevator up from the Nice end of the train station and follow signs, tel. 00-377/93 15 29 80, www.jardin-exotique.com.

▲Monte Carlo Casino (Casino de Monte-Carlo)

Monte Carlo, which means "Charles' Hill" in Spanish, is named for the prince who presided over Monaco's 19th-century makeover.

In the mid-1800s, olive groves stood here. Then, with the construction of casino and spas, and easy road and train access (thanks to France), one of Europe's poorest countries was on the Grand Tour map—*the* place for the vacationing aristocracy to play. Today, Monaco has the world's highest per-capita income.

Count the counts and Rolls-Royces in front of the casino and **Hôtel de Paris.** The hotel was built at the same time as the casino to house gamblers—transportation back to Nice was not as fast as it is today (visitors allowed in the hotel, no shorts). The odd bubble-like structures that line the parkway above the casino are temporary, and house high-end boutiques relocated from nearby for a long-term construction project. Ignore the tacky American-style casino that hides behind the outdoor café across from the hotel.

The Monte Carlo casino is intended to make you feel comfortable while losing your retirement nest egg. Charles Garnier designed the place (with an opera house inside) in 1878, in part to thank the prince for his financial help in completing Paris' Opéra Garnier (which the architect also designed). The central doors provide access to slot machines, gaming rooms, and the opera house. The gaming rooms occupy the left wing of the building. Cruise ship visitors can jam the entry during afternoons.

Cost and Hours: Tightwads can view the atrium entry, classy bar/café, and slot-machine room for free; daily 9:00-late. Touring the casino costs €17 (€12 off-season); daily 9:00-12:15; you'll see the atrium area and inner-sanctum gaming rooms with an audioguide, take photos, and have your run of the joint. Gamblers pay €10; daily 14:00 until the wee hours, must be 18 and show ID; no shorts, T-shirts, hoodies, tennis shoes, or torn jeans. Whether you gamble or not, expect lines at the entrance from May through September; tel. 00-377/92 16 20 00, www.montecarlocasinos.com.

Visiting the Casino: Enter through sumptuous **atrium.** This is the lobby for the 520-seat opera house (open Nov-April only for performances). A model of the opera house is at the far-right side

MONACO

Le Grand Prix Automobile de Monaco

The Grand Prix de Monaco focuses the world's attention on this little country. The race started as an enthusiasts' car rally by the Automobile Club de Monaco (and is still run by the same group, more than 80 years later). The first race, held in 1929, was won by a Bugatti at a screaming average speed of...48 mph (today's cars triple that speed). To this day, drivers consider this one of the most important races on their circuits. The race takes place every year toward the end of May (www.acm.mc).

By Grand Prix standards, it's an unusual course, running through the streets of this tiny principality, sardined between mountains and sea. The hilly landscape means that the streets are narrow, with tight curves, steep climbs, and extremely short straightaways. Each lap is about two miles, beginning and ending at the port. Cars climb along the sea from the port, pass in front of the casino, race through the commercial district, and do a few dandy turns back to the port. The race lasts 78 laps, and whoever is still rolling at the end wins (most don't finish).

The Formula 1 cars look like overgrown toys that kids might pedal up and down their neighborhood street (if you're here a week or so before the race, feel free to browse the parking structure below Monaco-Ville, where many race cars are kept). Time trials to establish pole position begin three days before the race, which is always on a Sunday. More than 150,000 people attend the gala event; like the nearby film festival in Cannes, it's an excuse for yacht parties, restaurant splurges, and four-digit bar tabs at luxury hotels. During this event, hotel rates in Nice and beyond rocket up (even for budget places).

Fans wanting to touch the storied past of this race can window-shop the Automobile Club de Monaco's headquarters and patronize its boutique next door (on the port at 23 Boulevard Albert 1er).

of the room, near the bar-café. The **first gambling rooms** (Salle Renaissance, Salon de l'Europe, and Salle des Amériques) offer European and English roulette, plus Trente et Quarante, Punto Banco—a version of baccarat—and slot machines. The more glamorous **game rooms** (Salons Touzet, Salle Medecin, and Terrasse Salle Blanche) have those same games and Ultimate Texas Hold 'em poker, but you play against the cashier with higher stakes.

The scene, flooded with camera-toting tourists during the day, is great at night—and downright James Bond-like in the private rooms. This is your chance to rub elbows with some high rollers. The **park** behind the casino is a peaceful place with a good view of the building's rear facade and of Monaco-Ville.

Eating: The casino has two dining options. The **$$$$ Train Bleu** restaurant is for deep pockets for whom price is no object and elegance is everything. **$$$ Le Salon Rose** offers brasserie food—big salads and pasta dishes in a classy setting. If you paid to tour the casino or to gamble, show your ticket for a discount.

Take the Money and Run: The stop for buses returning to Nice and Villefranche-sur-Mer, and for local buses #1 and #2, is on Avenue de la Costa, at the top of the park above the casino (at the small shopping mall; for location, see the "Monaco" map). To reach the train station from the casino, take bus #1 or #2 from this stop, or find Boulevard Princesse Charlotte (parallels Avenue de la Costa one block above) and walk 15 minutes.

Sleeping and Eating in Monaco

Sleeping: Centrally located in Monaco-Ville, **$$ Hôtel de France**** is comfortable, well run by friendly Sylvie and Christoph, and reasonably priced—for Monaco (includes breakfast, air-con, no elevator; exit west from train station, 10-minute walk to 6 Rue de la Turbie, tel. 00-377/93 30 24 64, www.hoteldefrance.mc, hoteldefrance@monaco.mc).

Eating on the Port: Several cafés serve basic, inexpensive fare (day and night) on the port. Troll the places that line the flowery and traffic-free Rue Princesse Caroline between Rue Grimaldi and the port. **$$$ Huit et Demi** is a reliable choice, with a white-tablecloth-meets-director's-chair ambience and good outdoor seating (closed Sun, 7 Rue Princesse Caroline, tel. 00-377/93 50 97 02). A few blocks below, **$$ Bella Vita**—an easygoing place for salads, Italian fare, and classic French dishes—has a large terrace and modern interior (daily, serves nonstop from morning to late, 21 Rue Princesse Caroline, tel. 00-377/93 50 42 02).

Eating in Monaco-Ville: You'll find sandwiches—including the massive *pan bagnat*, basically *salade niçoise* on country bread—and quiche at the yellow-bannered **$ Boulangerie** (daily until 19:00, near Place du Palais at 8 Rue Basse). At **$$ U Cavagnetu**, just a block from Albert's palace, you'll dine cheaply on specialties from Monaco—pizza and such (daily, serves nonstop 11:00-23:00, 14 Rue Comte Félix Gastaldi, tel. 00-377/97 98 20 40). Monaco-Ville has other pizzerias, *crêperies,* and sandwich stands, but the neighborhood is dead at night.

Monaco Connections

BY TRAIN

For a comparison of train and bus connections, see the "Public Transportation in the French Riviera" sidebar on page 10. Most trains heading west will stop in Villefranche-sur-Mer, Nice, and Antibes (ask). The last train leaves Monaco for Villefranche-sur-Mer and Nice at about 23:30.

From Monaco by Train to: Villefranche-sur-Mer, Nice, Antibes, or **Cannes** (2/hour).

BY BUS

Frequent **bus #100,** which runs along the Low Corniche back to **Nice** (1 hour), and **Villefranche-sur–Mer** (40 minutes) is often slammed. For a better chance of securing a seat, board at the stop near the TI on Avenue de la Costa (see the "Monaco" map earlier in this chapter) rather than the stop near Place d'Armes. The last bus leaves Monaco for Nice at about 21:30. In the other direction bus #100 goes to **Menton** (30 minutes). For bus details, including tickets, routes, frequencies, and travel times, see the "Getting Around the Riviera" section in the French Riviera chapter.

Bus #112, which goes along the scenic Middle Corniche to **Eze-le-Village** then on to Nice (6/day Mon-Sat, none on Sun, 20 minutes to Eze), departs Monaco from Place de la Crémaillère, one block above the main TI and casino park. Walk up Rue Iris with Barclays Bank to your left, curve right, and find the bus shelter across the street at the green La Crémaillère café.

Bus #11 to **La Turbie** (9/day Mon-Sat, 5/day Sun, 30 minutes) stops in front of the TI (same side of street).

Bus #110 express takes the freeway from the Place d'Armes stop to **Nice Airport** (2/hour, 50 minutes, €22).

BY CRUISE SHIP

Cruise ships tender passengers to the end of Monaco's yacht harbor, a short walk from downtown. It's a long walk or a short bus ride to most sights in town. To reach other towns, such as Villefranche-sur-Mer or Nice, you can take public transportation. To summon a taxi (assuming none are waiting when you disembark), look for the gray taxi call box near the tender dock—just press the button and wait for your cab to arrive.

Getting into Town: To reach **Monaco-Ville,** which towers high over the cruise terminal, you can either hike steeply and scenically up to the top of the hill, or walk to Place d'Armes and hop on bus #1 or #2, which will take you up sweat-free. It's a 15-minute, level walk to the bus stop from the port. Cross Boulevard Albert

I, follow green *Gare S.N.C.F./Ferroviare* signs, and take the public elevator to Place d'Armes.

The ritzy skyscraper zone of **Monte Carlo** is across the harbor from the tender dock, about a 25-minute walk. You can also ride the little electric "bateau bus" shuttle boat across the mouth of the harbor (works with a bus ticket). To reach the upper part of Monte Carlo—with the TI and handy bus stops (including for Eze-le-Village and La Turbie)—catch bus #1 or #2 at the top of the yacht harbor, along Boulevard Albert I.

Getting to Sights Beyond Monaco: Monaco is connected to most nearby sights by both train and bus. See the "Arrival in Monaco" section earlier in this chapter as well as the bus and train connection information in this section for details.

The train station is about a 20-minute walk from the tender harbor—first walk to Place d'Armes (directions above under "Getting into Town"), then follow Rue Grimaldi to find stairs and an elevator to the station. For buses, see earlier for bus stop locations and frequencies. If taking bus #112 to Eze-le-Village or bus #11 to La Turbie, first ride bus #1 or #2 to the TI and casino, then follow the directions above.

Menton

If you wish the Riviera were less glitzy and more like a place where locals take their families to lick ice cream and make sand castles, visit Menton (east of Monaco). Menton feels like a poor man's Nice. It's unrefined and unpretentious, with lower prices, fewer rentable umbrellas, and lots of Italians day-tripping in from right over the border (five miles away). There's not an American in sight.

Getting There: While trains serve Menton regularly (35 minutes from Nice, 10 minutes from Monaco), the station is a 15-minute walk from the action. Buses are much slower (1.5 hours from Nice, 30 minutes from Monaco) but they drop visitors right on the beach promenade (bus #100; see the "Getting Around the Riviera" section in the French Riviera chapter for details). If coming from a day trip via Monaco, take the bus here and train back to your home base.

Visiting Menton: Menton's TI is at 8 Avenue Boyer (tel. 04 92 41 76 76, www.tourisme-menton.fr). Though a bit rough, the Menton waterfront is a joy. An inviting promenade lines the beach, and seaside cafés serve light meals and salads at good prices. A snooze or stroll here is a fine Riviera experience. From the promenade, a pedestrian street leads through town. Small squares are alive with jazz bands playing crowd-pleasers under palm trees.

Stepping into the old town—which blankets a hill capped by a fascinating cemetery—you're immersed in a pastel-painted, yet dark-and-tangled Old World scene with (strangely) almost no commerce. A few elegant restaurants dig in at the base of the towering centuries-old apartment flats. The richly decorated Baroque St. Michael's Church (midway up the hill, Mon-Fri 10:00-12:00 & 15:00-17:15, closed to visitors Sat-Sun) is a reminder that, until 1860, Menton was a thriving part of the larger state of Monaco. Climbing past sun-grabbing flower boxes and people who don't get out much anymore, the steep stepped lanes finally deposit you at the ornate gate of a grand cemetery that fills the old castle walls. Explore the cemetery, which is the final resting place of many aristocratic Russians (buried here in the early 1900s) and offers breathtaking Mediterranean views.

MONACO

ANTIBES & NEARBY

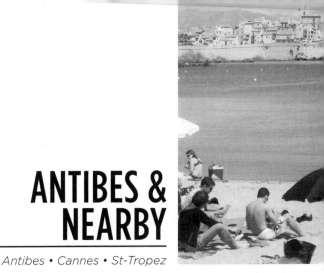

Antibes • Cannes • St-Tropez

The Riviera opens up west of Nice with bigger, sandier beaches and an overabundance of tasteless beachfront development. Ancient Antibes and superficial Cannes buck the slap-it-up high-rise trend, both with thriving centers busy with pedestrians and yachts. Glamorous St-Tropez, a scenic 1.5-hour drive from Antibes, marks the western edge of the French Riviera.

PLANNING YOUR TIME

Antibes works well by car, bus, or train. You can day-trip in from Nice or, better, sleep here (hotels outside the town center have easier parking than in Nice or Villefranche-sur-Mer, and train/bus service to nearby destinations is efficient). Allow a full day for Antibes sights (two nights is good). Antibes also works as a base for day trips: Cannes is a short hop away by bus, train, or car (train is best); the Inland Riviera hill towns of St-Paul-de-Vence, Vence, and Grasse (all covered in the next chapter) are also easy by car and doable by bus and/or train—Grasse has the best train service. St-Tropez—a 1.5-hour drive from Antibes—is best visited on your way in or out of the Riviera.

Antibes

Antibes has a down-to-earth, easygoing ambience. Its old town is a warren of narrow streets and red-tile roofs rising above the blue Med, protected by twin medieval towers and wrapped in extensive ramparts. Visitors making the short trip from Nice can browse Europe's biggest yacht harbor, snooze on a sandy beach, loiter through an enjoyable old town, and hike along a sea-swept trail. The town's

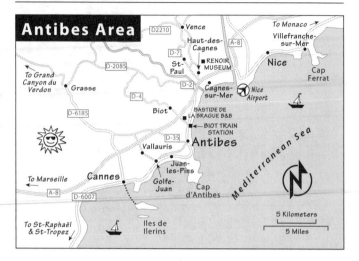

cultural claim to fame, the Picasso Museum (closed on Mondays), shows off its appealing collection in a fine old building.

Though much smaller than Nice, Antibes has a history that dates back just as far. Both towns were founded by Greek traders in the fifth century BC. To the Greeks, Antibes was "Antipolis"— the town *(polis)* opposite *(anti)* Nice. For the next several centuries, Antibes remained in the shadow of its neighbor. By the turn of the 20th century, the town was a military base—so the rich and famous partied elsewhere. But when the army checked out after World War I, Antibes was "discovered" and enjoyed a particularly roaring '20s—with the help of party animals like Rudolph Valentino and the rowdy (yet silent) Charlie Chaplin. Fun seekers even invented water-skiing right here in the 1920s.

Orientation to Antibes

Antibes' old town lies between the port and Boulevard Albert I and Avenue Robert Soleau. Place Nationale is the old town's hub of activity. Stroll above the sea between the old port and Place Albert I (where Boulevard Albert I meets the water). Good beaches lie just beyond Place Albert I, and the walk there leads to fine views. Fun play areas for children are along this path

and on Place des Martyrs de la Résistance (close to recommended Hôtel Relais du Postillon).

TOURIST INFORMATION

The TI is a few blocks from the train station at 42 Avenue Robert Soleau (July-Aug daily 9:00-19:00; Sept-June Mon-Sat 9:00-12:30 & 14:00-18:00, Sun 9:00-13:00; shorter hours and closed Sun in winter; tel. 04 22 10 60 10, www.antibes-juanlespins.com). Hikers should get the free tourist map of the Sentier Touristique de Tirepoil hike (see "Sights in Antibes," later).

ARRIVAL IN ANTIBES

By Train: Bus #14 runs frequently (except Sun) from below the train station along Avenue de la Libération to the city bus station (*gare routière;* near several recommended hotels and the old town), and continues to the fine Plage de la Salis, with quick access to the Phare de la Garoupe trail (2/hour, none on Sun, bus stop 100 yards to right as you exit train station). **Taxis** usually wait in front of the station.

To **walk** from the station to the port, the old town, and the Picasso Museum (15 minutes), cross the street in front of the station, skirting left of the café, and follow Avenue de la Libération downhill as it bends left. At the end of the street, head to the right along the port. If you walk on the water's edge, you'll see the yachts get bigger as you go.

To walk directly to the TI and recommended hotels in the old town, turn right out of the station and walk down Avenue Robert Soleau.

There's no baggage check in Antibes. The last train back to Nice leaves at about midnight.

By Bus: Antibes has two bus stations—one mostly for regional buses and one only for city buses. **Regional buses** (#200 & #250) use the bus station behind the train station (called the *Pôle d'Echange;* take the pedestrian overpass from behind the train station to reach it). Buses to and from Nice stop at the far right (east) end (info office open Mon-Fri 7:00-19:00, Sat 9:00-12:30 & 14:00-17:00, closed Sun). Bus #200 also stops in front of the train station (find the shelter 50 yards to the right as you leave the station) and near Place de Gaulle.

Some **city buses** use the *Pôle d'Echange* (like handy bus #2), but all serve the bus station in the old town on Place Guynemer, a block below Place Général de Gaulle (info desk open Mon-Fri 7:30-19:00, Sat 8:30-12:00 & 14:30-17:30, closed Sun, www.envibus.fr).

By Car: Day-trippers follow signs to *Centre-Ville,* then *Port Vauban.* The easiest place to park is a convenient but pricey underground parking lot located outside the ramparts near the archway leading into the old town (€10/4 hours, €24/12 hours, just south of Port Vauban—see the "Antibes" map in this chapter). A free lot is

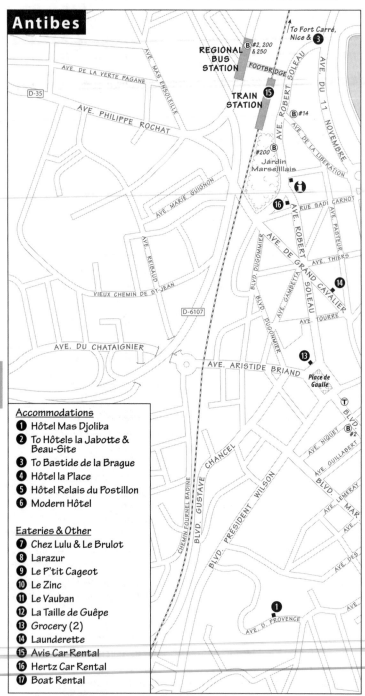

Antibes

Accommodations
1 Hôtel Mas Djoliba
2 To Hôtels la Jabotte & Beau-Site
3 To Bastide de la Brague
4 Hôtel la Place
5 Hôtel Relais du Postillon
6 Modern Hôtel

Eateries & Other
7 Chez Lulu & Le Brulot
8 Larazur
9 Le P'tit Cageot
10 Le Zinc
11 Le Vauban
12 La Taille de Guêpe
13 Grocery (2)
14 Launderette
15 Avis Car Rental
16 Hertz Car Rental
17 Boat Rental

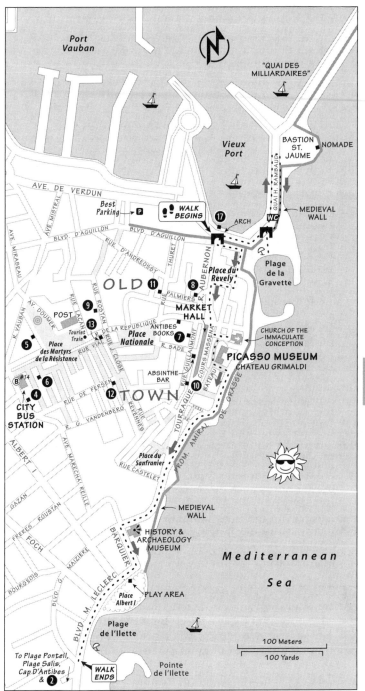

Port Vauban

"QUAI DES MILLIARDAIRES"

Vieux Port

BASTION ST. JAUME

NOMADE

AVE. DE VERDUN

Best Parking

WALK BEGINS

ARCH

WC

MEDIEVAL WALL

BLVD. D'AGUILLON

RUE D'ANDREOSSY

RUE D'AGUILLON

Plage de la Gravette

AVE. MISTRAL

AVE. MIRABEAU

OLD

Place du Revely

PALMIERS

MARKET HALL

CHURCH OF THE IMMACULATE CONCEPTION

RUE AUBERNON

THURET

AV. DOUMER

POST

RUE ROSTAN

RUE TACAN

RUE DE LA RÉPUBLIQUE

Tourist Train

Place Nationale

Antibes BOOKS

R. SADE

PICASSO MUSEUM
CHATEAU GRIMALDI

RUE VIAN

Place des Martyrs de la Résistance

RUE CLOSE

ABSINTHE BAR

RUE GUILLAUMONT

COURS MASSENA

BATEAU

RUE DE GRASSE

B #14

CITY BUS STATION

RUE DE FERSEN

TOWN

RUE REVENNES

TOURRAQUE

ROM. AMIRAL

ALBERT I

R. G. VANDENBERG

Place du Sanfranier

RUE CASTELET

Mediterranean

GAZAN

AVE. MARECHAL REILLE

FRERES ROUSTAN

MEDIEVAL WALL

Sea

FOCH

HISTORY & ARCHAEOLOGY MUSEUM

BOURGEOIS

BLVD. G.

BLVD. M. LECLERC

BARQUIER

MAIZIERE

Place Albert I

PLAY AREA

Plage de l'Ilette

100 Meters

100 Yards

To Plage Ponteil, Plage Salis, Cap D'Antibes &

WALK ENDS

Pointe de l'Ilette

ANTIBES & NEARBY

available opposite Fort Carré (north of the port). It's a 15-minute walk to the old town from here; you can also catch bus #14. Street parking is free Monday through Friday (12:00-14:00 & 19:00-8:00), and all day Saturday and Sunday.

If you're sleeping in Antibes, follow *Centre-Ville* signs, then signs to your hotel. The most appealing hotels in Antibes are best by car, and Antibes works well for drivers—compared with Nice, parking is easy, traffic is minimal, and it's a convenient springboard for the Inland Riviera. Pay parking is available at Antibes' train station, so drivers can ditch their cars here and day-trip from Antibes by train.

HELPFUL HINTS

Markets: Antibes' old-time market hall (Marché Provençal) hosts a vibrant produce market (daily until 13:00, closed Mon Sept-May), and a lively antiques/flea market fills Place Nationale and Place Audiberti, next to the port (Thu and Sat 7:00-18:00). A clothing market winds through the streets around the post office on Rue Lacan (Thu 9:00-18:00).

English Bookstore: With a welcoming vibe, **Antibes Books** has a good selection of new and used books; check out their many guidebooks—including mine (13 Rue Georges Clemenceau, tel. 04 93 61 96 47, www.antibesbooks.com).

Laundry: There's a launderette at 19 Avenue du Grand Cavalier (daily 8:00-20:45).

Bike Rental: The TI has a list of places where you can rent bikes (including electric bikes). Bikes are a good way for nondrivers to reach the hikes described later in this chapter.

Taxi: Tel. 04 93 67 67 67.

Car Rental: The big-name agencies have offices in Antibes (closed Mon-Sat 12:00-14:00 and all day Sun). The most central are **Avis** (at the train station, tel. 04 93 34 65 15) and **Hertz** (a few blocks from the train station at 52 Avenue Robert Soleau, tel. 04 92 91 28 00).

Boat Rental: You can motor your own seven-person yacht thanks to **Antibes Bateaux Services** (€100/half-day, at the small fish market on the port, mobile 06 15 75 44 36, www.antibes-bateaux.com).

GETTING AROUND ANTIBES

Antibes' buses (Envibus) cost €1 and are handiest for carless travelers wanting access to Cap d'Antibes. **Bus #14** links the train station, city bus station, old town, and Plage de la Salis. It also takes you to Fort Carré, where free parking is available. **Bus #2** provides access to the best beaches, the path to La Phare de la Garoupe, and the Cap d'Antibes trail. It runs from the Pôle d'Echange bus station (behind the train station) through the city center and down Boulevard Albert I (daily 7:00-19:00, every 40 minutes). Pick up a schedule at the bus station.

Antibes Walk

This 40-minute self-guided walk will help you get your bearings, and works well day or night.

• *Begin at the old port (Vieux Port) at the southern end of Avenue de Verdun. Stand at the port, across from the archway with the clock.*

Old Port: Locals claim that this is Europe's first and biggest pleasure-boat harbor, with 1,600 stalls. That star-shaped stone structure crowning the opposite end of the port is **Fort Carré,** which protected Antibes from foreigners for more than 500 years.

The pathetic remains of a once-hearty **fishing fleet** are moored in front of you. The Mediterranean is pretty much fished out. Most of the seafood you'll eat here comes from fish farms or the Atlantic.

• *With the port on your left, walk a block past the sorry fleet and duck under the first open arch to the shell-shaped...*

Plage de la Gravette: This normally quiet public beach is tucked right in the middle of old Antibes. Walk out onto the paved

area. Consider the scale of the ramparts that protected this town. Because Antibes was the last fort before the Italian border, the French king made sure the ramparts were top-notch. The twin towers crowning the old town are the church's bell tower and the tower topping Château Grimaldi (today's Picasso Museum). As you face the old town, forested Cap d'Antibes is the point of land in the distance to the left. Is anyone swimming? Locals don't swim much in July and August because of jellyfish—common now in warmer water. Throughout the Mediterranean, you'll see red flags warning of dangerous storms or tides. Many beaches now also have white flags with jellyfish symbols warning that swimming might be a stinging experience.

• For a close-up look at the megayachts and a walk along the ramparts, follow this fun detour. Otherwise, skip ahead to the "Old Antibes" directions.

Antibes' Megayacht Harbor: Take a three-block detour to the north as you leave Plage de la Gravette for a glimpse at the epitome of conspicuous consumption. You'll walk along the harbor under the ramparts known as Bastion St. Jaume.

You'll eventually reach a restricted area harboring massive yachts. Climb the ramparts on your right and make your way to the **modern white sculpture.** *Nomade*—a man of letters looking pensively out to sea—was created in 2010 by the Spanish artist Jaume Plensa (find the posted English explanations nearby). You can sit in the sculpture and ponder how human communication forms who we are and links all people. Looking north, the Alps make a beautiful backdrop when it's clear.

Browse the line of huge pleasure craft stern-tied to the pier (which was built in the 1970s with financial aid from mostly Saudi Arabian yacht owners, who wanted a decent place to tie up). Locals call this the **Quai des Milliardaires** ("billionaire's dock"). The Union Jacks fluttering above most of the boats show that they're registered in the Cayman Islands (can you say tax dodge?). The crews you see keep these toys shipshape all year long—even though many of them are used for just a few days a year. Today, Antibes is the haunt of a large community of English, Irish, and Aussie boaters who help crew these giant yachts. (That explains the Irish pubs and English bookstores.)

Old Antibes: Return along the upper walkway, then enter Antibes' old town through the arch under the clock.

• You can walk directly up the main street to get to our next stop, but here's a more scenic option: Passing through the gate, turn immediately left, and then walk up the steps in the small square. Walk straight through the arch at #14 and into picturesque Place du Revely. Cross Place du Revely to the right, and go down the ramp under several arches, then turn left when you reach the main drag into the old town and Antibes' market hall, Le Marché Provençal.

Market Hall: Antibes' market hall bustles under a 19th-century canopy, with flowers, produce, Provençal products, and beach accessories. The market wears many hats: produce until 13:30 (daily except closed Mon Sept-May), handicrafts most afternoons (Thu-Sun), and fun outdoor dining in the evenings, on Cours Masséna.

ANTIBES & NEARBY

On the right (at the corner of Rue Sade), a pretty shop hides an atmospheric **absinthe bar** in its ninth-century vaulted cellar. You're welcome to go through the shop (or enter via Rue Sade) and descend to find an amazing collection of absinthe fountains, the oldest dating from the 1860s. The owner will gladly show you his memorabilia. You can even taste the now-legal drink to better understand Picasso's paintings. On Friday and Saturday nights, the basement is transformed into an absinthe-infused jazz bar lounge with 1920s ambience.

• *Double back to the entry of the market and find Rue Christian Chessel leading uphill to the pretty pastel…*

Church of the Immaculate Conception: Built on the site of a Greek temple, this is worth a peek inside. A church has stood on this site since the 12th century. This one served as the area's cathedral until the mid-1200s. The stone bell tower standing in front of the church predates it by 600 years, when it was part of the city's defenses. Many of those heavy stones were pillaged from Antibes' Roman monuments.

• *Looming above the church on prime real estate is the white-stone…*

Château Grimaldi: This site was home to the acropolis of the Greek city of Antipolis and later a Roman fort. Later still, the château was the residence of the Grimaldi family (a branch of which still rules Monaco). Today it houses Antibes' Picasso Museum. Its proximity to the cathedral symbolized the sometimes too-cozy relationship between society's two dominant landowning classes: the Church and the nobility. (In 1789, the French Revolution changed all that.)

• *After visiting the **Picasso Museum** (see "Sights in Antibes," next), work your way through the warren of pretty lanes, then head out to the water, turn right along the ramparts, and find a sweeping sea view. As you walk, you'll pass a charming neighborhood (La Commune Libre du Safranier) on your right, making a lovely return route. As you wander, look for forested **Cap d'Antibes** (to the south), crowned by its lighthouse and studded with mansions (a proposed hike here is described later). The Cap was long the refuge of Antibes' rich and famous, and a favorite haunt of F. Scott Fitzgerald and Ernest Hemingway.*

*The rampart walk leads to the **History and Archaeology Museum**. After taking a quick spin through its galleries (see "Sights in Antibes," next), continue hugging the shore past Place Albert I until you see the smashing views back to old Antibes. Benches and soft sand await. You're on your own from here—energetic walkers can continue on the trail, which leads to the lighthouse (see "Hikes," later in this chapter); others can return to old Antibes and wander around in its peaceful back lanes.*

Sights in Antibes

▲▲Picasso Museum (Musée Picasso)

Sitting serenely where the old town meets the sea, this compact three-floor museum offers a manageable collection of Picasso's paintings, sketches, and ce-

ramics. Picasso lived in this castle for part of 1946, when he cranked out an amazing amount of art (most of the paintings you'll see are from this short but prolific stretch of his long and varied career). He was elated by the end of World War II, and his works show a celebration of color and a rediscovery of light after France's long nightmare of war. Picasso was also reenergized by his young and lovely companion, Françoise Gilot (with whom he would father two children). The resulting collection (donated by Picasso) put Antibes on the tourist map. For more on Picasso's life, see the sidebar.

Cost and Hours: €6; Tue-Sun 10:00-18:00, July-Aug Wed and Fri until 20:00, mid-Sept-mid-June closed Tue-Sun 13:00-14:00, closed Mon year-round; tel. 04 92 90 54 20.

Visiting the Museum: After buying your ticket, go through the glass door. Before heading inside, pause in the **sculpture garden** to appreciate Picasso's working environment (and wonder why he spent only a few months here).

The museum's interior is a calm place of white walls, soft arches, and ample natural light—a great space for exhibiting art. Tour the museum clockwise, noticing the focus on sea creatures, tridents, and other marine themes (*oursin* is a sea urchin, *poulpe* is an octopus, and *poisson* is, well, fishy). *Nature morte* means still life, and you'll see many of these in the collection. Each room has helpful English explanations posted. Expect some changes to these descriptions as the collection is shuffled periodically.

The **ground floor** houses a cool collection of paintings by Norwegian artist Ann-Eva Bergmen and her husband, Hans Hartung, who spent their last years in Antibes. The **first floor** up holds temporary exhibitions (usually related to Picasso) and a small collection of intriguing paintings by Nicholas de Stael, whose style was greatly influenced by southern France and artists such as Henri Matisse (the painting of Antibes' Fort Carré is mood altering).

The museum's highlight is on the **top floor,** where you'll find the permanent collection of Picasso's works. Visitors are greeted by a large image of Picasso and a display of photographs of the artist at work and play during his time in Antibes. Times were tough in 1946. Artists had to improvise. Picasso experimented with materials and surfaces like industrial paint on recycled canvases, random pieces of plywood, and even concrete. Try not to analyze too much. He's happy and in the French Riviera. Remember: The war's over and he's in love—this is pure happiness.

The first gallery room (up the small staircase to your left) houses several famous works, including the lively, frolicking, and big-breasted *La Joie de Vivre* painting (from 1946). This Greek bacchanal sums up the newfound freedom in a just-liberated France and sets the tone for the rest of the collection. You'll also see the colorless, three-paneled *Satyr, Faun and Centaur with Trident* and several ceramic creations. As you leave this room don't miss the adorable (pregnant?) goat.

Throughout, you'll see both black-and-white and colorful ink sketches that challenge the imagination—these show off Picasso's skill as a cartoonist and caricaturist. Look also for the cute Basque fishermen (*Pecheur attablé*) and several Cubist-style nudes *(nus couchés)*, one painted on plywood.

Near the end, don't miss the wall devoted to Picasso's ceramic plates. In 1947, inspired by a visit to a ceramics factory in nearby Vallauris, Picasso discovered the joy of this medium. He was smitten by the texture of soft clay and devoted a great deal of time to exploring how to work with it—producing over 2,000 pieces in one year. In the same room, the wall-sized painting *Ulysses and the Sirens* screams action and anxiety. Lashed to the ship mast, Ulysses survives the temptation of the sirens.

History and Archaeology Museum (Musée d'Histoire et d'Archéologie)

More than 2,000 years ago, Antibes was the center of a thriving maritime culture. It was an important Roman commercial port with aqueducts, theaters, baths, and so on. This museum—the only place to get a sense of the city's ancient roots—displays Greek, Roman, and Etruscan odds and ends in two simple halls but sadly, no English descriptions. Your visit starts at an 1894 model of Antibes and continues past displays of Roman coins, cups, plates, and scads of amphorae. The lanky lead pipe connected to a center box was used as a bilge pump; nearby is a good display of Roman anchors made of lead. In a later exhibit, the orange stones hanging from strings are from a Roman loom.

Cost and Hours: €3; Tue-Sun 10:00-12:00 & 14:00-18:00, shorter hours off-season, closed Mon year-round, on the water between Picasso Museum and Place Albert I, tel. 04 92 95 85 98.

ANTIBES & NEARBY

Pablo Picasso (1881-1973)

Pablo Picasso was the most famous and, for me, the greatest artist of the 20th century. Always exploring, he became the master of many styles (Cubism, Surrealism, Expressionism) and of many media (painting, sculpture, prints, ceramics, assemblages). Still, he could make anything he touched look unmistakably like "a Picasso."

Born in Málaga, Spain, Picasso was the son of an art teacher. At a very young age, he quickly advanced beyond his teachers. Picasso's teenage works are stunningly realistic and capture the inner complexities of the people he painted. As a youth in Barcelona, he fell in with a bohemian crowd that mixed wine, women, and art.

In 1900, at age 19, Picasso started making trips to Paris. Four years later, he moved to the City of Light and absorbed the styles of many painters (especially Henri de Toulouse-Lautrec) while searching for his own artist's voice. His paintings of beggars and other social outcasts show the empathy of a man who was himself a poor, homesick foreigner. When his best friend, Spanish artist Carlos Casagemas, committed suicide, Picasso plunged into a **Blue Period** (1901-1904)—so called because the dominant color in these paintings matches their melancholy mood and subject matter (emaciated beggars, hard-eyed pimps).

In 1904, Picasso got a steady girlfriend (Fernande Olivier) and suddenly saw the world through rose-colored glasses—the **Rose Period.** He was further jolted out of his Blue Period by the "flat" look of the Fauve paintings being made around him. Not satisfied with their take on 3-D, Picasso played with the "building blocks" of line and color to find new ways to reconstruct the real world on canvas.

At his studio in Montmartre, Picasso and his neighbor Georges Braque worked together in poverty so dire they often didn't know where their next bottle of wine was coming from. And then, at age 25, Picasso reinvented painting. Fascinated by the primitive power of African tribal masks, he sketched human faces with simple outlines and almond eyes. Intrigued by his girlfriend's body, he sketched Fernande from every angle, then experimented with showing several different views on the same canvas. A hundred paintings and nine months later, Picasso gave birth to a monstrous canvas of five nude, fragmented prostitutes with mask-like faces—*Les Demoiselles d'Avignon* (1907).

This bold new style was called **Cubism.** With Cubism, Picasso shattered the Old World and put it back together in a new way. The subjects are somewhat recognizable (with the help of the titles), but they're built with geometric shards (let's call them "cubes")—it's like viewing the world through a kaleidoscope of brown and gray. Cubism presents several different angles of the subject at once—say, a woman seen from the front and side simultaneously, resulting in two eyes on the same side of the nose. Cubism showed the traditional three dimensions, plus Einstein's new fourth dimension—the time it takes to walk around the subject to see other angles.

In 1918, Picasso married his first wife, Olga Kokhlova. He then traveled to Rome and entered a **Classical Period** (1920s) of more realistic, full-bodied women and children, inspired by the three-dimensional sturdiness of ancient statues. While he flirted with abstraction, throughout his life Picasso always kept a grip on "reality." His favorite subject was people. The anatomy might be jumbled, but it's all there.

Though he lived in France and Italy, Picasso remained a Spaniard at heart, incorporating Spanish motifs into his work. Unrepentantly macho, he loved bullfights, seeing them as a metaphor for the timeless human interaction between the genders. The horse—clad with blinders and pummeled by the bull—is just a pawn in the battle between bull and matador. To Picasso, the horse symbolizes the feminine, and the bull, the masculine. Spanish imagery—bulls, screaming horses, a Madonna—appears in Picasso's most famous work, *Guernica* (1937). The monumental canvas of a bombed village summed up the pain of Spain's brutal civil war (1936-1939) and foreshadowed the onslaught of World War II.

At war's end, Picasso left Paris, his wife, and his emotional baggage behind, finding fun in the **south of France.** Sun! Color! Water! Freedom! Senior citizen Pablo Picasso was reborn, enjoying worldwide fame. He lived at first with the beautiful young painter Françoise Gilot, mother of two of his children, but it was another young beauty, Jacqueline Roque, who became his second wife. Dressed in rolled-up white pants and a striped sailor's shirt, bursting with pent-up creativity, Picasso often cranked out a painting a day. Picasso's Riviera works set the tone for the rest of his life. They're sunny, lighthearted, and childlike; filled with motifs of the sea, Greek mythology (fauns, centaurs), and animals; and freely experimental in their use of new media. The simple drawing of doves Picasso made at this time became emblematic of the artist and an international symbol of peace.

Picasso made collages, built "statues" out of wood, wire, ceramics, papier-mâché, or whatever, and even turned everyday household objects into statues (like his famous bull's head made of a bicycle seat with handlebar horns). **Multimedia** works like these have become so standard today that we forget how revolutionary they once were. His last works have the playfulness of someone much younger. As it is often said of Picasso, "When he was a child, he painted like a man. When he was old, he painted like a child."

Fort Carré

This impressively situated, mid-16th-century citadel, on the headland overlooking the harbor, protected Antibes from Nice (which until 1860 wasn't part of France). You can tour this unusual star-shaped fort for the fantastic views over Antibes, but there's little to see inside (€3, Tue-Sun 10:00-12:30 & 13:30-18:00, until 16:30 off-season, closed Mon year-round).

▲Beaches *(Plages)*

Good beaches stretch from the south end of Antibes toward Cap d'Antibes. They're busy but manageable in summer and on weekends, with cheap snack stands and good views of the old town. The closest beach to the old town is at the port (Plage de la Gravette), which seems calm in any season.

HIKES

I list two good hikes below. Orient yourself from the seaside rampart walk below the Picasso Museum or from bottom of Boulevard Albert I (where it meets the beach). That tower on the hill is your destination for the first hike. The longer Cap d'Antibes hike begins over that hill, a few miles farther away. The two hikes are easy to combine by bus, bike, or car.

▲▲Chapelle et Phare de la Garoupe Hike

The territorial views—best in the morning, skippable if it's hazy—from this viewpoint more than merit the 20-minute uphill climb from Plage de la Salis (a few blocks after Maupassant Apartments, where the road curves left, follow signs and the rough, cobbled Chemin du Calvaire up to lighthouse tower). An orientation table explains that you can see from Nice to Cannes and up to the Alps.

Getting There: Take bus #2 or bus #14 to the Plage de la Salis stop and find the trail a block ahead. By car or bike, follow signs for *Cap d'Antibes*, then look for *Chapelle et Phare de la Garoupe* signs.

▲▲Cap d'Antibes Hike
(Sentier Touristique de Tirepoil)

Cap d'Antibes is filled with exclusive villas and mansions protected by high walls. Roads are just lanes, bounded on both sides by the high and greedy walls in this home of some of the most expensive real estate in France (and where "public" seems like a necessary evil). But all the money in the world can't buy you the beach in France, so a thin strip of rocky coastline forms a two-mile long,

parklike zone with an extremely scenic, mostly paved but often rocky trail (Sentier Touristique de Tirepoil).

As you walk, you'll have fancy fences with security cameras on one side and dramatic sea views on the other. The public space is rarely more than 50 yards wide and often extremely rocky—impassible if not for the paved trail carved out of it for the delight of hikers.

At a fast clip you can walk the entire circle in just over an hour. Don't do the hike without the tourist map (available at hotels or the TI). You can do it in either direction (or in partial segments; see "Getting There," below). I've described the walk starting at its western end going counter-clockwise.

From the La Fontaine bus stop walk five minutes down Avenue Mrs. L. D. Beaumont to the gate of the Villa Eilenroc. Enter through the gate to the trail skirting the villa on your left, and walk five more minutes to the rocky coastal trail. Now turn left and follow the trail for nearly an hour around Cap Gros. There's no way to get lost without jumping into the sea or scaling villa security walls. You return to civilization at a tiny resort (Plage de la Garoupe), with an expensive restaurant, a fine beach (both public and private), and a fun and inexpensive beachside bar/café. From here it's a 10-minute walk up Avenue André Sella to your starting point and the bus stop. With a car (or bike), you could start and end at Plage de la Garoupe. For a shorter version, walk from Plage de la Garoupe to Cap Gros and back.

Getting There: Drivers will find parking easier at the trail's eastern end (Plage de la Garoupe), though some street parking is available a few blocks from the trail's western end (look near Hôtel Beau-Site). Pedestrians should start at the trail's western end. Take bus #2 from Antibes for about 15 minutes to the La Fontaine stop at Rond-Point A. Meiland (next to the recommended Hôtel Beau-Site), then follow the route described above.

NEAR ANTIBES
Juan-les-Pins Town

The low-rise town of Juan-les-Pins, sprawling across the Cap d'Antibes isthmus from Antibes, is where the action is...after hours. It's a modern waterfront resort with good beaches, plenty of lively bars and restaurants, and a popular jazz festival in July. The town is also known for its clothing boutiques that stay open until midnight (people are too busy getting tanned to shop at normal hours). As locals say, "Party, sleep in, shop late, party more."

Getting There: Buses and trains (see "Getting Around Antibes," earlier) make the 10-minute trip to and from Antibes constantly.

Renoir Museum (Musée Renoir)

Halfway between Antibes and Nice, above Cagnes-sur-Mer, Pierre-Auguste Renoir found his Giverny. Here, the artist spent the last 12 years of his life (1907-1919) tending his gardens, painting, and even dabbling in sculpture (despite suffering from rheumatoid arthritis). In fact, there are more sculptures than paintings here—all on the basement floor. His home was later converted into a small museum. Visitors get a personal look into Renoir's later years but very little art. You'll see his studio, wheelchair, and bedroom; take a stroll in his gardens; and enjoy several of his and other artists' paintings of people and places around Cagnes-sur-Mer. It's a pleasant place and an enjoyable pilgrimage for his fans.

Cost and Hours: €6, Wed-Mon 10:00-12:00 & 14:00-18:00, Oct-April until 17:00, closed Tue year-round, Chemin des Collettes, tel. 04 93 20 61 07.

Getting There: It's complicated by public transport (and not worth the trouble for most), but manageable by car: Go to Cagnes-sur-Mer, then follow brown *Musée Renoir* signs.

Biot Village

The artsy pottery and glassblowing village of Biot is popular with aesthetic types and home to the Fernand Léger Museum.

Getting There: Biot is easy to reach on bus #10 from Antibes' city bus station (2/hour). Parking des Bâchettes is free and allows quick access to its pretty pedestrian street.

Sleeping in Antibes

Several sleepable options are available in the town center, but my favorite Antibes hotels are farther out and most convenient for drivers.

OUTSIDE THE TOWN CENTER

$$ Hôtel Mas Djoliba* is a traditional manor house with chirping birds and a flower-filled moat. While convenient for drivers, it's workable for walkers (10-minute walk to Plage de la Salis, 15 minutes to old Antibes). Bigger rooms are worth the additional cost, and several rooms come with small decks (several good family rooms, no elevator but just three floors, *boules* court and loaner balls; 29 Avenue de Provence—from Boulevard Albert I, look for gray signs two blocks before the sea, turn right onto Boulevard Général Maizière, and follow signs; tel. 04 93 34 02 48, www.hotel-djoliba.com, contact@hotel-djoliba.com, Delphine).

$$ Hôtel la Jabotte** is a cozy little hotel hidden along an ignored alley a block from the best beaches and a 20-minute walk from the old town. Run with panache by Nathalie, the hotel's rich colors and decor show a personal touch. The immaculate rooms have smallish bathrooms and individual terraces facing a cute, central garden where you'll get to know your neighbor (no TVs, free breakfast for Rick Steves readers, sauna, bikes, and a kayak available; 13 Avenue Max Maurey, take the third right after passing Hôtel Josse, tel. 04 93 61 45 89, www.jabotte.com, info@jabotte.com). The hotel can shuttle clients to the train station, hiking trails, restaurants, etc. in their small tuk-tuk vehicle for a small fee.

$$ Hôtel Beau-Site,*** my only listing on Cap d'Antibes, is a 10-minute drive from town. It's a terrific value if you want to get away...but not *too* far away. (Without a car, you'll feel isolated.) Helpful Nathalie and Francine welcome you with a pool, a comfy patio garden, and secure pay parking. Rooms are spacious and comfortable, and several have balconies (electric bikes available, 141 Boulevard Kennedy, tel. 04 93 61 53 43, www.hotelbeausite.net, contact@hotelbeausite.net). The hotel is a 10-minute walk from Plage de la Garoupe on the Cap d'Antibes loop hike (described earlier).

$ Bastide de la Brague is an easygoing bed-and-breakfast hacienda up a dirt road a 10-minute drive east of Antibes. The fun-loving family (wife Isabelle, who speaks English, and hubby Franck) rent seven rooms—the best rooms are upstairs; several are ideal for families, and breakfast is included (55 Avenue No. 6, tel. 04 93 65 73 78, www.labastidedelabrague.com, bastidebb06@gmail.com). Antibes bus #10 drops you five minutes away, and if arranged in advance, they can pick you up at the Biot or Antibes train station.

IN THE TOWN CENTER

$$$ Hôtel la Place*** is central, pricey, and cozy. It overlooks the ugly bus station with tastefully designed rooms and a comfy lounge (no elevator, 1 Avenue 24 Août, tel. 04 97 21 03 11, www.la-place-hotel.com, contact@la-place-hotel.com).

$ Hôtel Relais du Postillon,** is a mellow, central place above a peaceful café with 16 impeccable rooms at very fair rates. The furnishings are tasteful, and several rooms have small balconies or terraces (tiny elevator, pay parking, 8 Rue Championnet, tel. 04 93 34 20 77, www.relaisdupostillon.com, relais@relaisdupostillon.com).

$ Modern Hôtel,** in the pedestrian zone behind the city bus station, is suitable for budget-conscious travelers. The 17 standard-size rooms are simple and spick-and-span (no elevator, 1 Rue Four-millière, tel. 04 92 90 59 05, www.modernhotel06.com, modern-hotel@wanadoo.fr).

Eating in Antibes

Antibes is a fun and relaxed place to dine out. But there are pre-ciously few really good options in Antibes, and those get booked up on weekends in particular (when you're smart to book a day ahead). All but one of my recommendations are within a few blocks of each other, so it's easy to comparison shop.

Antibes' **Market Hall** (Marché Provençal) has great ambience and is popular with budget-minded diners each evening after the market stalls close. It's not *haute cuisine*, but prices are usually rea-sonable, and slurping mussels under a classic 19th-century canopy can make for a great memory. To start your soirée, consider a glass of wine from one of several wine bars that call the market hall home.

$$ Try **Chez Lulu** for an ultimate family-style dining ad-venture that seems utterly out of place on the Riviera. Diners fork over €27 and settle in, while charismatic owner Frank (who speaks flawless English), his wife Alice, and—when they're busy—their granddaughter dish out charcuterie, salads, soups, a main course, and desserts to be shared. Tables seat 6-10, and the setting is warm and convivial. Don't come for a romantic meal. You'll be on a first-name basis with your neighbors, cut your own bread, and serve your own soup (fun!). Book a day ahead or arrive early (from 19:00, closed Sun-Mon, tel. 04 89 89 08 92, 5 Rue Frédéric Isnard).

$$$$ **Larazur** is the love child of a young couple who both worked as chefs at Michelin-starred restaurants and wanted a qui-eter life in the south. Lucas does the cooking while Jeanne runs the restaurant. The setting is relaxed yet elegant, and the attention to quality is obvious (book ahead, closed Mon-Tue, 8 Rue des Palm-iers, tel. 04 93 34 75 60, www.larazur.fr).

$$ **Le P'tit Cageot** is a find. The chef makes delicious Medi-terranean cuisine affordable. The place is tiny, just 25 seats inside and out, so book ahead (closed Wed and Sun, 5 Rue du Docteur Rostan, tel. 04 89 68 48 66).

$$ **Le Zinc** is a cool little wine-bar bistro at the upper end of the market hall serving a limited selection of tasty cuisine. Book ahead or arrive early for an outside table (closed Mon, 15 Cours Masséna, tel. 04 83 14 69 20).

$$$ **Le Vauban** is a traditional and dressy place with red-velvet chairs and serious service. It's popular with locals for special events and its seafood (closed for lunch Mon and Wed, closed all day Tue, opposite 4 Rue Thuret, tel. 04 93 34 33 05, www.levauban.fr).

$$ **Le Brulot,** an institution in Antibes, is known for its Provençal cuisine and meat dishes (most cooked over an open fire). It's a small, rustic place with tables crammed every which way (big, splittable portions, come early or book ahead, closed Sun, 2 Rue Frédéric Isnard, tel. 04 93 34 17 76, www.brulot.fr).

$$$ **La Taille de Guêpe** is family-run by Olivier in the kitchen and Katy in the relaxing garden-like dining room. The chef has worked for several years with flowers; the colorful varieties you find on your plate are all edible and add a twist to the fresh, fine, and light food. The *moëlleux au chocolat* is a perfect way to end your meal. *Menus*, enjoyed with cheap and good local wine, are a good deal (reservations recommended, closed Sun-Mon, 24 Rue de Fersen, tel. 04 93 74 03 58).

Picnic on the Beach or Ramparts: Romantics on a shoestring can find grocery stores open until late in Antibes and assemble their own picnic dinner to enjoy on the beach or ramparts. There's a good **Carrefour City** market at 44 Rue de la République and a **Monoprix** on Place Général de Gaulle—both open late.

Antibes Connections

For a comparison of train and bus connections, see the "Public Transportation in the French Riviera" sidebar on page 10.

From Antibes by Train: TGV and local trains deliver great service to Antibes' little station. Trains go to **Cannes** (2/hour, 15 minutes), **Nice** (2/hour, 20 minutes), **Grasse** (1/hour, 40 minutes), **Villefranche-sur-Mer** (2/hour, 40 minutes), **Monaco** (2/hour, 50 minutes), and **Marseille** (hourly, 2.5 hours).

By Bus: All the buses listed below serve the Pôle d'Echange regional bus station (behind the train station). Handy **bus #200** ties everything together from Cannes to Nice, but runs at a snail's pace when traffic is bad. It goes west to **Cannes** (35 minutes) and east to near **Biot** village (15 minutes—bus #10 is better, see the Biot village listing under "Near Antibes," earlier), **Cagnes-sur-Mer**

(25 minutes), and **Nice** (1.5 hours). For bus details, including info on tickets, routes, frequencies, and travel times, see the "Getting Around the Riviera" section in the French Riviera chapter. **Bus #250** runs to **Nice Airport** (2/hour, 40 minutes).

Cannes

Cannes (pronounced "can"), famous for its May film festival, is the sister city of Beverly Hills. That says it all. When I asked at the TI for a list of museums and sights, they just smiled. Cannes—with big, exclusive hotels lining mostly private stretches of perfect, sandy beach—is for strolling, shopping, dreaming of meeting a movie star, and lounging on the seafront. Cannes has little that's unique to offer the traveler...except a mostly off-limits film festival and quick access to two undeveloped islands. You can buy an ice-cream cone at the train station and see everything before you've had your last lick. Money is what Cannes has always been about—wealthy people come here to make the scene, and there's always enough *scandale* to go around. The king of Saudi Arabia purchased a serious slice of waterfront just east of town and built his compound with no regard to local zoning regulations. Money talks on the Riviera...and always has.

GETTING TO CANNES

Don't sleep or drive in Cannes. Day-trip here by train or bus. It's a breeze, as frequent trains and buses link to Cannes from sea-front cities like Antibes (15 minutes by train) and Nice (30 minutes; longer by bus). For details, see the transportation chart in the "Getting Around the Riviera" section in the French Riviera chapter. From Grasse, you can take a direct train or bus to Cannes. Buses stop next to the train station. A car is a headache best avoided in Cannes, though there's a darn scenic drive just west of Cannes (from Fréjus on D-6098).

Orientation to Cannes

Buses stop in front of the train station, where you'll find a TI (to the left as you exit the train station), baggage storage (to the right as you exit), and a handy train-information desk with maps of the

Handy Cannes and St-Tropez Phrases

Where is a movie star?	*Où est une vedette?*
I am a movie star.	*Je suis une vedette.*
I am rich and single.	*Je suis riche et célibataire.*
Are you rich and single?	*Etes-vous riche et célibataire?*
Are those real?	*Ils sont des vrais?*
How long is your yacht?	*Quelle est la longeur de votre yacht?*
How much did that cost?	*Combien coûtait-il?*
You can always dream...	*On peut toujours rêver...*

city. If you must drive, store your car at the parking garage next to the train station.

Tourist Information: Cannes' main TI is located in the Film Festival Hall at 1 Boulevard de la Croisette (daily July-Aug 9:00-20:00, Sept-June 10:00-19:00). Another TI is next to the train station (same hours, 4 Place de la Gare).

Cannes Walk

This self-guided cancan will take you to Cannes' sights in a level, one-hour walk at a movie-star pace.

• *Walk straight out of the train station, crossing the bus station/street in front and turn left. Make a quick right on Rue des Serbes, and stroll for five unglamorous minutes to the beachfront. Cross the busy Boulevard de la Croisette, turn left on the promenade, and walk a few blocks down until you're about opposite the Marriot Casino. Now get familiar with...*

The Lay of the Land: Cannes feels different from its neighbors to the east. You won't find the pastel oranges and pinks of Old Nice and Villefranche-sur-Mer. Cannes was never part of Italy—and its architecture and cuisine remind me more of Paris than Nice.

Face the water. The land jutting into the sea on your left is actually two islands, St-Honorat and Ste-Marguerite. St-Honorat has

been the property of monks for over 500 years; today its abbey, vineyards, trails, and gardens can be visited by peace-seeking travelers. Ste-Marguerite, which you also can visit, is famous for the stone prison that housed the 17th-century Man in the Iron Mask (whose true identity remains unknown). For more on visiting these islands, see the boat excursions listed under "Activities in Cannes," later.

ANTIBES & NEARBY

Now look far to your right. Those striking mountains sweeping down to the sea are the Massif de l'Esterel. Their red-rock outcrops oversee spectacular car and train routes (see "Cannes Connections," later). Closer in, the hill with the medieval tower caps Cannes' old town (Le Suquet). This hilltop offers grand views and pretty lanes—and the only place in Cannes where you feel its medieval past. Below the old town, the port welcomes yachts of all sizes...provided they're really big.

Face inland. Closer, on the left, find the unexceptional, cream-colored building with the tinted windows overlooking the sea. That convention-center-like structure is home of the famous film festival (we'll visit there soon). Back the other way, gaze up the boulevard. That classy building with twin black-domed roofs is Hôtel Carlton, our eventual target and as far as we'll go together in that direction.

• *Continue with the sea on your right and stroll the...*

Promenade (La Croisette): You're walking along Boulevard de la Croisette—Cannes' famed two-mile-long promenade. First popular with kings who wintered here after Napoleon fell, the elite parade was later joined by British aristocracy. Today, Boulevard de la Croisette is fronted by some of the most expensive apartments and hotels in Europe. If it's lunchtime, you might try one of the beach cafés.

• *Stop when you get to...*

Hôtel Carlton: This is the most famous address on Boulevard de la Croisette (small double room–€1,500, more spacious double–€7,000). Face the beach.

The iconic Cannes experience is to slip into a robe (ideally, monogrammed with your initials), out of your luxury hotel (preferably this one), and onto the beach or pier. While you may not be doing the "fancy hotel and monogrammed robe" ritual on this Cannes excursion, you can—for about €25—rent a chair and umbrella and pretend you're tanning for a red-carpet premiere. Cannes has a few token public beaches, but most beaches are private and run by hotels like the Carlton. You could save money by sunning among the common folk, but the real Cannes way to flee the rabble and paparazzi is to rent a spot on a private beach.

Cross over and wander into the hotel—you're welcome to

browse (harder during the festival). Ask for a hotel brochure, verify room rates, check for availability. How do people afford this? Groupon? Imagine the scene here during the film festival. An affordable café (considering the cost of a room) lies just beyond the champagne lounge.

• *You can continue your stroll down La Croisette, but I'm doubling back to the cream-colored building that is Cannes'...*

Film Festival Hall: Cannes' film festival (Festival de Cannes), staged since 1946, completes the "Big Three" of Riviera

events (with Monaco's Grand Prix and Nice's Carnival). The hall where the festival takes place—a busy-but-nondescript convention center that also hosts the town TI—sits plump on the beach. You'll recognize the formal grand entryway (most likely without the famed red carpet). Find the famous (Hollywood-style) handprints in the sidewalk nearby (also by the entry to the TI). To get inside during the festival, you have to be a star (or a photographer—some 3,000 paparazzi attend the gala event, and most bring their own ladders to get above the crowds).

The festival originated in part as an anti-fascist response to Mussolini's Venice Film Festival. Cannes' first festival was due to open in 1939, on the very day Hitler invaded Poland. Because of World War II, the opening was delayed until 1946. Cannes' film festival is also famous as the first festival to give one vote per country on the jury (giving films from smaller countries a better chance).

Though generally off-limits to curious tourists, the festival is everything around here—and is worth a day trip to Cannes if you happen to be in the region when it's on. The town buzzes with megastar energy, press passes, and revealing dresses. Locals claim that it's the world's third-biggest media event, after the Olympics and the World Cup (soccer). The festival prize is the Palme d'Or (like the Oscar for Best Picture). The French press can't cover the event enough, and the average Jean in France follows it as Joe would the World Series in the States. The festival celebrated its 70th anniversary in 2017. American actors Jessica Chastain and Will Smith served on the main jury, and the Palme d'Or went to a Swedish film, *The Square*. And in 2018, the Japanese film *Shoplifters* took the top prize at a politically charged festival that also saw films (and protests) focused on women's empowerment, racial tension, and the lives of refugees.

• *Around the other side of the festival hall is the port (Gare Maritime).*

The Port and Old Town (Le Suquet): The megayachts line up closest to the Film Festival Hall. After seeing these amazing boats,

Yachters' Itinerary

If you're visiting Cannes on your private yacht, here's a suggested itinerary:

1. Take in the Festival de Cannes and the accompanying social scene. Organize an evening party on your boat.
2. Motor over to Monte Carlo for the Grand Prix, scheduled—conveniently for yachters—just after the film festival.
3. On your way back west to St-Tropez, deconstruct events from the film festival and Grand Prix with Brigitte Bardot.
4. Drop down to Porto Chervo on Sardinia, one of the few places in the world where your yacht is "just average."
5. Head west to Ibiza and Marbella in Spain, where your friends are moored for the big party scene.

everything else looks like a dinghy. Boat service to St-Tropez and the nearby islands of St-Honorat and Ste-Marguerite depart from the far side of the port (at Quai Laubeuf; for boat info, see "Activities in Cannes," later).

Cannes' oldest neighborhood, Le Suquet, crowns the hill past the port. Locals refer to it as their Montmartre. Artsy and charming, it's a steep 15-minute walk above the port, with little of interest except the panoramic views from its ancient church, Notre-Dame-de-l'Espérance (Our Lady of Hope).

• *To find the views in Le Suquet, aim for its clock tower and start by passing the bus station at the northwest corner of the port, then make your way up cobbled Rue Saint-Antoine (next to the Café St. Antoine). Turn left on Place du Suquet, and then follow signs to* Traverse de la Tour *for the final leg.*

Cue music. Roll end credits. Our film is over. For further exploration, look for Cannes' "underbelly" between Le Suquet and the train station—narrow lanes with inexpensive cafés and shops that regular folks can afford.

Activities in Cannes

Shopping

Cannes is made for window shopping (the best streets are between the station and the waterfront). For the trendiest boutiques, stroll down handsome Rue d'Antibes (parallel to the sea about three blocks inland). Rue Meynadier anchors a pedestrian zone with more affordable shops closer to the port. To bring home a real surprise, why not consider cosmetic surgery? Cannes is well known as *the* place on the Riviera to have your face (or other parts) realigned.

ANTIBES & NEARBY

Boat Excursions to St-Honorat and Ste-Marguerite Islands

Two boat companies ferry tourists 15 minutes from the Quai Laubeuf dock in Cannes' port to twin islands just offshore: St-Honorat and Ste-Marguerite. Both outfits charge the same (€15 round-trip) and run every half hour (daily 9:00-18:00). There's no ferry between the two islands. For the Ste-Marguerite schedule, go to TransCoteAzur.com; for St-Honorat hours, it's CannesIlesDelerins.com.

The islands offer a refreshing change from the town scene, with almost no development, good swimming, and peaceful walking paths. On Ste-Marguerite you can hike, visit the castle (part of which is now a youth hostel) and the cell where the mysterious Man in the Iron Mask was imprisoned (with a good little museum with decent English explanations featuring cargo from a sunken Roman vessel), and tour the Musée de la Mer's ancient collection and underwater exhibits. On St-Honorat you can hike seafront trails and visit the abbey where monks have lived and prayed for 16 centuries. Today they make fine wines in their free time. St-Honorat also has a few shops and a restaurant.

Cannes Connections

From Cannes by Train to: Antibes (2/hour, 15 minutes), **Nice** (2/hour, 30 minutes), **Monaco** (2/hour, 70 minutes), **Grasse** (hourly, 30 minutes).

By Bus: Bus #200 heads east from Cannes along the Riviera, stopping at **Antibes** (35 minutes) and **Nice** (2 hours; trip duration depends on traffic; for bus details, see the "Getting Around the Riviera" section in the French Riviera chapter). **Bus #210** runs from the train station express on the freeway to **Nice Airport** (1-2/hour, 50 minutes, €20). Both buses stop at the Cannes train station.

By Boat: Trans Côte d'Azur runs boat excursions from Cannes to **St-Tropez** (€50 round-trip, 1 hour each way; July-Aug daily 1/day; June and Sept 1/day Tue, Thu, and Sat-Sun only; no service Oct-May; tel. 04 92 98 71 30, www.trans-cote-azur.com). This boat trip is popular—book a few days ahead from June to September.

By Cruise Ship: Ships tender passengers to the west side of Cannes' port. From here, it's an easy walk into town: Head inland, with the port on your right-hand side. Note that the tender dock is near the end of my "Cannes Walk"; if planning to follow it, you can either start the walk here and do it in reverse or stroll about 10 minutes around the port to the walk's starting point (see "Cannes Walk," earlier). If heading to points beyond Cannes, it takes about 15 minutes to walk from the tender dock to the train station, where you can catch a train for Antibes, Nice, or Villefranche-sur-Mer.

ANTIBES & NEARBY

St-Tropez

St-Tropez is a busy, charming, and traffic-free port town smoth-
ered with fashion boutiques,
elegant restaurants, and luxury
boats. If you came here for history or quaintness, you caught
the wrong yacht. But if you have
more money than you know
what to do with, you're home.
There are 5,700 year-round residents...and more than 100,000
visitors daily in the summer. If
St-Tropez is on your must-visit
list, hit it on your way to or from Provence—and skip it altogether
in summer and on weekend afternoons.

As with lots of now-famous villages in southern France, St-
Tropez was "found" by artists. Paul Signac brought several of his
friends to St-Tropez in the late 1800s, giving the village its first
whiff of popularity (get rid of the yachts filling the harbor, and the
town would resemble what it looked like then). But it wasn't until
Brigitte Bardot made the scene here in the 1956 film...*And God
Created Woman* that St-Tropez became synonymous with Riviera
glamour. Since then, it's the first place that comes to mind when
people think of the jet set luxuriating on Mediterranean beaches.
For many, the French Riviera begins here and runs east to Menton,
on the Italian border.

The village is the attraction here; the nearest big beach is miles
away. Window shopping, people-watching, tan maintenance, and
savoring slow meals fill people's days, weeks, and, in some cases,
lives. Here, people dress up, size up one another's yachts or cars,
and troll for a partner. While the only models you'll see are in the
shop windows, Brigitte Bardot still hangs out on a bench in front
of the TI signing autographs (Thu 15:00-17:30, and if you believe
that...).

Wander the harborfront, where fancy yachts moor stern-in,
their carefully coiffed captains and first mates enjoying *pu-pus* for
happy hour—they're seeing and being seen. Take time to stroll the
back streets (the small lanes below La Citadelle are St-Tropez's
most appealing) while nibbling a chocolate-and-Grand Marnier
crêpe. Find the big Place des Lices (good cafés and local hangout),
and look for some serious games of *pétanque (boules)*.

St-Tropez lies between its famous port and the hilltop Citadelle (with great views). The network of lanes between the port and
Citadelle are strollable in a Carmel-by-the-Sea sort of way. The

main **TI** is on the starboard side of the port (to the right as you face the sea), where Quai Suffren and Quai Jean Jaurès meet (tel. 08 92 68 48 28, www.sainttropeztourisme.com). Pick up their helpful walking tour brochure, ask about events in town, and get maps and bus information if you plan to hike along the coast.

Getting There: With no trains to St-Tropez, buses and boats are your only options without a car. Varlib **buses** connect to St-Tropez from nearby train stations. From the east, catch bus #7601 from behind St-Raphaël's train station (70 minutes, goes via Ste-Maxime); from the west, take bus #7801 or #7802, 1.5 hours from Toulon's train station (if arriving at either station by train, check bus schedules to St-Tropez in advance to ensure you make the connection; www.varlib.fr).

Boats connect to St-Tropez from St-Raphaël twice daily (tel. 04 94 95 17 46, www.bateauxsaintraphael.com) and from Ste-Maxime about hourly (tel. 04 94 49 29 39, www.bateauxverts. com). For boats connecting St-Tropez with Nice, see page 69; with Cannes, see "Cannes Connections," earlier.

If arriving by **car,** prepare for traffic in any season—worse on weekends (forget driving on Sunday afternoons), always ugly during summer, and downright impossible between St-Tropez and Ste-Maxime on weekends. You can avoid this bottleneck by taking the autoroute to Le Luc and following the windy D-558 to St-Tropez from here (via La Garde-Freinet and Port Grimaud). The last few miles to St-Tropez are along a too-long, two-lane road with one way in, one way out, and too many people going exactly where you're going. There are two main parking lots: Parking des Lices (near recommended hotels) and Parking du Port (best for day-trippers).

Visiting St-Tropez: Use the TI's self-guided walking tour brochure to connect the following highlights.

The **port** has been a key player in St-Tropez's economy since the 18th century, when it saw a brisk trade in wine, cork, and lumber. St-Tropez's shipyards were famous for their three-mast ships, which could carry more than 1,000 barrels of wine. Today's port is famous for its big boats. There's something bizarre about the size of those boats, stern-tied tightly in such a small harbor. While strolling around, you'll see busy deckhands (hustling before their captains arrive) and artists competing for room. The red-tabled **Le Sénéquier,** by the TI, is one of the town's most venerated cafés—and has long attracted celebrities, including the philosopher Jean-Paul Sartre. High-end cafés and restaurants line the port from here to the jetty—it doesn't seem to matter that you can't see the sea for the big yachts. The bulky **Tour du Portalet** tower at the port's end has views across the bay to the town of Ste-Maxime and out to sea. A plaque honors the American, British, and French troops who

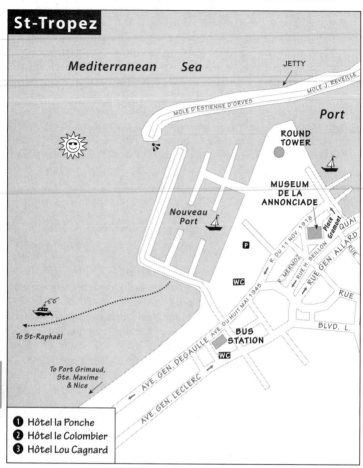

St-Tropez

Mediterranean Sea

JETTY

MOLE J. REVEILLE

MOLE D'ESTIENNE D'ORVES

Port

ROUND TOWER

MUSEUM DE LA ANNONCIADE

Place Gramont

QUAI

Nouveau Port

R. DU 11 NOV. 1918

R. MERMOZ

RUE H. SEILLON

RUE GEN. ALLARD

RUE

BLVD. L.

WC

RUE DU HUIT MAI 1945

To St-Raphaël

BUS STATION

AVE. GEN. DEGAULLE

WC

To Port Grimaud, Ste. Maxime & Nice

AVE. GEN. LECLERC

1 Hôtel la Ponche
2 Hôtel le Colombier
3 Hôtel Lou Cagnard

ANTIBES & NEARBY

liberated Provence on August 15, 1944. Climb the jetty for great views over the port.

The **Museum of the Annonciade,** though generally ignored, houses an enchanting collection of works from the Post-Impressionist and Fauvist artists who decorated St-Tropez before Brigitte. Almost all canvases feature St-Tropez sights and landscapes. You'll see colorful paintings by Paul Signac, Henri Matisse, Georges Braque, Pierre Bonnard, Maurice de Vlaminck, and more. Gaze out the windows and notice how the port has changed since they were here (tel. 04 94 17 84 10).

The scenic **Sentier du Littoral coastal path,** originally patrolled by customs agents, runs past the 1558 Citadelle fortress (which houses a maritime museum) and continues for 12 miles along the coast. The trail is marked with yellow dashes on the pavement, walls, and trees. Leave St-Tropez along the road below

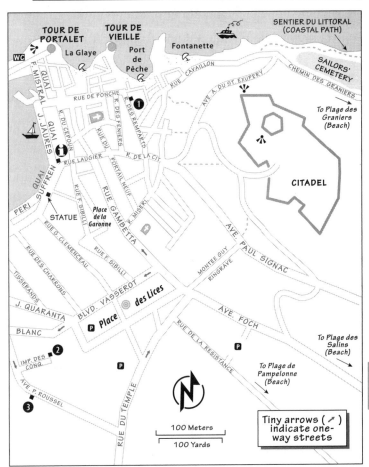

the Citadelle, pass the Sailors' Cemetery, and you'll join the path before long.

Several companies offer mildly interesting **boat tours** of the surrounding coastline. You'll learn a smidgen about St-Tropez's history and a lot about the villas of the rich and famous (details at TI).

The vast *pétanque (boules)* **court** on Place des Lices is worth your attention. Have a drink at Le Café and take in the action.

Nearby: Although more modern than St-Tropez, **Port Grimaud** (located a few miles toward Ste-Maxime) is no less attractive or upscale. This "Venice of Provence" was reclaimed from a murky lagoon about 40 years ago and is now lined with four miles of canals, lovely homes, and moorage for thousands of yachts. It's a fascinating look at what clever minds can produce from a swamp. Park at the lot across from the town entry (TI next to the parking lot, www.grimaud-provence.com), and cross the barrier and bridge into a beautiful world of privilege. Climb the church bell tower for a good panorama view.

Sleeping in St-Tropez: If you're spending the night here, remember that high season in St-Tropez runs from June through September, and weekends are busy year-round. Hotels worth considering include: **$$$$ Hôtel la Ponche****** (central and luxurious, 3 Rue des Remparts, tel. 04 94 97 02 53, www.laponche.com); **$$ Hôtel le Colombier**** (small, adorable, and on a quiet street—Impasse des Conquêtes, reservations by phone only, tel. 04 94 97 05 31, lecolombierhotel.free.fr); and **$$ Hôtel Lou Cagnard**** (pretty courtyard garden, 18 Avenue Paul Roussel, tel. 04 94 97 04 24, www.hotel-lou-cagnard.com).

INLAND RIVIERA

*St-Paul-de-Vence • Vence •
Grasse • Inland Riviera Drive •
Grand Canyon du Verdon*

For a verdant, rocky, fresh escape from the beaches, head inland and upward. Some perfectly perched hill towns and splendid scenery hang overlooked in this region more famous for beaches and bikinis. A short car or bus ride away from the Mediterranean reaps big rewards: lush forests, deep canyons, and swirling hilltop villages. It's easy to link the main sights and towns of this region in a day's drive from Nice. A longer drive brings you to Europe's greatest canyon, the Grand Canyon du Verdon.

PLANNING YOUR TIME

With one full day, rent a car and do my Inland Riviera Drive (described later in this chapter). Start in Nice (or Antibes) and arrive in St-Paul-de-Vence as early as you can to minimize crowds (or just skip it). Do visit Fondation Maeght, then head to nearby Vence for lunch, then take an ice cream stroll through unspoiled Tourrettes-sur-Loup. End your day with a visit to the perfume city of Grasse. (This same trip can be done by bus if you depart early in the morning and forgo Grasse.)

With two days (and a car), conclude your driving tour with an overnight in Vence, then spend your second day visiting the Grand Canyon du Verdon (ideally ending in the Luberon, Cassis, or Aix-en-Provence).

GETTING AROUND THE INLAND RIVIERA

By Car: Driving is the best way to tour this area, though weekend traffic and parking challenges will test your patience. You can rent a car for a day from Nice or Antibes.

By Bus: Buses get you to many of the places in this chapter. Vence, St-Paul-de-Vence, and Grasse are well served by bus from Nice (#94 Nice/Vence, #400 Nice/St-Paul-de-Vence/Vence, #500

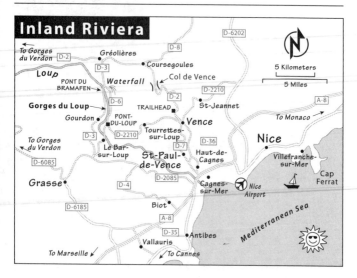

Inland Riviera

Nice/Grasse, about 2/hour). Grasse is also connected by trains from Nice, Antibes, and Cannes (there's also a bus connection between Grasse and Cannes, #600). Within the area, bus #510/511 runs from Vence to Grasse via Tourrettes-sur-Loup and Le Bar-sur-Loup (6/day, 50 minutes, buy tickets in these towns at *tabacs* (not from drivers). Bus connections for the Gorges du Loup, the village of Gourdon, or the Gorges du Verdon are either too complicated or nonexistent. For schedules, see www.lignesdazur.com.

With a Local Guide: The owners of the recommended Frogs' House in St-Jeannet, Benoît and Corinne, are happy to organize cooking classes, wine tastings, hiking trips, and other excursions around their native area (see their listing under "Sleeping in and near Vence," later in this chapter).

See page 12 for guides with cars who can get you to places you would not find yourself.

St-Paul-de-Vence

This most famous of Riviera hill towns is also the most-visited village in France. I believe it. This incredibly situated village—with views to the sea and the Alps—is understandably popular. Every cobble and flower seems just so, and the setting is postcard-perfect. But it can also feel like an overrun and over-restored artist's shopping mall. Avoid visiting between 11:00 and 18:00, particularly on weekends. Beat the crowds by skipping breakfast at your hotel to get here early, or come for dinner and experience the village at its tranquil best.

Orientation to St-Paul-de-Vence

Tourist Information: The helpful TI, just through the gate into the old town on Rue Grande, has maps with minimal explanations of key buildings, and rental *boules* for *pétanque* on the square (daily 10:00-18:00, June-Sept until 19:00, closes for lunch on weekends, tel. 04 93 32 86 95, www.saint-pauldevence.com).

Arrival in St-Paul-de-Vence: Pay to park close to the village, or park for free along the road to Fondation Maeght (look for *Parking Conseillé* signs) and walk down to the village. Free parking is also available at the entry to Fondation Maeght (a 20-minute walk from town). Bus #400 (connecting Nice and Vence) stops on the main road, just above the village.

However you arrive, if the traffic-free lane leading into the old town is jammed, walk along the road that veers up and left just after Café de la Place, and enter the town through its side door.

Sights in St-Paul-de-Vence

The Old Town

St-Paul's old town has no essential sights, though its perfectly cobbled lanes and peekaboo views delight most who come. You'll pass two vintage eateries before piercing the walls of the old town. The recommended **La Colombe d'Or** is a good spot for a meal. Back when the town was teeming with artists, this historic hotel/restaurant served as their clubhouse. Its walls are covered with paintings by Picasso, Miró, Braque, Chagall, and others who traded their art for free meals. **Café de la Place** is a classic spot to have a coffee and croissant while watching waves of tourists crash into town (daily from 7:00). On the square, serious *boules* competitions take place. Find the cool *boules* sculpture there.

After entering the walls of St-Paul, meander deep to find its quieter streets and panoramic views. How many art galleries can this village support? Imagine the time it took to create the intricate stone patterns in the street you're walking along. Visit **Marc Chagall's grave** in the cemetery at the opposite end of town, a 10-minute walk keeping straight along the main drag (from the cemetery entrance, turn right, then left to find Chagall's grave). Walk up the stairs to the **view platform** above the cemetery and try to locate the hill town of Vence at the foot of an impressive mountain. Is the sea out there—somewhere?

INLAND RIVIERA

▲Fondation Maeght

This inviting, pricey, and far-out private museum is situated a steep walk or short drive above St-Paul-de-Vence. Fondation Maeght (fohn-dah-shown mahg) offers an excellent introduction to modern Mediterranean art by gathering many of the Riviera's most famous artists under one roof. There are no English explanations for the interior displays.

Cost and Hours: €16, daily 10:00-18:00, July-Sept until 19:00, audioguide-€3 (covers primarily art in the gardens), great gift shop and cafeteria, tel. 04 93 32 81 63, www.fondation-maeght.com.

Getting There: The museum is a steep uphill 20-minute walk from St-Paul-de-Vence and the bus stop. Parking is usually available (and free) at the sight and in lower lots, signed *Parking Conseillé*.

Visiting the Museum: The founder, Aimé Maeght, long envisioned the perfect exhibition space for the artists he supported and befriended as an art dealer. He purchased this arid hilltop, planted 35,000 plants, and hired the Catalan architect José Luis Sert to enact his vision.

A sweeping lawn laced with amusing sculptures and bending pine trees greets visitors. On the right, a chapel designed by Georges Braque—in memory of the Maeghts' young son, who died of leukemia—features a moving purple stained-glass work over the altar. The unusual museum building is purposely low profile to let its world-class modern art collection take center stage. Works by Fernand Léger, Joan Miró, Alexander Calder, Georges Braque, Marc Chagall, and many others are thoughtfully arranged in well-lit rooms (the permanent collection is sometimes replaced by special thematic shows). Outside, in the back, you'll find a Gaudí-esque sculpture labyrinth by Miró and a courtyard filled with the wispy works of Alberto Giacometti—both designed by the artists for these spaces.

Eating in St-Paul-de-Vence

$$ Le Tilleul is a good place to dine well in St-Paul, either at inviting tables on the broad terrace or in its pleasant interior (daily, near the TI on Place du Tilleul, tel. 04 93 32 80 36, www.restaurant-letilleul.com).

Book well ahead for **$$$$ La Colombe d'Or,** a veritable institution in St-Paul where the menu hasn't changed in 50 years (see description earlier). Dine on good-enough cuisine inside by the fire to best feel its pulse (closed Nov-Dec, tel. 04 93 32 80 02, www. la-colombe-dor.com; for reservations, email contact@la-colombe-dor.com).

Vence

Vence, an appealing town set high above the Riviera, sees a fraction of the crowds that you'll find in St-Paul. While growth has sprawled beyond Vence's old walls and cars jam its roundabouts, the traffic-free lanes of the old city are a delight, the mountains are front and center, and the breeze is fresh. Vence bubbles with workaday life—and ample tourist activity in the day—but it's quiet at night, with far fewer visitors and cooler temperatures than along the coast. You'll also find terrific choices for affordable hotels and restaurants. Vence makes a handy base for travelers wanting the best of both worlds: a hill-town refuge near the sea. Some enjoy the Grand Canyon du Verdon as a long day trip from Vence (see the route described at the end of this chapter).

Orientation to Vence

Tourist Information: Vence's fully loaded and helpful TI is at the southwest corner of the main square, Place du Grand Jardin (in the Villa Alexandrine, Mon-Sat 9:00-19:00, Sun 10:00-18:00; Nov-March 10:00-17:00 and closed Sun, tel. 04 93 58 06 38, www. vence-tourisme.fr). Pick up the city map with a well-devised self-guided walking tour, a list of art galleries, bus schedules, or *pétanque* instructions, and ask about guided walking tours in English (officedetourisme@ville-vence.fr).

    Arrival in Vence: Bus #94 (fastest bus from Nice, about an hour) or #400 (from Nice, Cagnes-sur-Mer, and St-Paul-de-Vence, just over an hour) drops you at the Ara bus stop just off the roundabout at Place Maréchal Juin, a 10-minute walk to the town center (along Avenue Henri Isnard or Avenue de la Résistance). If arriving by **car,** follow signs to *cité historique* and park in the underground Parking Grand Jardin, near the TI.

    Helpful Hints: Market days are Tuesdays and Fridays until 13:00 on the Place du Grand Jardin and in the *cité historique* around Place Clemenceau. A big all-day antiques market is on Place du Grand Jardin every Wednesday. If you miss market day, a Monoprix **supermarket** is on Avenue de la Résistance, across from the entrance to the Marie Antoinette parking lot (grocery store upstairs, Mon-Sat 8:30-20:00, Sun 9:00-13:00). For a **taxi,** call 04 93 58 11 14.

Sights in Vence

Explore the narrow lanes of the old town using the TI's worthwhile self-guided tour map. Connect the picturesque streets, enjoy a drink on a quiet square, inspect an art gallery, and find the small 11th-century cathedral with its colorful Chagall mosaic of Moses. And, of course, visit Matisse's Chapel of the Rosary. If you're in Vence later in the day, enjoy the *boules* action across from the TI.

Château de Villeneuve

This 17th-century mansion, adjoining an imposing 12th-century watchtower, bills itself as one of the Riviera's high temples of modern art, with a rotating collection. Check with the TI to see what's showing in the temple. The museum offers a loaner guide with English explanations of the collection.

Cost and Hours: €7, Tue-Sun 11:00-18:00, closed Mon, 2 Place du Frêne, tel. 04 93 58 15 78.

▲Chapel of the Rosary (Chapelle du Rosaire)

The chapel—a short drive or 20-minute walk from town—was designed by an elderly and ailing Henri Matisse as thanks to a Dominican nun who had taken care of him (he was 81 when the chapel was completed). While the chapel is the ultimate pilgrimage for his fans, the experience may underwhelm others. (Picasso thought it looked like a bathroom.) The chapel's design may seem basic—white porcelain tiles, simple black designs, and floor-to-ceiling windows—but it's a space of light and calm that only a master could have created.

Cost and Hours: €7; Tue, Thu, and Fri 10:00-12:00 & 14:00-18:00, Wed and Sat 14:00-18:00 (Nov-March until 17:00), closed Sun-Mon and mid-Nov-mid-Dec, 466 Avenue Henri Matisse, tel. 04 93 58 03 26, www.chapellematisse.fr.

Getting There: On foot, it's a 20-minute walk from Place du Grand Jardin. Walk down Avenue Henri Isnard all the way to the traffic circle. Turn right across the one-lane bridge on Avenue

Henri Matisse, following signs to *St-Jeannet*. **By car,** follow signs toward *St-Jeannet*, cross the bridge, and start looking for parking—the chapel is about 400 yards after the bridge toward St-Jeannet.

Visiting the Chapel: The modest chapel holds a simple series of charcoal black-on-white tile sketches and uses three symbolic colors as accents: yellow (sunlight and the light of God), green (nature), and blue (the Mediterranean sky). Bright sunlight filters through the stained-glass windows and does a cheery dance across the sketches.

Your entry ticket includes a 20-minute tour from one of the kind nuns who speak English. In the little museum, you'll find pictures of the artist, displays of the vestments Matisse designed for the priests, his models of the chapel, and sketches. Outside, there's a terrace with terrific views toward Vence.

Matisse was the master of leaving things out. Decide for yourself whether Matisse met the goal he set for himself: "Creating a religious space in an enclosed area of reduced proportions and to give it, solely by the play of colors and lines, the dimensions of infinity."

Sleeping in and near Vence

These places tend to close their reception desks between 12:00 and 16:00. Make arrangements in advance if you plan to arrive during this time.

$$$ La Maison du Frêne, centrally located behind the TI, is a modern, art-packed B&B with four sumptuous suites. Energetic and art-crazy Thierry and Guy make fine hosts (RS%, includes good breakfast, kids under 12 free; next to the Château de Villeneuve at 1 Place du Frêne; tel. 04 93 24 37 83, www.lamaisondufrene.com, contact@lamaisondufrene.com).

$ Hôtel La Victoire is a solid value right on the main square next to the TI. Rooms are small but have all the comforts; it's warmly run and well maintained by Pierre (elevator one floor up, 1 Place du Grand Jardin, tel. 04 93 24 15 54, www.hotel-victoire.com, contact@hotel-victoire.com).

$ Auberge des Seigneurs feels medieval. Located in a 17th-century building, it has six simple but spacious rooms over a well-respected restaurant (Wi-Fi in lobby, no air-con, no elevator, 1 Rue du Docteur Binet, tel. 04 93 58 04 24, http://auberge-seigneurs.fr, sandrine.rodi@wanadoo.fr).

NEAR VENCE

$ The Frogs' House is situated in the untouristed hill town of St-Jeannet, a 15-minute drive from Vence. (It's so quiet, it's hard to believe a Riviera beach is only 10 miles away.) Benôit and Corinne

Vence

Accommodations
1. La Maison du Frêne
2. Hôtel La Victoire
3. Auberge des Seigneurs
4. To The Frogs' House

Eateries & Other
5. Les Agapes
6. La Litote
7. La Michel Ange
8. Bistro du Peyra
9. Monoprix Grocery

← To Matisse Chapel (on foot)
To ❹ , Place M. Juin (Bus Stop), Col de Vence via D-2 & Chapel of the Rosary
AVENUE HENRI ISNARD

CHATEAU DE VILLENEUVE MODERN ART MUSEUM

RUE DU DR. BINET

← To Place M. Juin (Bus Stop), Tourettes-sur-Loup via D-2210 & St. Paul via D-7
AVENUE DE LA RESISTANCE

PLACE DU GRAND JARDIN

TOWER →

PORTE DU PEYRA

Marie Antoinette

Place du Grand Jardin

Grand Jardin

WC

RUE DES ARCS

RUE MASSENA

RUE GAMBETTA

INLAND RIVIERA

welcome travelers with a full menu of good rooms, cooking lessons, restaurant recommendations, hikes in the area, and day trips. If you don't have wheels, they'll pick you up at the train station or airport. Rooms are small but sharp (includes hearty breakfast, some rooms with balconies, family rooms, full-house rentals available in winter, mobile 06 28 06 80 28, www.thefrogshouse.fr, info@ thefrogshouse.com). Park in the lot at the bottom of St-Jeannet, a few blocks from this small hotel.

Eating in Vence

Tempting outdoor eateries litter the old town. Lights embedded in the cobbles illuminate the way after dark. The restaurants I list have similar prices and quality, and all have outside dining options.

At **$$ Les Agapes**, Chef Jean-Philippe goes beyond the standard fare with lavish presentations, creative food combinations, and moderate (for the Riviera) prices. Try the *sphere chocolat* dessert

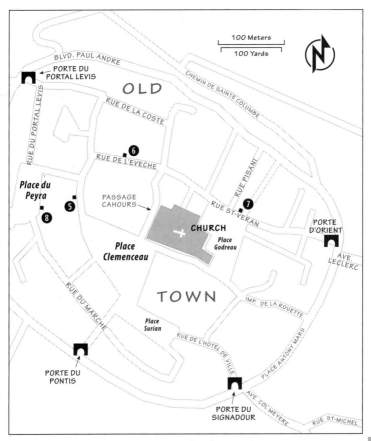

to round out your meal (closed Mon year-round, closed Sun off-season, reservations smart, 4 Place Clemenceau, tel. 04 93 58 50 64, www.les-agapes.net).

$$ La Litote is a favorite, with outdoor tables on a quiet, hidden square, a cozy interior, and traditional cuisine (closed Sun year-round, closed Mon off-season, 7 Rue de l'Evêché, tel. 04 93 24 27 82).

$ Le Michel Ange is a sweet, kid-friendly place on an adorable square serving excellent-value cuisine from pizza to pasta, as well as tasty, well-presented *plats du jour* (closed Sun-Mon, 1 Place Godeau, tel. 04 93 58 32 56).

For inexpensive, casual dining, head to Place du Peyra, where you'll find ample outdoor seating and early dinner service. At the basic **$$ Bistro du Peyra,** enjoy a relaxed dinner salad or pasta dish outdoors to the sound of the town's main fountain (closed Mon-Tue off-season, 13 Place du Peyra, tel. 04 93 58 67 63).

Grasse

The historic and contemporary capital of perfume, Grasse offers a contrast to the dolled-up hill towns above the Riviera. Though famous for its pricey product, Grasse is an unpolished but intriguing collection of walking lanes, peekaboo squares, and vertical staircases. Its urban center feels in need of a graffiti facelift and a jobs program for its large immigrant population. For me, Grasse is refreshingly real. Its historic alliance with Genoa explains the Italian-esque look of the old city. Still, the only good reasons to visit Grasse are if you care about perfume, or if you're heading to or from the Grand Canyon du Verdon.

Orientation to Grasse

All sights in Grasse cluster near the Cours Honoré Cresp, also referred to as Place du Cours.

Tourist Information: The TI is a 10-minute walk from the center on Place de la Buanderie, where buses from Nice and Cannes stop (daily July-mid-Sept 9:00-12:00 & 13:00-19:00, shorter hours off-season, tel. 04 93 36 66 66, www.grassetourisme.fr). Pick up a map with a simple, self-guided tour of the old city. If heading to the Grand Canyon du Verdon, get specifics here.

Arrival in Grasse: Buses from Cannes (#600) and Nice (#500) are better than trains, as they are cheap and run directly to the town center (stopping at the TI and the *gare routière*).

To reach the town center from the TI, walk out to Avenue Thiers, turn left, and merge onto Boulevard du Jeu de Ballon (where you'll soon find the stop for bus #510/511 to Vence).

Fifteen **trains** a day connect Grasse with Nice (1 hour), Antibes (40 minutes), and Cannes (30 minutes). Taxis usually wait at the station and are the best option to reach the town center. From the train station, bus #5 runs to the TI; buses #A, #B, and #C take you to the old town center (€1.50 round-trip, none on Sun, schedules at www.sillages.paysdegrasse.fr).

Those arriving by **car** are confounded by Grasse's size, hilly terrain, and inconsistent signage. Follow signs to *Centre-Ville,* then *Office de Tourisme,* and park at Parking Notre Dame des Fleurs (under the TI, direct access to the old town) or at Parking Honoré Cresp (follow *Sortie Parfumerie* signs directly to the Fragonard Perfume Factory).

INLAND RIVIERA

Fragrant Grasse

Grasse has been at the center of the fragrance industry since the 1500s, when it was known for its scented leather gloves. The cultivation of aromatic plants around Grasse slowly evolved to produce ingredients for soaps and perfumes, and by the 1800s, Grasse was recognized as the center for perfume—thanks largely to its flower-friendly climate.

It can take a ton of carefully picked petals—that's about 10,000 flowers—to make about two pounds of essence. A damaged flower petal is bad news. Today, perfumes are made from as many as 500 different scents; most are imported to Grasse from countries around the world. The "blender" of these scents and the perfume mastermind is called the "nose" (who nose best). The five master "noses" who work here must study their profession longer than a doctor goes to med school (seven years). They must show that they have the gift before entering "nose school" (in Versailles), and they cannot drink alcohol, ever.

Skip the outlying perfumeries with French-only tours. Only three factories out of forty open their doors to visitors, and only one is worth visiting: Fragonard Perfume in Grasse.

Sights in Grasse

▲International Museum of Perfume
(Musée International de la Parfumerie, MIP)

This city museum is a magnificent—if overwhelming—tribute to perfume, providing a thorough examination of its history and production from ancient Greece until today. The well-designed museum, with excellent English explanations, a good audioguide, and impressive multimedia exhibits, could keep a perfume fan busy for days. Start in the Sensorial Room, where you'll get mellow while preparing your senses for the visit. The three floors below—organized chronologically—teach you everything there is to know about perfume. Your visit ends with a cool display of perfume packaging for every year since 1900 and a chance to sniff 32 key perfume ingredients. Allow at least one hour to see everything.

Cost and Hours: €4.50, keep ticket for 50 percent off at the gardens (see next); daily 10:00-19:00, Oct-April 10:30-17:30, audioguide-€1, two blocks above Fragonard Perfume at 2 Rue Jeu de Ballon, tel. 04 97 05 58 00, www.museesdegrasse.com.

Perfume Gardens (Les Jardins du MIP): You can also visit the museum's terraced gardens, about five miles from Grasse, with acres of plants and flowers used in perfume production (€4.50, 50 percent off with perfume museum ticket, includes videoguide, same hours as museum, see website or ask at museum for location).

INLAND RIVIERA

Fragonard Perfume Factory (Visite de l'Usine)

This historic but still-functioning factory, located dead-center in Grasse, provides frequent, fragrant, informative 20-minute tours and an interesting "museum" to explore while you wait. Pick up the English brochure describing what's in the museum cases, then drop down to where the tour begins. You'll learn the difference between perfume, eau de toilette, and cologne (it's only a matter of perfume percentages); how the product is made today; and how it was made in the old days (by pressing flowers in animal fat). The tour ends with a whiff in the elegant gift shop.

Cost and Hours: Free guided tour, daily 9:00-18:00, closes for lunch Nov-Jan, just off Cours Honoré Cresp at 20 Boulevard Fragonard, tel. 04 93 36 44 65, www.fragonard.com.

Museum of Provençal Costume and Jewelry (Musée Provençal du Costume et du Bijou)

This small, dimly lit museum, a few steps from the Fragonard factory, displays traditional dresses and jewelry from the 18th and 19th centuries, giving a sense of the lives of the high- and low-born women of Grasse.

Cost and Hours: Free, daily 10:00-13:00 & 14:00-18:30, closed Sun in winter, a block above the *parfumerie* on the pedestrian street at 2 Rue Jean Ossola, tel. 04 93 36 44 65, www.fragonard.com.

Fragonard Museum (Musée Fragonard)

This free, air-conditioned museum houses paintings by three of Grasse's most famous artists: Jean-Honoré Fragonard, Marguerite Gérard, and Jean-Baptiste Mallet. Ask for the English explanations at the welcome desk.

Cost and Hours: Free, daily 10:00-18:00, just a few doors down from the costume museum, 14 Rue Jean Ossola, tel. 04 93 36 02 07, www.fragonard.com.

Old Grasse

Just above Fragonard Perfume, Rue Jean Ossola leads into the labyrinthine ancient streets that form an intriguing pedestrian area. To get a good taste of old Grasse, you can follow the TI's minimalist self-guided tour with your map (takes an hour at a brisk pace, read the posted information plaques as you go) or, better, wander at will and read the plaques when you see them.

Start by strolling up Rue Jean Ossola (just above Boulevard Fragonard), then turn right down Rue Gazan to find the Romanesque cathedral opposite an unusual WWI monument (it's worth peering into the cathedral to see its tree-trunk columns and austere decor). Find the view terrace behind the cathedral. Double back to Rue Jean Ossola, turn right, then make a left up bohemian Rue de l'Oratoire and pop out onto a terrific square, making a left just after 27 Place aux Aires (with good eating options).

Inland Riviera Drive

NICE TO GRASSE LOOP

This splendid loop drive takes you from the Riviera up to inland villages and through a rocky gorge before returning you to the coast. The basic route connects Nice (or Antibes) to St-Paul-de-Vence, Vence, Tourrettes-sur-Loup, and Grasse.

Planning Your Drive: This route adds up to about 2.5 hours of driving and 70 zigzagging round-trip miles, but allow plenty of extra time for stops along the way. Once you are inland, each stop is only minutes away from the next, but allow 45 minutes to drive from Nice (or Antibes) to the first village, St-Paul-de-Vence. Start early to see St-Paul-de-Vence without the mobs. Be prepared for twisty mountain roads, and be aware of bicyclists sharing the road, particularly on weekends.

Route Options: With more time (or if you are staying in Vence), consider taking the beautiful long way around from Vence via the Col de Vence (see the alternate route outlined below). Hardy day-trippers or those leaving the Riviera altogether can opt to extend the drive through the Grand Canyon du Verdon to reach Provence (see "Grand Canyon du Verdon Drive" at the end of this chapter).

Nice to Grasse (via Tourrettes-sur-Loup)

The major towns—St-Paul-de-Vence, Vence, and Grasse—on this drive are described earlier in this chapter. The remaining inland villages and sights you'll see are described later, under "Inland Riviera Towns and Sights".

Leaving Nice, you'll drive west, through Cagnes-sur-Mer (passing the Renoir Museum—see page 134), then follow *Vence* and *St-Paul-de-Vence* signs into the village of **St-Paul-de-Vence.** Consider having breakfast there (at the Café de la Place just before the town walls), then explore the village and visit the Fondation Maeght.

From St-Paul-de-Vence, continue a few miles to **Vence,** with many good lunch options and Matisse's famous **Chapel of the Rosary** (closed Sun-Mon, sparse parking). The best views of Vence are a mile beyond the chapel, where there's a turnaround.

Next, from Vence, follow D-2210 through slippery-sloped **Tourrettes-sur-Loup** (great views of Tourrettes-sur-Loup a quarter-mile after you pass through the town). Before long, you'll see views of Le Bar-sur-Loup, clinging to its hillside in the distance. (Sugar addicts can detour quickly down to Pont-du-Loup and visit the small candied-fruit factory of Confiseries Florian).

INLAND RIVIERA

Follow *Gourdon* and *Gorges du Loup* signs to the right along D-6 and climb into the teeth of a rocky canyon, the **Gorges du Loup.** It's a mostly low-gear road that winds between severe rock faces above a surging stream. Several miles into the gorge, you can visit the Cascades du Saut du Loup **waterfall,** which may have you thinking you've made a wrong turn onto Hawaii (€1, easy walk down).

The drive passes all too quickly to where the road hooks back, crossing Pont du Bramafen and around toward Gourdon on D-3. As you climb above the canyon you just drove through, you'll watch the world below miniaturize. At the top, the Shangri-La village of **Gourdon**—known as the "Eagle's Nest" (2,400 feet)—waits for tourists with shops, good lunch options, and grand panoramas.

From Gourdon, slide downhill (stopping at pullouts for views back and up to Gourdon) toward **Grasse.** Enjoy sensational views down to (literally) overlooked Le Bar-sur-Loup. Follow signs to *Grasse,* then *Centre-Ville,* then *Office de Tourisme* (park under the TI at Parking Notre Dame des Fleurs).

After mastering your scent in Grasse—the capital of perfume—return to your Riviera home base (allow 45 minutes back to Nice or 30 minutes to Antibes), or continue to the Grand Canyon du Verdon (see the end of this chapter).

Nice to Grasse (Col de Vence Alternate)

This dilly of a route is ideal if you're staying in Vence (it adds about 25 miles and an hour of driving time to the basic route): Follow the route described above until **Vence,** then find D-2 just before the bridge that leads to St-Jeannet, and follow signs for *Col de Vence* (the Vence pass) and *Coursegoules.* The road rises beyond the tree line into a barren landscape to the pass in about 15 minutes. From the pass (3,000 feet), continue on D-2, trading rocky slabs for lush forests, pastures, and vast canyons.

You'll soon pass the postcard-perfect village of **Coursegoules** (worth a photo but not a detour), then follow signs to *Gréolières.* At a roundabout just before Gréolières, find D-3, which leads to Nice, Gorges du Loup, and Gourdon. But first, continue a few minutes past **Gréolières** to the pullout barely above the village, with stirring views of its ruined castle. Consider a coffee break in Gréolières before backtracking to the roundabout, following signs to *Gourdon.* After visiting **Gourdon,** you can continue to Grasse, or return to Nice or Antibes.

INLAND RIVIERA TOWNS AND SIGHTS
Tourrettes-sur-Loup

This unspoiled and picturesque town, hemmed in by forests, looks like it's ready to skid down its hill. Stroll the beautifully preserved, narrow medieval lanes, admire the wall-to-wall homes (built for defense, not the view), have an ice cream, and finish with a view drink. Many prefer this peaceful hill town to St-Paul-de-Vence. Known as the *Cité des Violettes,* this small village produces more violets than anywhere else in France, most of which end up in perfume. In early March, Tourrettes-sur-Loop fills with almost 10,000 visitors (hard to imagine) for the annual Violet Festival.

Park in the lot just outside the village center, on Place de la Libération, where you'll also find the **TI** (Mon-Sat 9:30-13:00 & 14:00-18:00, closed Sun, tel. 04 93 24 18 93, www.tourrettessurloup.com). Wednesday is **market day** on Place de la Libération (you'll be forced to park elsewhere if you arrive before 13:30).

If it's lunchtime, consider sitting outside at the **Les Gourmandises** *pâtisserie* on the square, which has delicious *pissaladière* (pizza-like dough topped with onions, olives, and anchovies) and the filling *tourte de Blettes* (Swiss chard tart).

Enter the medieval village under the clock tower (just off the square's right corner) onto Grande Rue. Stroll in a counterclockwise direction, ending up back at the parking lot. Along the way, you'll find a smattering of arts and crafts boutiques as well as a handful of other places to eat or take a break.

Tom's Ice Cream may entice you with its violet-flavored scoops or tasty coffee (daily from 12:00, 25 Grand Rue, tel. 04 93 24 12 12). Or finish your walk with a glass of wine on the tiny back terrace at **La Cave de Tourrettes.** This small wine bar serves salads and quiches, with a daily by-the-glass selection and vast cellar. The sliver-sized balcony has panoramic views (closed Mon, near St. Grégoire church and the parking lot, 8 Rue de la Bourgade, tel. 04 93 24 10 12).

Confiseries Florian in Pont-du-Loup

This candied-fruit factory hides between trees down in Pont-du-Loup (though their big, bright sign is hard to miss). Frequent 10-minute tours of the factory cover the candied-fruit process and explain the use of flower petals (like violets and jasmine) in their products. Everything they make is fruit-filled—even their chocolate (with oranges). The tour ends with a tasting of the *confiture* in the dazzling gift shop.

INLAND RIVIERA

Cost and Hours: Tours are free, daily 9:00-12:00 & 14:00-18:30, gift shop stays open during lunch in summer, tel. 04 93 59 32 91, www.confiserieflorian.com.

Gorges du Loup

The Inland Riviera is crawling with spectacular canyons only miles from the sea. Slotted between Grasse and Vence, the Gorges du Loup is the easiest to reach and works well on a day trip from the Nice area. You can drive about five miles right up into the canyon (on D-6)—passing numerous waterfalls, deep pools, and sheer rock walls. Circling back on the gorge's rooftop (on D-3) to the village of Gourdon gives magnificent vistas and a complete change of scenery.

Gourdon

This 2,400-foot-high, cliff-topping hamlet features grassy picnic areas, a short lineup of tourist shops, and a few good lunch options (there's an upper parking lot that reduces some of the uphill walk). The village's most famous building is its château, which is best enjoyed from the outside. Walk out to the broad terrace for the splendid view (TI in the far corner). A trail (Chemin du Paradis) leads down those cliffs from the far left side of the village to Le Bar-sur-Loup (1 hour)—now

that's steep (you'll pass the trailhead as your enter the village). This part of the village features fabulous vistas, a tiny Romanesque church, and a nice option for lunch with a view, **$$ La Taverne Provençale,** which boasts a popular spread of outdoor tables for pizza, pasta, and salads (daily, tel. 04 93 09 68 22). The building below on the left, Le Nid de l'Aigle ("The Eagle's Nest"), was until a few years ago the region's greatest view restaurant (now closed).

INLAND RIVIERA

Grand Canyon du Verdon Drive

Two hours north of Nice and three hours east of Avignon lies the Parc Naturel Régional du Verdon. This immense area of natural

beauty is worth ▲▲▲—even to Arizonans. The park, far more than just its famous canyon, is a vast area mixing alpine scenery with misty villages, meandering streams, and seas of gentle meadows. The Grand Canyon du Verdon (a.k.a. Gorges du Verdon) is the heart of the park, where colossal slabs of white and salmon-colored limestone plunge impossible distances to the snaking Verdon River.

For millions of years, this region was covered by the sea. Over time, sediments and the remains of marine animals were deposited here, becoming thick layers of limestone as they were buried. Later, plate tectonics uplifted the limestone and erosion exposed it, and the Verdon River—with help from Ice Age glaciers—carved out the gorges and its side canyons. At their deepest points, the gorges drop 2,200 feet to the river. At the bottom, the canyons narrow to as little as 26 feet across, while at the top, the canyon walls spread as far as 4,700 feet apart.

The Verdon River is named for its turquoise-green hue (it's derived from *vert*, the French word for green). The striking color comes from very fine particles of rock suspended in the water, pulverized by glaciers high at the river's source. It's a sight that has inspired visitors since Ligurian Celts ruled the region.

PLANNING YOUR DRIVE
The Grand Canyon du Verdon offers a magnificent route between the Riviera and Provence. You'll need a car, ample time, and a lack of vertigo to enjoy this area.

The canyon itself is located between the villages of Moustiers-Ste-Marie and Aiguines to the west and Castellane to the east. Roads crawl along both sides of the canyon. The most scenic driving segments are along the south side (Rive Gauche), between Aiguines and the Balcon de la Mescla, and the north side (Rive Droite) between Moustiers-Ste-Marie and the Point Sublime overlook. The Rive Gauche works best for most, though both sides are spectacular. Thrill seekers head for the Castellane area, where the whitewater rafting, climbing, and serious hiking trails are best.

When to Go: The canyon can be overrun with cars in summer and on weekends, but is quiet most days in the off-season. If you

INLAND RIVIERA

are traveling in summer or on holiday weekends, go really early or skip it.

The Basic Route: You'll drive from the coast through Grasse and toward Castellane, then turn off to hit the canyon at the Balcon de la Mescla. After seeing the canyon's most scenic stretch, you can either split off (after Aiguines) to return to the Riviera, or continue through Moustiers-Ste-Marie and on to Provence. (For drivers coming *from* Provence, this tour works in reverse, west to east; see "Approaching the Canyon from Provence," at the end of the tour.)

Length of This Drive: Figure seven hours and about 150 miles with modest canyon time between Nice and the Luberon or Aix-en-Provence.

Here are some rough driving times: Riviera to Grasse—1 hour, Grasse to Balcon de la Mescla—1.5 hours, Balcon de la Mescla to Aiguines—1.5 hours with photo stops, Aiguines to Moustiers-Ste-Marie—25 minutes, Moustiers-Ste-Marie to Manosque (en route to Provence)—1.5 hours.

Driving Tips: Fill your tank before leaving Grasse or Moustiers-Ste-Marie. Don't expect US National Park conditions—you won't see a ranger, signage is minimal, and the road rarely has a shoulder.

There are fewer pullouts and viewpoints than you'd expect, but picnickers will find some good choices for the perfect lunch stop. Just be sure to stock up on provisions before you hit the canyon area—stores are scarce on this route.

Hiking in the Canyon: Hikes into the canyon are long and pretty steep. Most visitors are better off walking along the main road for a bit, or detouring down some of the short paths scattered alongside the road. Your best bet for a canyon hike is the **Cavaliers trail,** which leads down to the river from a spot near the Hôtel-Restaurant Grand Canyon du Verdon (details later, under "Along the Canyon, from Balcon de la Mescla to Aiguines").

Overnighting in the Canyon: If you get a late start or just want to savor the canyon, overnighting en route works well (see suggestions later in this chapter).

Round-Trip Option from Nice: You can reach the canyon on a very long round-trip drive from the Nice area if you leave early. From Nice, figure on five hours of driving without stops and about 175 miles round-trip (easier if staying in Vence or Antibes). To do this, take the most direct route to or from the canyon and make it a one-way loop (from Nice take the route via Grasse to Balcon de la Mescla, as outlined later, tour the canyon in the westbound direction, leave the route just before the Lac de Ste-Croix, and connect to the autoroute back to Nice; details below under "Aiguines").

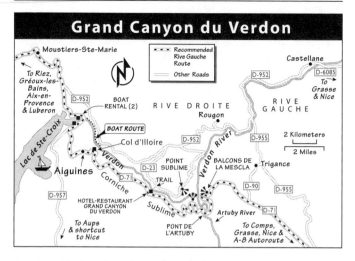

FROM THE RIVIERA TO PROVENCE

For drivers connecting the Riviera with Provence via the canyon, this self-guided drive along the Rive Gauche offers the most accessible and most scenic tour of the gorges. You'll be driving the canyon from east to west in the outside lane, which is best for views.

Cannes to Balcon de la Mescla

The most direct route from the Riviera follows D-6185, which starts near Cannes (A-8 autoroute from Nice to Cannes saves time) and passes through Grasse, changing to D-6085 and continuing north toward Digne and Castellane. You'll turn left off D-6085 about 25 kilometers before Castellane, following signs to the *Gorges du Verdon* and *Draguignan* (an impressive medieval bridge stands just north of the road, about 3 kilometers before Comps-sur-Artuby, signed *La Souche*). Turn right onto D-71 at Comps-sur-Artuby, following signs to *Gorges du Verdon, Rive Gauche* (not *Rive Droite*). In a few minutes, you'll reach a pullout with a good view of the village of Trigance.

Driving along D-71, you'll soon arrive at the canyon rim at the Balcon de la Mescla. Park just below **Le Relais de Balcon** café/gift shop, and find the steps down to a memorable lookout above the river bend. The café/gift shop has a small selection of maps and books, and a big selection of drinks.

Along the Canyon, from Balcon de la Mescla to Aiguines

From here, follow the canyon lip for about 90 serpentine minutes (including ample stops). You'll drive at an escargot's pace, navigating hairpin turns while enjoying views of rocky masses and vanishing-point views up the canyon. There are small pullouts along the route that come without warning.

A little beyond the Balcon de la Mescla, you can amble across Europe's second-highest bridge, the **Pont de l'Artuby,** and imagine working on its construction crew. There's a large parking lot at the far end of the bridge; get out and breathe here. About 3 kilometers past the bridge, you'll find a dirt road and pullout on the north side of the road; drive down 50 yards and you can park easily. A five-minute stroll along the dirt road (push straight through some bushes at end) leads to good views of the canyon and acres of limestone to scramble over—and no car noise. It's a rare chance to lose the road and be alone with the canyon.

About 10 minutes beyond the bridge, you'll reach the recommended cliffhanger **Hôtel-Restaurant Grand Canyon du Verdon.** This funky, concrete place looks slapped together, but the café terrace has tables with stupendous views (drinks, snacks, and meals available at fair prices). If your driver feels cheated about missing the views, make sure you stop here for a break. Just below the hotel, the **Cavaliers trail** is your best chance to hike into the canyon. For those in reasonable shape, it's a 90-minute round-trip hike on a well-maintained path to the river and back.

Back along the main road, you'll pass some of the canyon's most stunning views along the next stretch. Notice small red and white markers along the guardrails at pullouts. These are trail markers, where you can hop over the guardrail, if you dare, for better views. The **Col d'Illoire**—the last pass before leaving the canyon—provides sweeping views from the western portal, including your first peek at **Lac de Ste-Croix.** Park in the large pullout, where you'll find a few picnic tables scattered above and some good rock-scampering just below.

Aiguines

Just west of the canyon, the small village of Aiguines squats below waves of limestone and overlooks the long turquoise Lac de Ste-Croix. This unspoiled village has a handful of shops, recommended hotels, and cafés. It's an outdoorsy, popular-with-hikers place that most canyon visitors cruise right through. Detour onto the grounds of the 15th-century château for the view over Aiguines (with picnic benches and a play area for kids;

château interior closed to the public). Aiguines' **TI** is on the main drag (July-Aug daily 8:30-18:00; Sept-June Mon-Fri 9:00-12:00

& 14:00-17:00, closed Sat-Sun; Allée des Tilleuls, tel. 04 94 70 21 64, www.aiguines.com). Have lunch at the recommended **Hôtel du Vieux-Château's** café on charming Place de la Fontaine (described later under "Sleeping and Eating near the Grand Canyon du Verdon").

For more views over Aiguines and the lake, stroll north of Place de la Fontaine, then head right and up one of the staircases to find the small **Chapelle St. Pierre.** From here, you can walk up the small road five minutes to the campground café, with nice tables on its broad view terrace (ideal for a predinner drink or morning coffee).

Returning to the Riviera: If you're day-tripping from the Riviera rather than continuing to Provence, this is your turnaround point: Follow signs for *Aups* (D-957) as you leave Aiguines, then *Draguignan*, then *Nice* via A-8.

Aiguines to Moustiers-Ste-Marie

Barely 50 years old, the man-made **Lac de Ste-Croix** is about six miles long and is the last stop for water flowing out of the Gorges du Verdon. For a fun lake/river experience, rent a canoe or a pedal boat at either side of the low bridge halfway between Moustiers and Aiguines (no motor boats are allowed). You can paddle under the bridge, then follow the aquamarine inlet upstream as far as 2.5 miles, tracing the river's route up the gorge on its final journey to the lake.

Moustiers-Ste-Marie

Here's another pretty Provençal face lined with boutiques—though this one comes with an impressive setting, straddling a small stream at the base of the limestone cliffs of the Grand Canyon du Verdon. The town is busy, as tourists clamoring for the locally famous china compete with hikers. Parking can be difficult, especially in high season (use one of the signed lots, and expect a fair walk to the village center). The **TI** is in the center, next to the church (daily 10:00-12:30 & 14:00-18:00, no midday break July-Aug, Place de l'Eglise, tel. 04 92 74 67 84, www.moustiers.fr).

You can escape some of the crowds by climbing 20 minutes on a steep, ankle-twisting path (262 steps) to the **Chapelle Notre-Dame de Beauvoir**—a simple chapel that has attracted pilgrims for centuries. A notebook in the

INLAND RIVIERA

chapel allows travelers to pen a request for a miracle for a loved one. For most, the chapel does not warrant the effort, though you'll get great views over the village by walking a short way up the path.

Moustiers-Ste-Marie to Provence

From here it's another 1.5 to 2 hours to most Provençal destinations. From Moustiers-Ste-Marie, head for Riez, then Gréoux-les-Bains. From Gréoux-les-Bains, follow signs for *Manosque,* then *Apt* for the Luberon and Avignon; or use A-51 south to reach Aix-en-Provence, Lourmarin in the Luberon, Cassis, Marseille, or Arles.

APPROACHING THE CANYON FROM PROVENCE

Drivers coming from Provence can reverse the above tour, traveling from west to east (Moustiers-Ste-Marie to the Balcon de la Mescla).

All roads from Provence pass through Gréoux-les-Bains, an hour northeast of Aix-en-Provence. Those coming from Cassis, Aix-en-Provence, the southern Luberon, and Arles will find A-51 north the fastest path; those coming from the central Luberon and Avignon should take D-900 via Apt (turns into D-4100), then follow signs for *Manosque*. From Gréoux-les-Bains, follow signs to *Riez, Moustiers-Ste-Marie,* and *Aiguines* before entering the Grand Canyon du Verdon (Rive Gauche). Ignore the *Grand Canyon du Verdon* signs as you leave Moustiers-Ste-Marie—they lead to the Rive Droite. Follow the *Aiguines* signs instead to make sure you are going to the Rive Gauche.

Leave the canyon after the Balcon de la Mescla. To get to Nice, follow signs for *Comps-sur-Artuby* (and *Draguignan* for a short distance), then *Grasse* and *Nice*. The fastest way from Grasse to Nice is via Cannes and A-8.

SLEEPING AND EATING NEAR THE GRAND CANYON DU VERDON

These places are listed in the order you'll reach them on the self-guided driving tour from east to west. Most hotels in this area want you to take half-pension, but it is rarely required outside of high season. Budget-minded travelers will find lots of places to picnic, but bring groceries with you as stores are scarce (grocery stores and bakeries are in Gréoux and Moustiers if coming from the west, but there's not much if coming from the east—stock up before you head out).

Midway Through the Canyon

$ Hôtel-Restaurant Grand Canyon du Verdon** is housed in a funky structure that must have been grandfathered-in to own such an unbelievable location—2,500 feet high on the Corniche Sub-

lime. The hotel rents 14 b
on the canyon side and ma
10, well worth reserving
April, tel. 04 94 76 91 31,
gd.canyon.verdon@wanado

In Aiguines

$ Hôtel du Vieux-Châtea
and is Aiguines' most cha
lish-speaking Fred and Eu
spotless, and tastefully app
hearty fare (great goat-chee
elevator, Place de la Fontain
22 95, www.hotelvieuxchate

$ Hôtel Altitude 823,*
fers a fair deal with good roo
ers (no air-con, no elevator, «
altitude823-verdon.com, alt

In Moustiers-Ste-Mari

$ Le Mas du Loup is a fine-
ute walk below town. Charm
bedroom *bastide*, where roo
and come with private patio
parking, tel. 04 92 74 65 61, w
hotmail.fr).

¢ Restaurant/Chambre
less rooms that are available f
good for families and indivi
de Blacas, in the village cent
church, tel. 04 92 77 29 30).

Eating: There is no shor
Ste-Marie. The simple $ Res
inexpensive and simple meals
door and outdoor tables. $$$
steps south of the old town, v
views, and good cuisine at fair
day Tue, tel. 04 92 74 68 91). $
the stream and is the place to e
lovely atrium room (closed We
de l'Eglise, tel. 04 92 74 64 31)

PRACTICALITIES

This section covers just the basics on traveling in the French Riviera (for much more information, see the latest edition of *Rick Steves Provence & The French Riviera*). You'll find free advice on specific topics at www.ricksteves.com/tips.

THE LANGUAGE

In France, it's essential to acknowledge the person before getting down to business. Start any conversation, or enter any shop, by saying: *"Bonjour, madame (*or *monsieur)."* To ask if they speak English, say, *"Parlez-vous anglais?",* and hope they speak more English than you speak French (most do). See "Survival Phrases" at the end of this chapter.

MONEY

France uses the euro currency: 1 euro (€) = about $1.20. To convert prices in euros to dollars, add about 20 percent: €20 = about $24, €50 = about $60. (Check www.oanda.com for the latest exchange rates.)

The standard way for travelers to get euros is to withdraw money from an ATM *(distributeur)* using a debit card, ideally with a Visa or MasterCard logo. To keep your cash, cards, and valuables safe, wear a money belt.

Before departing, call your bank or credit-card company: Confirm that your card(s) will work overseas, ask about international transaction fees, and alert them that you'll be making withdrawals in Europe. Also ask for the PIN number for your credit card—you may need it for Europe's "chip-and-PIN" payment machines (see below; allow time for your bank to mail your PIN to you).

Dealing with "Chip and PIN": Most credit and debit

cards now have chips that authenticate and secure transactions. European cardholders insert their chip card into the payment slot, then enter a PIN. (Until recently, most US cards required a signature.) Any American card with a chip will work at Europe's hotels, restaurants, and shops—although often the clerk may ask for a signature. But some self-service payment machines—such as those at train stations, toll roads, or unattended gas pumps—may not accept your card, even if you know the PIN. If your card won't work, look for a cashier who can process the transaction manually—or pay in cash.

Dynamic Currency Conversion: If merchants or hoteliers offer to convert your purchase price into dollars (called dynamic currency conversion, or DCC), refuse this "service." You'll pay extra in fees for the expensive convenience of seeing your charge in dollars. If an ATM offers to "lock in" or "guarantee" your conversion rate, choose "proceed without conversion." Other prompts might state, "You can be charged in dollars: Press YES for dollars, NO for euros." Always choose the local currency.

STAYING CONNECTED

The simplest solution is to bring your own device—mobile phone, tablet, or laptop—and use it just as you would at home (following the tips below, such as connecting to free Wi-Fi whenever possible).

To call France from a US or Canadian number: Whether you're phoning from a landline, your own mobile phone, or a Skype account, you're making an international call. Dial 011-33 and then the local number, omitting the initial zero. (The 011 is our international access code, and 33 is France's country code.) If dialing from a mobile phone, you can enter + in place of the international access code—press and hold the 0 key.

To call France from a European country: Dial 00-33 followed by the local number, omitting the initial zero. (The 00 is Europe's international access code.)

To call within France: Just dial the local number (including the initial zero).

To call from France to another country: Dial 00 followed by the country code (for example, 1 for the US or Canada), then the area code and number. If you're calling European countries whose phone numbers begin with 0, you'll usually have to omit that 0 when you dial.

Tips: If you bring your own mobile phone, consider signing up for an international plan; most providers offer a global calling plan that cuts the per-minute cost of phone calls and texts, and a flat-fee data plan.

Use Wi-Fi whenever possible. Most hotels and many cafés offer free Wi-Fi, and you'll likely also find it at tourist information offices (TIs), major museums, and public-transit hubs. With Wi-Fi you can use your device to make free or inexpensive domestic and international calls via a calling app such as Skype, FaceTime, or Google+ Hangouts. When you can't find Wi-Fi, you can use your cellular network to connect to the Internet, send texts, or make voice calls. When you're done, avoid further charges by manually switching off "data roaming" or "cellular data."

Without a mobile device, you can make calls from your hotel and get online using public computers (there's usually one in your hotel lobby or at local libraries). Most hotels charge a high fee for international calls—ask for rates before you dial.

For more on phoning, see www.ricksteves.com/phoning. For a one-hour talk on "Traveling with a Mobile Device," see www.ricksteves.com/travel-talks.

SLEEPING

I've categorized my recommended accommodations based on price, indicated with a dollar-sign rating (see sidebar). I recommend reserving rooms in advance, particularly during peak season. Once your dates are set, check the specific price for your preferred stay at several hotels. You can do this either by comparing prices on sites such as Hotels.com or Booking.com, or by checking the hotels' own websites. To get the best deal, contact French hotels directly via their website, by phone, or by email. French hotels recently won the right to undercut Booking.com and Hotels.com prices on their websites; virtually all offer lower rates if you book direct. If the price they quote is higher than the offer on a booking site, let the hotel know, and they'll usually adjust the rate.

For complicated requests, send an email with the following information: number and type of rooms; number of nights; arrival date; departure date; and any special requests. Use the European style for writing dates: day/month/year. Hoteliers typically ask for your credit-card number as a deposit.

Some hotels are willing to make a deal to attract guests: Try emailing several hotels to ask for their best price. In general, hotel prices can soften if you do any of the following: offer to pay cash, stay at least three nights, or travel off-season.

The French have a simple hotel-rating system based on amenities (zero through five stars, indicated in this book by * through *****). Two- and three-star hotels are my mainstay. Other accommodation options include bed-and-breakfasts (*chambres d'hôtes*, usually more affordable than hotels), hostels, campgrounds, or even homes (*gîtes*, rented by the week). For a list of over 16,000

PRACTICALITIES

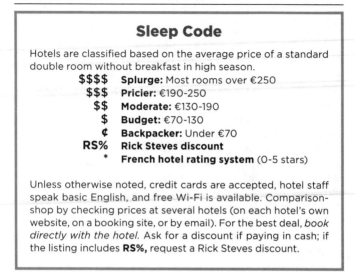

Sleep Code

Hotels are classified based on the average price of a standard double room without breakfast in high season.

$$$$	**Splurge:**	Most rooms over €250
$$$	**Pricier:**	€190-250
$$	**Moderate:**	€130-190
$	**Budget:**	€70-130
¢	**Backpacker:**	Under €70
RS%	**Rick Steves discount**	
*	**French hotel rating system**	(0-5 stars)

Unless otherwise noted, credit cards are accepted, hotel staff speak basic English, and free Wi-Fi is available. Comparison-shop by checking prices at several hotels (on each hotel's own website, on a booking site, or by email). For the best deal, *book directly with the hotel.* Ask for a discount if paying in cash; if the listing includes **RS%,** request a Rick Steves discount.

chambres d'hôtes throughout France, check www.chambres-hotes. fr. To find an apartment or room in a private home, try Airbnb, Booking.com, and the HomeAway family of sites (HomeAway, VRBO, and VacationRentals).

EATING

I've categorized my recommended eateries based on price, indicated with a dollar-sign rating (see sidebar). The cuisine is a highlight of any French adventure. It's sightseeing for your palate. For a formal meal, go to a restaurant. If you want the option of lighter fare (just soup or a sandwich), head for a café or brasserie instead.

French restaurants usually open for dinner at 19:00 and are typically most crowded around 20:30. Last seating is usually about 21:00 or 22:00 (earlier in villages). If a restaurant serves lunch, it generally goes from about 11:30 to 14:00.

In France, an entrée is the first course, and *le plat* or *le plat du jour* is the main course with vegetables. If you ask for the *menu* (muh-noo), you won't get a list of dishes; you'll get a fixed-price meal—usually your choice of three courses (soup, appetizer, or salad; main course with vegetables; and cheese course or dessert). Drinks are extra. Ask for *la carte* (lah kart) if you want to see a menu and order à la carte, like the locals do. Request the waiter's help in deciphering the French.

Cafés and brasseries provide budget-friendly meals. If you're hungry between lunch and dinner, when restaurants are closed, go to a brasserie, which generally serves throughout the day. (Some cafés do as well, but others close their kitchens from 14:00 to 18:00.) Compared to restaurants, cafés and brasseries usually have

PRACTICALITIES

Restaurant Price Code

I've assigned each eatery a price category, based on the average cost of a typical main course. Drinks, desserts, and splurge items (steak and seafood) can raise the price considerably.

$$$$ **Splurge:** Most main courses over €30
$$$ **Pricier:** €25-30
$$ **Moderate:** €15-25
$ **Budget:** Under €15

In France, a crêpe stand or other takeout spot is **$**; a sit-down brasserie, café, or bistro with affordable *plats du jour* is **$$**; a casual but more upscale restaurant is **$$$**; and a swanky splurge is **$$$$**.

more limited and inexpensive fare, including salads, sandwiches, omelets, *plats du jour*, and more. Check the price list first, which by law must be posted prominently. There are two sets of prices: You'll pay more for the same drink if you're seated at a table *(salle)* than if you're seated or standing at the bar or counter *(comptoir)*.

Tipping: A 12-15 percent service charge *(service compris)* is always included in the bill. Most French never tip, but if you feel the service was exceptional, it's kind to tip up to 5 percent extra.

Breakfast: Most hotels serve an optional breakfast (generally €10-15). They almost all offer a buffet (cereal, yogurt, fruit, cheese, ham, croissants, juice, and hard-boiled eggs). Coffee is often self-serve from a machine or a thermos. If all you want is coffee or tea and a croissant, the corner café or bakery offers more atmosphere and is less expensive (though you get more coffee at your hotel).

TRANSPORTATION

By Train: Travelers who need to cover long distances in France by train can get a good deal with a Eurail France Pass, sold only outside Europe. To see if a rail pass could save you money, check www.ricksteves.com/rail. To research train schedules, visit Germany's excellent all-Europe website, www.bahn.com. The French rail website is www.sncf.com; for online sales, go to https://en.oui.sncf/en. You can also buy tickets at train-station ticket windows, SNCF boutiques (small, centrally located offices of the national rail company), and travel agencies. Travelers with smartphones have the option of saving tickets and reservations directly to their phones (see https://en.oui.sncf/en/mobile).

All **high-speed TGV trains** in France (also called "InOui") require a seat reservation—book as early as possible, as these trains fill fast, and some routes use TGV trains almost exclusively. This is especially true if you're traveling with a rail pass, as TGV pass-holder reservations are limited, and usually sell out well before other seat reservations do.

You are required to validate (*composter,* kohm-poh-stay) all train tickets and reservations when printed on official ticket stock; before boarding look for a yellow machine to stamp your ticket or reservation. Reserved tickets that are printed at home on plain paper and etickets on your phone don't need validation. Strikes (*grève)* in France are common but generally last no longer than a day or two; ask your hotelier if one is coming.

By Car: It's cheaper to arrange most car rentals from the US. For tips on your insurance options, see www.ricksteves.com/cdw, and for route planning, consult www.viamichelin.com. Bring your driver's license.

Local road etiquette is similar to that in the US. Ask your car-rental company for details, or check the US State Department website (www.travel.state.gov, search for France in the "Learn about your destination" box, then click on "Travel and Transportation").

France's toll road (*autoroute)* system is slick and speedy, but pricey; two hours of driving costs about €15 in tolls. Be aware that US credit cards may not work in toll machines (use the cash lanes and have coins or bills under €50). Your US credit cards also may not work at self-service gas pumps and automated parking garages—but if you know your PIN, try it anyway. The easiest solution is carrying sufficient cash.

A car is a worthless headache in cities—park it safely (get tips from your hotel or pay to park at well-patrolled lots; look for blue *P* signs). As break-ins are common, be sure your valuables are out of sight and locked in the trunk, or even better, with you or in your hotel room.

By Bus: Regional buses work well for many destinations not served by trains. Buses are almost always comfortable and air-conditioned. For dirt-cheap bus fares between cities in France, check out www.flixbus.com and www.ouibus.com.

HELPFUL HINTS

Emergency Help: In France, dial 112 for any **emergency**—ambulance, police, or fire. To replace a passport, call the **US Consulate and Embassy** in Paris (tel. 01 43 12 22 22, 2 Avenue Gabriel, Mo: Concorde, https://fr.usembassy.gov) or the **US Consulate** in Marseille (tel. 01 43 12 48 85). Canadians can call the **Canadian Consulate and Embassy** in Paris (tel. 01 44 43 29 00, 130 Rue du Faubourg Saint-Honoré, Mo: Saint-Philippe-du-Roule or Miromesnil, www.canadainternational.gc.ca/france) or the **Canadian Consulate** in Nice (tel. 04 93 92 93 22). For other concerns, get advice from your hotelier.

Theft or Loss: France has hardworking pickpockets, and they particularly target those coming in from Paris airports—wear a money belt. Assume beggars are pickpockets and any scuffle is simply a distraction by a team of thieves. If you stop for any commotion or show, put your hands in your pockets before someone else does.

To replace a passport, you'll need to go in person to an embassy or consulate (see above). Cancel and replace your credit and debit cards by calling these 24-hour US numbers collect: Visa—tel. 303/967-1096, MasterCard—tel. 636/722-7111, American Express—tel. 336/393-1111. In France, to make a collect call to the US, dial 08 00 90 06 24 and say "operator" for an English-speaking operator. For another option (with the same results), you can call these toll-free numbers in France: Visa (tel. 08 00 90 11 79) and MasterCard (tel. 08 00 90 13 87). File a police report either on the spot or within a day or two; you'll need it to submit an insurance claim for lost or stolen rail passes or travel gear, and it can help with replacing your passport or credit and debit cards. For more information, see www.ricksteves.com/help.

Time: France uses the 24-hour clock. It's the same through 12:00 noon, then keep going: 13:00, 14:00, and so on. France, like most of continental Europe, is six/nine hours ahead of the East/West Coasts of the US.

Business Hours: Most shops are open from Monday through Saturday (generally 10:00–12:00 & 14:00–19:00) and closed on Sunday, though some grocery stores, bakeries, and street markets are open Sunday morning until noon. In smaller towns, many businesses are closed on Monday until 14:00 and sometimes all day. Touristy shops are usually open daily.

Sights: Opening and closing hours of sights can change unexpectedly; confirm the latest times with the local tourist information office or its website. Some major churches enforce a modest dress code (no bare shoulders or shorts) for everyone, even children.

Holidays and Festivals: France celebrates many holidays, which can close sights and attract crowds (book hotel rooms ahead). For information on holidays and festivals, check France's website: http://us.france.fr. For a simple list showing major—though not all—events, see www.ricksteves.com/festivals.

Numbers and Stumblers: What Americans call the second floor of a building is the first floor in Europe. Europeans write dates as day/month/year, so Christmas 2020 is 25/12/20. Commas are decimal points and vice versa—a dollar and a half is 1,50, a thousand is 1.000, and there are 5.280 feet in a mile. France uses the metric system: A kilogram is 2.2 pounds; a liter is about a quart; and a kilometer is six-tenths of a mile.

RESOURCES FROM RICK STEVES

This Snapshot guide is excerpted from my latest edition of *Rick Steves Provence & the French Riviera*, one of many titles in my ever-expanding series of guidebooks on European travel. I also produce a public television series, *Rick Steves' Europe,* and a public radio show, *Travel with Rick Steves.* My website, www.ricksteves.com, offers free travel information, a forum for travelers' comments, guidebook updates, my travel blog, an online travel store, and information on European rail passes and our tours of Europe. If you're bringing a mobile device, my free Rick Steves Audio Europe app features dozens of self-guided audio tours of the top sights in Europe and travel interviews about France. You can get Rick Steves Audio Europe via Apple's App Store, Google Play, or the Amazon Appstore. For more information, see www.ricksteves.com/audioeurope.

ADDITIONAL RESOURCES

Tourist Information: http://us.france.fr
Passports and Red Tape: www.travel.state.gov
Packing List: www.ricksteves.com/packing
Travel Insurance: www.ricksteves.com/insurance
Cheap Flights: www.kayak.com or www.google.com/flights
Airplane Carry-on Restrictions: www.tsa.gov
Updates for This Book: www.ricksteves.com/update

HOW WAS YOUR TRIP?

To share your tips, concerns, and discoveries after using this book, please fill out the survey at www.ricksteves.com/feedback. Thanks in advance—it helps a lot.

PRACTICALITIES

French Survival Phrases

When using the phonetics, try to nasalize the n̲ sound.

English	French	Pronunciation
Good day.	Bonjour.	bohn̲-zhoor
Mrs. / Mr.	Madame / Monsieur	mah-dahm / muhs-yuh
Do you speak English?	Parlez-vous anglais?	par-lay-voo ahn̲-glay
Yes. / No.	Oui. / Non.	wee / nohn̲
I understand.	Je comprends.	zhuh kohn̲-prahn̲
I don't understand.	Je ne comprends pas.	zhuh nuh kohn̲-prahn̲ pah
Please.	S'il vous plaît.	see voo play
Thank you.	Merci.	mehr-see
I'm sorry.	Désolé.	day-zoh-lay
Excuse me.	Pardon.	par-dohn̲
(No) problem.	(Pas de) problème.	(pah duh) proh-blehm
It's good.	C'est bon.	say bohn̲
Goodbye.	Au revoir.	oh ruh-vwahr
one / two / three	un / deux / trois	uhn̲ / duh / trwah
four / five / six	quatre / cinq / six	kah-truh / sank̲ / sees
seven / eight	sept / huit	seht / weet
nine / ten	neuf / dix	nuhf / dees
How much is it?	Combien?	kohn̲-bee-an̲
Write it?	Ecrivez?	ay-kree-vay
Is it free?	C'est gratuit?	say grah-twee
Included?	Inclus?	an̲-klew
Where can I buy / find...?	Où puis-je acheter / trouver...?	oo pwee-zhuh ah-shuh-tay / troo-vay
I'd like / We'd like...	Je voudrais / Nous voudrions...	zhuh voo-dray / noo voo-dree-ohn̲
...a room.	...une chambre.	ewn shahn̲-bruh
...a ticket to ___.	...un billet pour ___.	uhn̲ bee-yay poor ___
Is it possible?	C'est possible?	say poh-see-bluh
Where is...?	Où est...?	oo ay
...the train station	...la gare	lah gar
...the bus station	...la gare routière	lah gar root-yehr
...tourist information	...l'office du tourisme	loh-fees dew too-reez-muh
Where are the toilets?	Où sont les toilettes?	oo sohn̲ lay twah-leht
men	hommes	ohm
women	dames	dahm
left / right	à gauche / à droite	ah gohsh / ah drwaht
straight	tout droit	too drwah
pull / push	tirez / poussez	tee-ray / poo-say
When does this open / close?	Ça ouvre / ferme à quelle heure?	sah oo-vruh / fehrm ah kehl ur
At what time?	À quelle heure?	ah kehl ur
Just a moment.	Un moment.	uhn̲ moh-mahn̲
now / soon / later	maintenant / bientôt / plus tard	man̲-tuh-nahn̲ / bee-an̲-toh / plew tar
today / tomorrow	aujourd'hui / demain	oh-zhoor-dwee / duh-man̲

In a French Restaurant

English	French	Pronunciation
I'd like / We'd like...	Je voudrais / Nous voudrions...	zhuh voo-dray / noo voo-dree-oh<u>n</u>
...to reserve...	...réserver...	ray-zehr-vay
...a table for one / two.	...une table pour un / deux.	ewn tah-bluh poor uh<u>n</u> / duh
Is this seat free?	C'est libre?	say lee-bruh
The menu (in English), please.	La carte (en anglais), s'il vous plaît.	lah kart (ah<u>n</u> ah<u>n</u>-glay) see voo play
service (not) included	service (non) compris	sehr-vees (noh<u>n</u>) koh<u>n</u>-pree
to go	à emporter	ah ah<u>n</u>-por-tay
with / without	avec / sans	ah-vehk / sah<u>n</u>
and / or	et / ou	ay / oo
special of the day	plat du jour	plah dew zhoor
specialty of the house	spécialité de la maison	spay-see-ah-lee-tay duh lah may-zoh<u>n</u>
appetizers	hors d'oeuvre	or duh-vruh
first course (soup, salad)	entrée	ah<u>n</u>-tray
main course (meat, fish)	plat principal	plah pra<u>n</u>-see-pahl
bread	pain	pa<u>n</u>
cheese	fromage	froh-mahzh
sandwich	sandwich	sahnd-weech
soup	soupe	soop
salad	salade	sah-lahd
meat	viande	vee-ahnd
chicken	poulet	poo-lay
fish	poisson	pwah-soh<u>n</u>
seafood	fruits de mer	frwee duh mehr
fruit	fruit	frwee
vegetables	légumes	lay-gewm
dessert	dessert	day-sehr
mineral water	eau minérale	oh mee-nay-rahl
tap water	l'eau du robinet	loh dew roh-bee-nay
milk	lait	lay
(orange) juice	jus (d'orange)	zhew (doh-rah<u>n</u>zh)
coffee / tea	café / thé	kah-fay / tay
wine	vin	va<u>n</u>
red / white	rouge / blanc	roozh / blah<u>n</u>
glass / bottle	verre / bouteille	vehr / boo-tay
beer	bière	bee-ehr
Cheers!	Santé!	sah<u>n</u>-tay
More. / Another.	Plus. / Un autre.	plew / uhn oh-truh
The same.	La même chose.	lah mehm shohz
The bill, please.	L'addition, s'il vous plaît.	lah-dee-see-oh<u>n</u> see voo play
Do you accept credit cards?	Vous prenez les cartes?	voo pruh-nay lay kart
tip	pourboire	poor-bwahr
Delicious!	Délicieux!	day-lees-yuh

For more user-friendly French phrases, check out *Rick Steves' French Phrase Book and Dictionary* or *Rick Steves' French, Italian & German Phrase Book*.

INDEX

Our website enhances this book and turns

Explore Europe

At ricksteves.com you can browse through thousands of articles, videos, photos and radio interviews, plus find a wealth of money-saving travel tips for planning your dream trip. And with our mobile-friendly website, you can easily access all this great travel information anywhere you go.

TV Shows

Preview the places you'll visit by watching entire half-hour episodes of Rick Steves' Europe (choose from all 100 shows) on-demand, for free.

your travel dreams into affordable reality

Radio Interviews

Enjoy ready access to Rick's vast library of radio interviews covering travel

tips and cultural insights that relate specifically to your Europe travel plans.

Travel Forums

Learn, ask, share! Our online community of savvy travelers is a great resource

for first-time travelers to Europe, as well as seasoned pros. You'll find forums on each country, plus travel tips and restaurant/hotel reviews. You can even ask one of our well-traveled staff to chime in with an opinion.

Travel News

Subscribe to our free Travel News e-newsletter, and get monthly updates from Rick on what's happening in Europe.

Audio Europe™

Rick's Free Travel App

Pack Light and Right

*Gear up for your
next adventure at
ricksteves.com*

Light Luggage

Pack light and right
with Rick Steves'
affordable, custom-
designed rolling carry-on
bags, backpacks, day
packs and shoulder bags.

Accessories

From packing cubes to
moneybelts and beyond,
Rick has personally
selected the travel
goodies that will help
your trip
go smoother.

Experience maximum Europe

Save time and energy

This guidebook is your independent-travel toolkit. But for all it delivers, it's still up to you to devote the time and energy it takes to manage the preparation and logistics that are essential for a happy trip. If that's a hassle, there's a solution.

Rick Steves Tours

A Rick Steves tour takes you to Europe's most interesting places with great

with minimum stress

guides and small groups of 28 or less. We follow Rick's favorite itineraries, ride in comfy buses, stay in family-run hotels, and bring you intimately close to the Europe you've traveled so far to see. Most importantly, we take away the logistical headaches so you can focus on the fun.

travelers—nearly half of them repeat customers—along with us on four dozen different itineraries, from Ireland to Italy to Athens. Is a Rick Steves tour the right fit for your travel dreams? Find out at ricksteves.com, where you can also request Rick's latest tour catalog. Europe is best experienced with happy travel partners. We hope you can join us.

Join the fun
This year we'll take thousands of free-spirited

A Guide for Every Trip

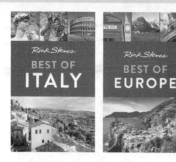

BEST OF GUIDES

Full color easy-to-scan format, focusing on Europe's most popular destinations and sights.

Best of England
Best of Europe
Best of France
Best of Germany
Best of Ireland
Best of Italy
Best of Spain

COMPREHENSIVE GUIDES

City, country, and regional guides with detailed coverage for a multi-week trip exploring the most iconic sights and venturing off the beaten track.

Amsterdam & the Netherlands
Barcelona
Belgium: Bruges, Brussels,
  Antwerp & Ghent
Berlin
Budapest
Croatia & Slovenia
Eastern Europe
England
Florence & Tuscany
France
Germany
Great Britain
Greece: Athens & the Peloponnese
Iceland
Ireland
Istanbul
Italy
London
Paris
Portugal
Prague & the Czech Republic
Provence & the French Riviera
Rome
Scandinavia
Scotland
Spain
Switzerland
Venice
Vienna, Salzburg & Tirol

HE BEST OF ROME

e, Italy's capital, is studded with
an remnants and floodlit-fountain
es. From the Vatican to the Colos-
with crazy traffic in between, Rome
derful, huge, and exhausting. The
, the heat, and the weighty history

of the Eternal City where Caesars walked
can make tourists wilt. Recharge by taking siestas, gelato breaks, and after-dark
walks, strolling from one atmospheric
square to another in the refreshing evening air.

*l Pantheon—which
l dome until the
2,000 years old
over 1,500).

Athens in the Vat-
es the humanistic

diators fought
ther, entertaining

ome ristorante.
at St. Peter's
riously

tos in a coin

Rick Steves guidebooks are published by Avalon Travel,
an imprint of Perseus Books, a Hachette Book Group company.

POCKET GUIDES

Compact, full color city guides with the essentials for shorter trips.

Amsterdam
Athens
Barcelona
Florence
Italy's Cinque Terre
London
Munich & Salzburg

Paris
Prague
Rome
Venice
Vienna

SNAPSHOT GUIDES

Focused single-destination coverage.

Basque Country: Spain & France
Copenhagen & the Best of Denmark
Dublin
Dubrovnik
Edinburgh
Hill Towns of Central Italy
Krakow, Warsaw & Gdansk
Lisbon
Loire Valley
Madrid & Toledo
Milan & the Italian Lakes District
Naples & the Amalfi Coast
Normandy
Northern Ireland
Norway
Reykjavík
Sevilla, Granada & Southern Spain
St. Petersburg, Helsinki & Tallinn
Stockholm

CRUISE PORTS GUIDES

Reference for cruise ports of call.

Mediterranean Cruise Ports
Scandinavian & Northern European
Cruise Ports

Complete your library with...

TRAVEL SKILLS & CULTURE

Study up on travel skills and gain insight on history and culture.

Europe 101
Europe Through the Back Door
European Christmas
European Easter
European Festivals
Postcards from Europe
Travel as a Political Act

PHRASE BOOKS & DICTIONARIES

French
French, Italian & German
German
Italian
Portuguese
Spanish

PLANNING MAPS

Britain, Ireland & London
Europe
France & Paris
Germany, Austria & Switzerland
Ireland
Italy
Spain & Portugal

Credits

CONTRIBUTOR
Gene Openshaw

 Gene has co-authored a dozen Rick Steves books, specializing in writing walks and tours of Europe's cities, museums, and cultural sights. He also contributes to Rick's public television series, produces tours for Rick Steves Audio Europe, and is a regular guest on Rick's public radio show. Outside of the travel world, Gene has co-authored *The Seattle Joke Book*. As a composer, Gene has written a full-length opera called *Matter* (soundtrack available on Amazon), a violin sonata, and dozens of songs. He lives near Seattle with his daughter, enjoys giving presentations on art and history, and roots for the Mariners in good times and bad.

Avalon Travel
Hachette Book Group
1700 Fourth Street
Berkeley, CA 94710

Printed in Canada by Friesens.
First Edition. First printing March 2019.

ISBN 978-1-64171-166-1

For the latest on Rick's talks, guidebooks, tours, public television series, and public radio show, contact Rick Steves' Europe, 130 Fourth Avenue North, Edmonds, WA 98020, 425/771-8303, www.ricksteves.com, rick@ricksteves.com.

Rick Steves' Europe

Managing Editor: Jennifer Madison Davis
Special Publications Manager: Risa Laib
Assistant Managing Editor: Cathy Lu
Editors: Glenn Eriksen, Julie Fanselow, Tom Griffin, Katherine Gustafson, Suzanne Kotz, Rosie Leutzinger, Jessica Shaw, Carrie Shepherd
Editorial & Production Assistant: Megan Simms
Editorial Interns: Nola Peshkin, Madeline Smith
Contributor: Gene Openshaw
Graphic Content Director: Sandra Hundacker
Maps & Graphics: David C. Hoerlein, Lauren Mills, Mary Rostad
Digital Asset Coordinator: Orin Dubrow

Avalon Travel

Senior Editor and Series Manager: Madhu Prasher
Editors: Jamie Andrade, Sierra Machado
Copy Editor: Denise Silva
Proofreader: Kelly Lydick, Patrick Collins
Indexer: Stephen Callahan
Production & Typesetting: Christine DeLorenzo, Lisi Baldwin, Rue Flaherty
Maps & Graphics: Kat Bennett
Cover Design: Kimberly Glyder Design

Front Cover: © Rostislav Glinsky | Dreamstime.com
Title page: © Dominic Arizona Bonuccelli
Additional Credits: 130 © Keystone Pictures USA/Alamy
Additional Photography: Dominic Arizona Bonuccelli, Rich Earl, Trish Feaster, Barb Geisler, Cameron Hewitt, David C. Hoerlein, Michaelanne Jerome, Paul Orcutt, Michael Potter, Carrie Shepherd, Steve Smith, Robyn Stencil, Rick Steves

Let's Keep on Travelin'

Your trip doesn't need to end.

Follow Rick on social media!

31901064745351